Who's Next?

Who's Next?

A memoir by

DERRICK SHERWIN

First published in 2014 by Fantom Films
fantomfilms.co.uk

A catalogue record for this book is available from the British Library.

Hardback edition ISBN: 978-1-78196-111-7

Typeset by Phil Reynolds Media Services, Leamington Spa
Printed and bound by CPI Group (UK) Ltd, Croydon, CR0 4YY

Jacket design by Stuart Manning

Contents

Acknowledgements

FOR THE LAST DECADE I have been kept alive and encouraged by my Thai wife, Ingsumon, without whom I would have joined my ancestors six feet under. With her care and encouragement I have got my life back together.

There have been many people who have influenced the way my life has developed whom I would like to thank. My ex-wife, Jane, who has suffered my inadequacies for over twenty-four years of our marriage and since, now remains – although divorced – a good friend, together with my three adopted children, Sam, Kate and Daniel.

In my chosen profession as writer and TV and film producer I have many people to thank: Nils Nilson; my old friend and artist, Zeesh; my previous agent Robin Lowe (all now unfortunately dead); my Buddhist doctor friend, Taweesilp; and all of the hundreds of people I have worked with in the business – good creative people.

My thanks to all – too numerous to mention.

Introduction

BEING RETROSPECTIVE ABOUT ONE'S LIFE for an autobiography requires absolute honesty, and although this can be damaging to one's ego it is essential for the truth to be paramount: for truth, more often than not, is stranger than fiction and more interesting to anyone else. At the same time truth can appear to others to be contentious since it can be a matter of personal opinion and damaging or libellous to others and the honest approach is a difficult road to tread. But tread it one must, carefully. To avoid offence real names may be avoided and not used, or not understandable to anyone other than those directly involved. However, seventy-seven years is a substantial lifespan, and many of those with whom I have been involved are either dead and gone or do not care!

Collecting together all of the relevant memories and details of my life would have been considerably easier had I been able to keep my annual diaries, but over my seventy-odd years I have moved around to so many different parts of the world that, in the process, many of my diaries suffered from decay or were lost. I must therefore rely on my ageing memory which at best finds it difficult to recall yesterday, never mind yesteryear!

'What's it all about, Alfie...?'

A good if somewhat trite title for a song of the 1960s, but a good question when reflecting on one's life and why it developed in the way it did.

I first began to consider the way in which my life had evolved when, in 1999, I realised that my normal mood of optimism about the future was seemingly changing for the worse.

Standing on London's Putney Bridge, looking downstream at the early morning sun trying vainly to break through the grey cloud of an October morning, glancing at the straggling commuters' grey faces as they lethargically plodded towards the City on their way to work, I wondered: *Is this how the rest of my life is going to be – grey? No colour?*

At sixty-something, nearing the 'old fart' OAP status, rejected as unemployable by the 'yoof' culture that seemed to have taken over my world of entertainment, I pondered the future. My bones may have been creaking, yes. My diabetes may have slowed me down a bit, and I was not capable of running a two-minute mile. Indeed I was no longer able to run a mile. However, my brain was still as active as ever it was and well developed creatively.

Why is anyone over fifty rejected as being unemployable? For 'retired', read 'retarded'. What a strange world it is where experience and acquired wisdom are treated not as an asset but as a stigma! Or maybe the 'yoof' are afraid of the competition from the experienced; afraid they may be shown up as naive, as lacking expertise and attempting to justify themselves simply by innovation. Who knows? Reality shows, another hideous import from America, had became popular fare but not a development that interested me. I am 'old school'.

With such depressing thoughts as these brewing in my mind, I determined not to spend what remained of my life watching daytime TV or attending OAP centres to play bingo to help those who had already given in to the state's answer to over-employment.

So this was where and how my reflections on my past life began; but, to determine why I had been reduced to such depression and despair, I must begin at the beginning.

Chapter One
THE FORMATIVE YEARS

I WAS BORN SLIGHTLY BEFORE the Second World War, in 1936, to working-class parents in High Wycombe in Buckinghamshire as an only child: no brothers or sisters, just me. Being an only child had its advantages and disadvantages.

The years between 1939 and 1945 were difficult for a young family, interrupting as they did normal family life since my father was recruited to serve in the Army, in the Royal Artillery. For this reason I didn't really know him until I was nine years old, except on his infrequent leaves when he returned to the fold; and therefore I was totally under the guidance and care of my mother.

She was a fair, loving but strict parent, and my first memory of our relationship is of her insisting that I attended the local Church of England junior school, which appealed neither to my independent spirit nor my lazy youthful attitude; my stubbornness was rewarded with an excruciating but effective whacking across the legs and buttocks with a seemingly innocent twig as she chased me all the way to school! My introduction to the realms of academe was therefore memorably painful, unwelcome but effective. It did nonetheless provide me with the basic skills of the three 'R's and a certain appreciation of personal discipline.

My years during the Second World War were peppered with the ever-present fear of German bombers dropping their remaining bombs over my home town following the raids on London, and of the hideous 'Doodlebug' rockets which hummed threateningly overhead without warning and fell on the terrified population below with devastating effect.

Air raids were frequent, and at school we were shown how to wear our gas-masks, and taught to hide under our desks for shelter when there was an air-raid warning. I also remember that, during a visit to my father, who was stationed in Hull, I lost my slipper whilst running for the air-raid shelter and, turning to recover it, I was spattered with shrapnel from above. The fact that I am here to tell the tale without a scratch is surely only by the intervention of a power from above – so there must have been some purpose in my survival!

War I did not understand then any more than I do today, and the memories and fear it invoked in my young brain still remain.

My mother and father, on his demobilisation from the Army following the end of the war, decided that their future lay in business, and in particular as landlord and landlady of a public house – a local boozer! In order to afford this they agreed to go into partnership with my grandparents on my father's side. I had little or no respect for either of my grandfathers since they were selfish, dictatorial and (in common with most men of that time) badly behaved towards their wives. My grandmothers on the other hand were gentle and considerate souls. My mother's family were pure Welsh stock from the Rhondda Valley but my maternal grandfather was, I was sure, bred of the Devil despite being an officer in the Salvation Army. He was a bully and a lazy indolent who left the responsibility of providing for his family to my ever-loving Granny Williams who, up until her last days, spent every day on her hands and knees as a cleaner in the local cinema.

Fortunately my Welsh grandfather died early, otherwise I am sure that when I grew up I would have given him what he deserved: a good thrashing. The last I remember of Granny Williams was when (as I did every Sunday morning prior to the obligatory attendance at Sunday School) I visited her, sat on the side of her bed and watched her as she lathered her chin with a shaving-brush coated with carbolic soap and shaved! What a character: much loved and sorely missed.

Most of my father's family had been on the periphery of the bookmaking business, and after the war my uncle set up the business properly. He did well and recruited a number of 'runners', of which I was one since the pub was a selected pick-up point for the punter's bets. Saturday was the busiest day for betting activity, when football matches and the biggest horse-racing events took place. Saturday night therefore was equally busy at my uncle's house, when all of the bets throughout the day had to be checked, the winners selected and the winnings calculated: an all-night exercise. One lesson I learned from participating in this was that the bookmaker always wins; my uncle became quite wealthy as a result, but he died prematurely owing to the nights working during which he smoked hundreds of cigarettes!

A public house was not conducive to a normal family life since it revolved around serving customers and it could not be considered as a family home with any privacy. Everywhere smelled of stale beer and cigarette smoke; the whole of the downstairs, with the exception of the small kitchen area, was open to the customers, and upstairs was a large licensed room which was ostensibly the family living room but which could also be used for special occasions by the paying customers. There was no bathroom and the toilets were outside for the use of customers and family alike – primitive to say the least. On bath day, Friday, I had to carry a zinc bath in from outside, put it in one of the rooms with a fire and fill it up with hot water so that my father could have the first bath, me second and finally my mother who would have to wallow in the murky depths. Once this weekly exercise was completed I would have to carry the full bath through the bar area and outside to empty it. On one fateful day I managed to drop the entire thing, spilling the grotty soapy contents throughout the bar! My one desire from the early days was to have an inside bathroom and toilet. I wasn't afforded that sort of luxury until much later when I left home to pursue my career.

Having no privacy, therefore, I spent almost this entire period outside of the house – outside of my 'home'. I had few friends so I was thrown back onto my own resources. I was a country boy and the surrounding countryside my playground. The Buckinghamshire hills with their beech trees and hillsides have remained dear to my heart ever since.

One development that particularly affected me from my childhood was when I began learning to play the piano. From my earliest days I have appreciated – no, *loved* – music, but practising my piano was difficult since the piano I used was downstairs in the lounge area of the bar and the only time I could practise was in the early morning around six o'clock. After a long day and night working in the pub this was irritating for my weary parents but they suffered it for many years. I showed great promise, studying at the local music school for some nine years until my interest in acting interrupted it. Although I had taken the Royal Schools of Music exams up to Grade Seven, I was told by my teacher that, if I wanted to continue and train as a concert pianist, I had to choose; I chose acting. I continued to play the piano, but no longer seriously – only for the customers in the pub every Friday night!

The Golden Fleece, the pub we lived in, had a substantial rear garden which, in good weather, was also open to the customers. I was charged with the task of caring for the lawns and gardens on a weekly basis to earn my pocket money. This I did, and also grew many flowers with which I supplemented my pocket money by producing posies for the male customers to purchase as gift offerings to their long-suffering wives, whose patience was rightly exhausted as they waited to serve the Sunday lunch! Thus everybody was happy – including me as I pocketed my well-earned subsidy in my Post Office savings account to provide for that inevitable rainy day. I also collected hundredweight sacks of coke on my back from the next-door gasworks to deliver to whoever had ordered them; each delivery earned me sixpence. This was my introduction to the world of financial self-sufficiency.

One of the perpetual consequences of living in a pub was dealing with the continual rows that erupted between my parents, brought on I am sure by the constant availability of and participation in booze. It is difficult to refuse to drink if you are serving it to customers: resisting an offer may appear to be unsociable or even unfriendly – not good for business. Both of my parents drank on a daily basis which led them to overindulgence and, when under the influence of alcohol with their inhibitions released, into arguments which were sometimes violent. Such arguments happened after closing time when I was in bed; more often than not, if I judged that they were becoming out of control, I would have to come downstairs into the bar to intervene. At eleven years of age this was an upsetting experience and sometimes a traumatic one, which I promised would never happen to me in my adult life; I determined then to be able to control my temper with an imposed coolness which I have tried to observe (not always successfully) ever since.

It's strange, thinking back all these years, with all of the difficulties, the rows and no real family home, how happy I was. Having spent my early teens in a working pub I became physically quite substantial from hauling around crates of beer bottles and eighteen-gallon barrels of beer and from my duties in the garden. I created a 'bolthole', my own private getaway in one of the two substantial buildings in the garden area. This became my refuge, my own private resort away from the non-existent family home, my escape from reality.

The second building housed Sally, a Shetland pony owned by my uncle which I was also charged with looking after: a not unpleasant task as I was allowed to exercise her in the saddle or in the trap around the local streets. Sally, being my silent confidante (and I lacking other friendly ears), heard, uncomplainingly, all of my fears and woes and indeed my ambitions. I also kept chickens, ducks and an assortment of other beasties which I had to learn to be able to slaughter for the pot when required; perhaps this is why they weren't as sympathetic to listening to my private reveries as Sally was.

Leading a lonely life had its advantages since I could concentrate more energy on those things which interested me and not be absorbed with the trivial pursuits that occupied most of the children of my age: sports, girls, smoking behind the toilets in the playground and other meaningful adventures!

In the summer months, once my chores were finished I would cycle the twenty-odd miles to Burnham Beeches, the nearest swimming pool, which, apart from bringing me into contact with other kids of my age, added to my physical development and gave me a feeling, at least, of social companionship and acceptability.

My schooldays were unspectacular since I did no more than was absolutely necessary to pass muster and be entered into the secondary modern school, and not the expected grammar school. The humiliation of this apparent academic failure, and the subsequent appalling experience that was my time at the secondary modern school, prompted me to apply myself a little more enthusiastically to my studies, resulting in an improvement in my academic status and an eventual offer of a place in the more prestigious College of Art and Technology, which allowed me to demonstrate my more acceptable practical abilities and skills as well as improving my academic talents.

The teachers at the secondary modern school seemed to delight in inflicting corporal punishment. One, who taught maths and gymnastics, had the pointless habit at the beginning of his class of hauling me and my fat friend Sam out in front of the class and whacking us on the backside with one of his gym slippers; just to get the attention of the class, so he said, but I suspect it was really to satisfy his sadistic personality! This is another of the people I would have loved to meet up with in a dark alley when I had grown sufficiently. That wouldn't have been long, since he, despite being our gym teacher, was what might now be called 'physically challenged' – in other words very small!

Another one with the same inclination was our woodwork teacher, who had the nasty but effective habit of throwing a narrow piece of oak with particular accuracy at the head of any misbehaving student; an effective deterrent but, I suspected, with motives identical to those of our maths teacher – sadism. This was my overall impression of secondary modern schools, in part due no doubt to the type of children into whom they had to try and pummel an education. I was happy to be upgraded.

My home town of High Wycombe is renowned, among other things, for furniture-making and cabinetry; and my new school, the Arts and Technical College, was aimed towards such skills. I learned, and enjoyed learning, to be a skilled woodworker and designer, making passable furniture. For my graduation I made a reproduction Chippendale ladder-back armchair, and was rewarded with a general Arts Certificate. Furniture design, it seemed, was to be my future; and indeed I was offered a job working as a hospital furniture designer, combining my design skills and practical applications as a chair-maker – not that my flair for reproduction Chippendale was required! It was a way of earning a living but was not exactly inspiring or what I wanted to spend the rest of my life doing. There had to be something else.

Luckily I did not have to take up the job offer, because it was during this period that I began to appreciate the pleasure of being involved in entertainment, and of having my amateur contributions appreciated, which was great for one's personal ego. I appeared in several Boys' Clubs amateur entertainment presentations at the local town hall and in several Gilbert and Sullivan operettas – not that I had a fantastic voice but I was young, looked good in tights and had a good appreciation of the music!

It was, I believe, my mother who nurtured my appreciation of the theatre by taking me to London for a day out to visit the Oxford Street shops (Derry and Toms I remember distinctly), then to Lyons Corner House for a meal (very posh!), then on afterwards to the big treat: a matinee at one of the various musicals on at the time in the fabulous West End. I was intrigued by this fascinating world of entertainment: the glamour, the make-believe of transporting us out of the mundane world of everyday life. This was a world of magic!

However, what really got me involved as an actor was being able to attend a summer course in theatre at a private school in Cranbourne, Kent. This was run by a Mr Anthony Thomas and his wife. They were excellent people, understanding and compassionate, the kind of couple I wished I had been blessed with as parents; but they were of a different class and with a more fortunate life and upbringing than my family. I spent two summer courses there, the second of which I worked my way through as a labourer to earn my presence there, stoking the house boilers. This heavy work led me, despite my healthy and physically advanced state, to having some kind of fever and being nursed back to health by the caring Mrs Thomas.

It was at these two joyful summer courses that I first appreciated the opposite sex, and I 'fell in love' with a gentle creature from Durham! I was besotted: not by her beauty but by her gentleness, her femininity and character. Most of my previous experiences with the opposite sex had been with the local High Wycombe girls of my age who appeared to differ from the boys only because they had longer hair and bumps in different places! They had no feminine attributes at all. My 'first love' was something else entirely. She was how I imagined an angel would be. It was over, of course, as soon as the summer course ended; but she left an indelible impression and remained in my memory as a template, my 'ideal'. It had nothing to do with what I later experienced as sexual attraction, since at that early age I could hardly understand the word 'sex'!

The experiences at Cranbourne and the caring and encouragement of the Thomas family nurtured in me the desire to pursue a life in the theatre and not as a furniture designer. I began to take private acting and voice production lessons to rid me of my Buckinghamshire accent, which was particularly 'yokel': not unattractive but certainly not the 'Queen's English' expected at that time in the acting profession. I also somehow wormed my way into an unpaid position helping out at the local repertory theatre in High Wycombe as assistant scenic artist and small 'bit' player and general dogsbody. This was it, the real theatre! Not the West End theatres that I had so enjoyed with my mother, but it allowed me to dream: to be a part of that make-believe world.

Chapter Two

DON'T PUT YOUR DAUGHTER ON THE STAGE, MRS WORTHINGTON

MY ATTENDANCE AT THE PRIVATE acting classes led to my taking exams at LAMDA – the London Academy of Music and Dramatic Art. I was terrified, but must have performed my audition piece more than adequately as, much to my surprise, I was offered a free scholarship there. Somebody obviously saw a talent in me… or perhaps again it was my ability to look good in tights! Or maybe it was because I was an accomplished liar, which after all is the essence of being an actor: being able to pretend to be something or someone you are not and to be able to convince others that your 'lie' is true.

LAMDA was, I suppose, a good place to learn from scratch the art of being an actor. However, I did not appreciate being back at school, having experienced the exciting world of real theatre, of weekly rep and the 'buzz' I got from appearing before an audience. Having achieved my Gold and Silver medals I assumed that I would learn more in the demanding world of real theatre; so I left LAMDA and accepted a job in the local rep, once again as assistant scenic artist. I also didn't want to be a classical actor: I was more inclined towards the 'method' acting that had begun in the USA – the Marlon Brando days.

I was lucky to enter the world of theatre when I did, for there were still forty or so repertory companies still operating on a weekly basis around the country, as well as several seasonal theatres in the summer months. This number has sadly diminished in recent years with the advent of television and movies, so where up-and-coming actors are getting their theatrical training I do not really know.

Weekly rep was something else: a seven-days-a-week job with a new play being rehearsed whilst still playing the current one every night. This was a serious task with six nightly performances and two matinees. After the two Saturday performances, the weekly turnaround began as the old sets were removed overnight and the newly painted sets were constructed for the following week's performances. Sunday was no day of rest for the actors, for they had to prepare for the dress rehearsal on Monday for the new play which opened Monday night! There was hardly time to draw breath, and since I was painting the scenery as well as acting there was little time to enjoy my teenage years; but at the age of seventeen I was as happy as Larry, doing exactly what I wanted to do and enjoying every moment. My parents were very understanding and proud that I had decided to remove myself from the kind of life which allowed for nothing other than being like everybody else, and had opted instead for being different and so gaining a modicum of respect. Deciding to be in the entertainment business was a decidedly eccentric decision in those days!

From High Wycombe Rep I went briefly to Amersham Rep and with them to a summer season in Bangor, Northern Ireland as juvenile lead and also as stage electrician. It was there that, after being blown off a thirty-foot gantry having touched the wrong terminal of a three-phase master, I learned to wear thick rubber gloves and not be so arrogantly stupid as to think I was indestructible!

I then undertook a scenic artist job with a fit-up somewhere in the outer reaches of East London. The problem with this new commission was that I had not been informed that the 'rake' on the theatre's stage was so steep; in consequence, all my scenery leaned at a precarious angle and I had to adjust everything accordingly! After this I took up an offer to help build and open a new theatre in South Shields in Northumberland, again as scenic artist and juvenile lead actor.

My carpentry and artistic skills had helped me enormously and I was certainly honing my skills as an actor. Then came the crunch when my call-up papers arrived for me to do my National Service. My career was about to be devastated by the unavoidable two years' interruption in my chosen profession; but then fate took a hand – or rather took away one of my hands.

My scenery dock was situated next door to a roller-skating rink; and, whilst carrying a scene flat across it, I slipped and broke a metacarpal in my left hand. The hospital mended the problem, and gave me another six weeks of freedom since every other day I rebroke it – not deliberately but owing to the nature of my work!

Nevertheless I was eventually dragged off to serve my time with the RAF Fighter Command, though not as a pilot because I failed the eye test as they decided I was colour-blind; me, a scenic artist, colour-blind! There was no arguing with them, so I was relegated to communications, and eventually served a good deal of my first year in Northern Ireland on a redundant and virtually deserted airbase. With little to do except pass the time playing cards with the equally bored commanding officer, I started writing, and chose to write an adaptation of Dostoyevsky's book *The Idiot*! What a time-consuming task; but then time was what I had on my hands, and I loved the characters and highly complex story. I had no option either but to write laboriously in longhand. This passed my time and encouraged me to continue writing.

I had been told by my English teacher previously that my overactive imagination prevented me from writing! Perhaps her idea of writing was limited to writing letters or perhaps journalism or marking the students' work with her cryptic remarks? I did, however, pursue my desire to write creatively; and, when my first television play *Yob and Nabob* was accepted some time later and broadcast by the BBC on December 26th 1965, directed by Lionel Harris with stars Emlyn Williams and Bill Fraser, to some considerable appreciation and praise, I had the satisfaction of communicating this to my old English teacher! I therefore continued at a later date to write drama, encouraged by the appreciation.

But I jump ahead, and I had to return to the real world as I was transferred to Headquarters Fighter Command where I was upgraded in status to acting corporal and put in charge of one area of communications, working mainly only nights and deep underground. This allowed me to travel back to my home town of High Wycombe and work (unofficially) during the days as scenic artist, at my original repertory theatre. Of course I couldn't act as well because I had to sleep some time! But I had at least made it back into my beloved theatre for the last six months of my National Service.

Once I was back in civvy street, my writing ambitions took a back seat as I had to concentrate on my job as a scenic artist and juvenile lead actor. My optimistic attitude to life continued unabated as I had also progressed in my earning power from the early days when I was paid seven shillings and sixpence a week to the high-blown wage of seven pounds a week; those were the days!

My scenic artist teacher, Jimmy Jackson (who also lived in a pub on the outer reaches of High Wycombe), had ambitions to produce a pantomime and offered that I join as assistant scenic artist and small-part player. I readily agreed since it was employment and I had always enjoyed pantomime before.

Two weeks into the run, which was going well, I was contacted by an actress I had known in rep, Margery Mason, who was also trying to produce a pantomime in a barn of a theatre in Walthamstow in London. She was in trouble because the scenic artist who was supposed to have been working for her had left her high and dry. She knew my ability to work under pressure, and as she was due to open in two days she implored me to help. It was a weekend and I had to wait until I had performed on the Saturday evening before I could travel to Walthamstow to try and fix her problem. That meant I only had Sunday and all day Monday before returning to appear in Basingstoke in the pantomime on Monday night. No sleep: just working on a massive and complicated backcloth and one large set. I was exhausted but Margery managed to open on the Monday as planned.

What I hadn't known was that the actor playing one of the Ugly Sisters in the Basingstoke pantomime had been struck down with flu over the weekend and I had been designated as unofficial understudy to take his place. Even though I knew the script (more or less) and the dance and comedy routines, I only had one hour on my return from Walthamstow in which to prepare. To add to the problem, I hadn't slept for two days and could hardly stand, let alone do complicated routines and songs that hadn't been rehearsed.

Perhaps it was just as well that I didn't know too much about what was going on, because the two-hour performance went by like a dream! The audience was aware that I was taking over the Ugly Sister role at short notice, and I received a standing ovation. After three or four days, by which time I had perfected my performance, the original actor returned and I had to go back to playing the small parts. The compensation of forty pounds helped ease my disappointment, but all the same it was a memorable achievement.

I determined that my career therefore had to be directed towards my other string as juvenile actor, and I signed up for a season at the theatre in Carlisle. Here I didn't have to paint scenery but could concentrate solely on my ability as an actor. I was on my way up!

Chapter Three

Climbing the Ladder

I RETURNED TO LONDON DETERMINED to find an agent to assist me in my new career. Up to this point in my life I had had little time for the normal teenage pursuit of romance, except for a brief relationship with a girl from my home town which collapsed when I met my future wife, Jane, with whom I worked at High Wycombe Rep.

Now, with time on my hands, the relationship blossomed as I worked hard at my career as an actor and supplemented my income by working as a stage hand with the London Festival Ballet, at the Royal Festival Hall on the South Bank. With my knowledge of scenery I was put in charge of the 'flies' – the area directly above the stage where the backcloths and other scenery are stored on counter-weighted pulleys and lowered or raised as required. This was physically demanding but required little other than the discipline of following an ordered sequence. Changing sets from one ballet to another again required long nights of arduous work, but this was something I was used to from my years in weekly rep.

The interesting part of this job was that, having to work late nights, I went home in the dawn hours through the deserted streets of London and witnessed the strange folk whose world this was: the street cleaners, the market traders, the office cleaners, milkmen, drunks, streetwalkers and revellers who inhabited this twilight world. It was a way for me to observe such characters and store such information in my memory for future use.

When the Festival Ballet Company went on tour I took another job, as a lighting assistant designing and preparing lighting rigs for West End productions which went on tour prior to opening in London, travelling with them and eventually setting up the lighting in the chosen West End theatre. I worked on such shows as the *Darling Buds of May* musical, *My Fair Lady* and the satirical comedy shows popular at that time like *Share My Lettuce.* It was a wonderful experience working with and meeting such talented people as Julie Andrews, Fenella Fielding and Kenneth Williams, whose blinding rows make me blush to recall them but nevertheless left me with profound admiration for their sublime creative comedy talents. That was my world, a world of which I wanted desperately to be a part – a world of escapism.

However, this world was still some way off, still somewhat beyond my grasp. I had a lot of learning to do yet, and the road to becoming such a consummate entertainer was littered with difficult pitfalls and mountainous obstacles which, alone, I could not climb. I needed an agent!

Jane had also secured a job working as a dresser and wardrobe mistress with the Festival Ballet Company, and we had determined that marriage was a good idea although we had not a penny to rub between us! She was a superb actress in the classical sense, but she didn't have that deep and persistent burning in her soul to succeed that I did, or my optimistic disposition; my fire was far more consuming than hers and my determination was directed towards being a recognised and successful actor. I needed an agent: someone who knew the ropes, who knew 'the business'; someone who could introduce me to the right people, the casting directors and so on who could ease my way up the vast mountain I had decided I must climb if they would only recognise my inherent but as yet still not fully developed talent.

I discussed my needs and desires with several potential agents, but none of them met with my standards as they were only interested in putting me to work to earn their percentage and not putting their efforts and experience into building my career. Such agents are the leeches of the business, and I learned to avoid them like the plague! My persistence paid off in the end, and an interview with a highly respected agent, Derek Marr, finally led to my being sent to some worthwhile auditions. Not that he agreed to take me on as my agent – that was something he would not do until I had proved myself.

Jane and I took this opportunity to marry, and we searched for a suitable place to live – not an easy task considering that very little was available within our miserable budget range, since we existed largely on unemployment benefit (the dole), about four pounds weekly between us! Faced with this problem, I made an offer of two pounds a week for a five-year lease on a derelict basement, and set about converting it into a habitable space at my own expense, employing my basic design skills and using only old junk that was being stored in the basement which, incidentally, was under a couple of feet of stinking waste water! My fit-up experience gained working in rep earlier in my career proved invaluable, for at four pounds a week income and two pounds a week rent we only had two pounds a week for everything else, including food. We therefore had to make do on a once-a-week visit to the local market to buy the barest minimum and scrounge the discarded vegetables! It was, however, a happy time and both Jane and I enjoyed the challenge.

I auditioned for many plays and even musicals, for Derek believed that I had a singing voice and even insisted that I take singing lessons. I was not a natural singer, although curiously it was this that led to my success at one of my auditions where it was necessary for me to use my Welsh background and my ability to speak with a credible Welsh accent – even in a cod Welsh language – for the writer/actor/director Emlyn Williams in his new play *Beth*. After several audition recalls, for the last of which it was required that I sing, I launched into a tenuous rendition of 'Old Man River' – a song for a bass voice which I had to pitch higher for my natural baritone to accommodate! To my surprise this convinced Emlyn and I was given the role.

We were to tour first to see if the production was up to standard for the West End: a six-week try-out around the country culminating in Brighton. It was at this last stop that Derek Marr came to see me perform and decided that he would take me on as a regular client.

Derek was known as an agent who represented many good-looking young actors and 'groomed' them for eventual stardom. I was the newest addition to his stable, his current success being Steven Boyd whom he had nurtured into a reasonably recognised movie actor. This and the fact that my salary had leaped to the giddy heights of twenty pounds a week convinced me that I was on my way!

Again, the best laid plans of mice and men crushed my high hopes; for, despite getting reasonable reviews and opening at the Apollo Theatre in Shaftesbury Avenue, under the management of the highly respected Tennant's organisation, we crashed after only a ten-day run. If at first you don't succeed...

Derek decided that perhaps the new medium of TV drama was my forte and proceeded to put me forward for several good parts in TV plays, one of which was the juvenile lead role of Raleigh in a television adaptation of the famous play *Journey's End*. It had a well-respected director, John Jacobs, and was broadcast in the BBC's top play slot. Success! The only problem was that, following transmission, my mother rang up in a panic because in the play I had 'died' under a heap of rubble in a First World War trench; she had totally believed what she had seen on the screen. Such was the power of television!

The play, and happily I, got rave reviews and this was indeed the first concrete foundation stone in my career move. Derek was delighted and encouraged enough to be even more adventurous, and secured several more good roles for me. I was now fortunately becoming an actor whose reputation was accepted, and directors actually sent scripts for me to consider.

Derek introduced me to several of the better known film casting agents and I began to cut my teeth on small 'B' feature films such as those produced by the Danziger Brothers, with a turnaround similar to that on which I had been nurtured in my early days in weekly rep – in other words, cheap and fast: learn your lines, don't fall over the furniture and a maximum of two takes to save the film stock! I was reliable, efficient and gave a good professional performance, which meant I was employed regularly at seven pounds a day playing many different parts.

Following my initial success with the Danziger Brothers I was then upgraded to play in their feature film, *The Spanish Sword*, a movie script compiled from several of their other scripts. I played the young blacksmith hero, again because I looked good in tights and could deliver a believable performance – and because I was cheap! They decided to make this movie in the summer break between shooting their TV films (*William Tell* I believe was their current series) because they didn't want to close their studio and undergo the expense of starting up again in the new season. Everything at Danzigers' was all about money without spending too much of it!

This then secured me work at the more prestigious film studios of Merton Park, making more 'B' feature movies such as the Edgar Wallace thrillers and a legal thriller series of which I made at least six, being given star billing in each of them. The advantage of working on such films was not only the experience gained and the improvement in my reputation and image with cinema audiences, but also the opportunity to work with good up-and-coming directors, who were climbing the same ladder to get recognition and would, if they appreciated me as an actor, give me work in far more prestigious films or TV shows in the future.

Merton Park feature-film making was always on a ten-day turnaround, and I played the juvenile lead in several, at a salary of £300 per picture and with star billing! Such work improved my standing in the industry but did not afford me entry yet into the 'A' feature market, apart from one film, *The Vengeance of She*, which only made the 'A' category because of the new craze for horror movies! I also appeared in many of the Second World War movies that were being made. Odd to remember that I was cast as a very English upper-class young officer considering my working-class background; it shows how effective my elocution lessons had been. In the meantime I continued to appear as a featured actor in TV plays and series such as the *Somerset Maugham Hour*, the *Blackmail* series of plays, Wednesday Plays for the BBC and *Armchair Theatre* plays for the new commercial companies. All good and interesting work which I enjoyed and which improved my reputation.

However, it was at this time that the commercially motivated American influence of cheap-to-buy-in drama series came onto our screens: flashy mindless stories and easy-to-watch, chewing-gum-for-the-eyes entertainment. Both the BBC and the commercial channels succumbed to the temptation and began to imitate them, and soap operas and crime-based home-grown drama began to take root in the UK, replacing the more creative dramas of earlier years. This led to typecasting; and I, as a lead actor, was offered the same character to play over and over again – very boring and uninspiring!

Jane was fortunate enough to land a part in Granada's *Skyport* series which provided a welcome boost to our virtually empty bank accounts. With this improvement in our financial fortunes, Jane and I had been planning a family; but it was discovered that, thanks to some quirk of nature with my genes, I couldn't produce the wherewithal, and she suggested that we adopt a family. Obviously the news that I was unable to produce my own children and that I was 'shooting blanks' was a blow to my masculinity, but I realised that this was a necessity for Jane and agreed, and we duly applied for consideration with the Church of England Adoption Society. Our application was given priority, for my father-in-law was a clergyman!

I hadn't given much thought to adopting children before this. I did not know anyone who had done so; and the idea had not, it appeared, widely been seen as 'acceptable' for some reason, probably because most families had enough difficulty sustaining themselves without taking on another mouth to feed. It was only couples like us who simply couldn't produce their own progeny to whom this was an attractive alternative. A baby is a baby – or is it?

I began to think a little more about this. Would the babies be like their birth parents, carrying the same genetic make-up, evolving into combined-clone copies? I thought, no: they would be brought up by Jane and me and nurtured in a different family environment, and would adopt those moral and ethical natures that they learned through us, their adopting parents. Wrong again! Our children grew up with a mixture of both, retaining their basic genetic attributes but absorbing some of the moral and ethical attitudes they were taught by us. My eldest son, Sam, had a much more developed academic brain, a mathematical brain, making him a good logical thinker. My daughter, Kate, being placed between two boys, had a hard time holding her own against two boisterous and genetically different brothers. Our third child, Benjamin, unfortunately died at around six months old and was immediately replaced by our adoption society with another child, Daniel.

The adoption society did their best to offer us children from 'like parents', but this was obviously a bit hit-and-miss since the best match they could make was with physical likeness and social status history. In essence, then, they were all three of them quite different in personality. They were all 'ours' and, as such, loved dearly; and thankfully they considered themselves, no matter how different individually, to be part of the same family and showed their love and appreciation in return.

In anticipation of our first adopted child, my mother-in-law offered that we should move into the newly converted top-floor flat in her substantial house in Holland Park, since our rented basement was hardly suitable for a new addition to the family. Her builders did the basic work of conversion and I applied my interior design talents to finish things off. Our first child, a boy whom we named Sam, arrived, and Jane was totally absorbed with this event.

During this period I was offered another chance to further my career on stage, acting in a play titled *Music at Midnight*, a religious saga for the campaigning organisation known as Moral Re-Armament (MRA). The part was the juvenile lead and was in London's West End playing opposite a group of well-known actors including Walter Fitzgerald; indeed, it was his taking the starring role that persuaded me to accept – that and the run at the Westminster Theatre to be followed by a tour in America! They also had plans to make a film of this subject on a small island on the Great Lakes between the USA and Canada. All in all this was to be a tour of some nineteen thousand miles, playing at many theatres along the way to, as I understood it, selected high-profile (for which read influential and rich) audiences whom they were trying to invite into the fold. The opportunity was impossible to resist and so, despite my objections to the blatant religious implications in the script, I accepted.

Returning home after the performance at the Westminster Theatre one Saturday night, I was confronted by massively dense smog so bad that one literally couldn't see beyond the end of one's nose. The only buses that were running were those returning to the depot – and they were being led by someone on foot! The trouble was that, being virtually blind, one could only make any progress on the home journey by literally feeling one's way along, from one street corner to the next, and crossing the road was very hazardous. This was the worst smog in the capital's history and led to the banning of coal fires in London.

The MRA were, in general, nice people with good intentions; but their methods for attracting converts, persuading them to part with all their worldly wealth, were anathema to my free spirit. Walter felt likewise, but he was more subtle with his opinions! I was the hothead with my own axe to grind and was the more difficult one to target as a convert. The short run at the Westminster Theatre was painless and Walter and I, as like souls, joined forces in order to resist the continuous onslaught of the MRA's efforts to convince us to become converts to their particular brand of religious fetishism.

My introduction to the unfamiliar culture of America was a shock to my left-wing inclinations. The sight of the countless nodding donkeys of the oil wells lining the highways along which we travelled on our seemingly never-ending coach journey through the various states annoyed me, as it indicated the constant flow of the greenback into a few pockets whilst others struggled to survive. These vast pockets of great wealth were what the MRA were targeting with their proselytising.

Our opening night was in a barn of a theatre in downtown Los Angeles and was celebrated by a dinner afterwards with prestigious guests such as Charlton Heston and others too numerous to name. In a future city stop (Palm Springs I believe it was), I met with Ike Eisenhower and Shirley Temple: both cracking on a bit but still big names in the public arena, which of course was what the MRA was interested in. This was to be the norm throughout the entire tour, because English actors also had their kudos – socially if not professionally!

At one such celebration dinner I found myself in a furious argument with a wealthy doctor, voicing my opinions about the value of the NHS over the private medicine of USA society, my left-wing tendencies firing up my rhetoric. The next morning, as we were preparing to board our Greyhound bus to the next venue, the doctor arrived in his very smart and expensive car, insisting that he wanted to continue our previous night's conversation and also that to do so he would fly me to the next city in his private airplane! It was a very pleasant and unusual flight, throughout which we continued our conversation, but I didn't persuade him of the virtues of the NHS, nor him me of the fiscal advantages of the private medical system which he practised. We did, however, part amicably as friends.

The pressure and continuous surveillance of the MRA drove Walter and me to seek privacy, and each night after the performance we repaired to the hotel room to indulge in a glass of mind-numbing whisky or ten! On one occasion we decided to fox our MRA 'tail' by venturing into the downtown low-life drinking area and, at an opportune moment, dodging into a strip-club and drinking there; of course our tail couldn't follow us into such a disreputable establishment. We employed many different such ruses to escape. The only extravagance that the members of the MRA seemed to indulge in was eating. Boy! How they could eat!

The part I was playing was supposed to be similar to Fidel Castro, which, when we played in Midland, Texas – the home of the ultra-right-wing John Birch Society – raised more than eyebrows. On the first night playing there, a group of these angry John Birch guys were waiting outside the stage door and seemed prepared to show their displeasure. Fortunately they didn't recognise me since my stage make-up was that of an unshaven angry young renegade. Without make-up I was a seemingly innocent youth and able to pass through their ranks without being recognised. That was one punch-up I was happy to avoid, knowing that most Texans observed the Second Amendment and would almost certainly be packing guns. Fidel Castro was not at all popular at the time!

We completed the tour of the States in Boston, and Jane and Sam, now one year old, joined me there with the intention of travelling onwards with me to Canada, to stay with friends during the spring and summer months while I completed the Canadian leg of the tour. Unfortunately the flight had upset Sam's body clock to such an extent that I had to spend the early mornings walking him around the Boston early-morning streets in his pushchair, waiting for him to fall asleep. Needless to say I got little sleep myself and had to resort to bedding down in my dressing room before the evening's performance.

The Canadian tour passed uneventfully for the most part, the only significant exception being in Montreal where, as an Englishman, my presence was not appreciated. At this time, the French contingent were agitating for independence from England, even going so far as to display their mood by blowing up the English red postboxes. They refused to speak English, and my less-than-adequate schoolboy French gave me away, resulting in several close encounters with furious French Canadians!

As I had been rejected from the cast to play in the film the MRA were to make (I think owing to my continuous rebellion and refusal to join their club), Jane and I decided to take a well-deserved rest by returning to the UK aboard the ocean liner Queen Elizabeth. Apart from Sam falling over and cracking his head during a particularly heavy storm, the cruise passed without incident and we were happy to be back in England. To some extent it was good to be back in the familiar grind of looking for work in London.

Chapter Four
CHANGING COURSE

DESPITE BEING AWAY FOR VIRTUALLY a year, my name and reputation still had some clout. Out of financial desperation I accepted an offer to star in a series entitled *United*, a football-based format for the BBC in which I had been asked to feature as the centre forward star player. It was so badly written and characterless that I was forced to rewrite much of my dialogue. Once again my ambition to write took over, and my efforts were so successful that when I refused to sign a new contract as an actor I was asked to join as lead writer!

So my writing career began again, albeit in a serial soap. I continued acting for a while; although the ever-present typecasting still bored me, I persevered in the vain hope that the broadcasters would see the result of their folly in attempting to climb onto the commercial American bandwagon. A vain hope indeed it proved to be, and I therefore leaned more towards a career change to becoming a full-time writer. In that way, hopefully, I could at least make some more substantial improvement in that area into which the business was inevitably travelling.

I began writing in earnest and wrote several plays for *Thirty-Minute Theatre*, most notably *The Timekeepers* and *'Twas on a Sunday Morning* starring Billie Whitelaw and Alec McCowen. My first major play, *Yob and Nabob*, which I wrote in a twenty-four-hour writing spate was accepted – verbatim. Not a word was changed. As I had been cast in Emlyn Williams' last stage play, so too was he cast in my first TV play! What a compliment. My play was greeted with great enthusiasm by the critics and I was immediately commissioned by the Head of BBC Drama to write another.

My second contribution was, however, far too adventurous philosophically. Called *Quietus*, it concerned those moments when one is about to die and one's life flashes before one in a subliminal rush. I was far too young as a writer to take on such a subject; and the BBC technology was, at that time, unable to realise satisfactorily the necessary visual images.

By this time Jane and I had adopted a second child – a girl, Kate – and were planning for a third, Benjamin. But despite my burgeoning writing career, times were tough; although I was still taking the odd acting role, we were always short of money. I therefore started to supplement my income by using another of my interests: fishing! I bought a boat and moored it in Folkestone harbour, near to where my in-laws had recently bought a clifftop Edwardian house. This house, appropriately named Abbotscliffe, had served during the Second World War as a radar station. I had to apply my building talents to repair the exterior walls: a difficult job since it all had to be done high up on a ladder. The other problem was that the house, being on top of the high cliffs, was wide open to the howling gales that frequented that area, and as fast as I applied the cement it blew off in my face! Also, part of the newly fitted conservatory blew off and was carried three miles or so, ending up in Dover in some poor unfortunate's back garden!

I ran the fishing boat at weekends, ferrying amateur anglers from London to Folkestone in a tatty Ford Transit van which I had converted as a minibus, taking them out to sea for the day and driving them back to London. This was a tough and exhausting job, but it was a living. If we had a good day at sea and a big catch I would purchase all of the newspapers from the local vendor and sell the catch to the public around the harbour. Thus my fishing customers got their day's entertainment for nothing and I made a little more profit. Another lesson from my enterprising childhood!

The chronology of this time now becomes a little blurred because a disastrous event happened which affected both Jane and me. Whilst I was away working on a documentary film on an aircraft carrier in Portsmouth, our third child, Benjamin, who was only six months old, contracted pneumonia and died in the middle of the night. I was recovering from a hard day's filming, but Jane's horrified calls for help woke me up fast enough. I tried to revive Benjamin with CPR but had to rush the infant to the hospital. I am sure they tried, as I had done, to breathe some life back into him; but he was eventually declared dead.

This threw me into a spiral of depression and confusion and effectively destroyed what little faith I had in the existence of a loving God. It didn't shake Jane's faith, but inevitably a rift began between us, particularly as I refused to attend the religious funeral. I preferred to stay at home with our other two children, not wishing to subject them – nor in truth myself – to the emotional ceremony.

The family had been hit so badly that I wanted to move out of the home where Benjamin had died. I found another dilapidated house, previously the home of Mabel Lucy Atwell, facing Barnes Common. This edifice was large enough to accommodate our ever-expanding family, but again it was a wreck. I would have to virtually gut it – and again drain out the flooded basement! It had a beautiful aspect overlooking the common and was ideal for the children. It was, however, another financial challenge: for, apart from the costs of the conversion, I had to take out a mortgage.

To provide financially for this I took on a commission as one of the team of writers on the soap *Crossroads*, which meant weekly journeys by train to the Midlands (over a breakfast of kippers and gin and tonic!) for story conferences as well as writing a weekly half-hour script. This and my other commissions for the BBC kept the ship afloat.

Writing a soap requires both creative skill and speed. *Crossroads* was no different although we three writers, Terrance Dicks, Peter Ling and I, developed a collaborative method of communicating by telephone our story and character developments, virtually acting as each other's editors and shaping the story between us. It was a great trio of writing talent with trusting participants, and somehow made a relatively tedious and boring job quite acceptable; the camaraderie was great fun.

At the same time I converted the lower ground floor of our house into a separate flat which I rented out.

Our children by this time were growing up rapidly and nearing the end of their local prep school period, and it was decided that they should go to more upmarket boarding schools to continue their education. Another hit, but a necessary one, on the pocket! This didn't appeal to Sam because he loved his home life, and within a year or so we had to remove him to a more convenient school in London where he thrived.

My parents at this time were nearing their 'sell-by' date and their business was suffering, as they were, from the overuse of alcohol, their hard life and now their approaching old age. I therefore decided they should give up being publicans and move into London into our ground-floor flat. They didn't want to do this but it was necessary and I had to force the situation.

I suppose, like all children of my era, I felt it was an obligation and a duty to look after my ageing parents, although I had little in common with them. I had developed an entirely different life of my own and, in a sense, had moved up in the social scale. I owned my own house, had worked my way up in my profession (not the easiest task), had earned a reasonable living, Jane and I had 'created' a family and chosen to educate them in private schools and so on; all things my parents couldn't achieve. I had a kind of filial love for them, but my responsibility was more one inspired by duty. I felt more like a parent than a child.

As it worked out it gave them a few extra years in comparative peace and security, although it only curbed their drinking habit and didn't cure it. However, they enjoyed a couple of years of relative retirement. Eventually my father died of lung cancer, obviously caused by his smoking the lethal Woodbines and the long years spent serving in his smoke-filled bar. My mother survived a year longer, but drank more and more and eventually died, having collapsed while trying to climb into the downstairs window in the flat, drunk, and died of exposure in the cold night air. I was woken in the early morning by neighbours who saw her, and I carried her inside and tried to revive her, unsuccessfully. I was used to seeing death by this time but always it was a shock; and I determined, if I could possibly help it, nobody should die alone.

Chapter Five
THE GOOD DOCTOR

BEFORE I EXPLAIN HOW I became involved with *Doctor Who* and describe my experience of working on the series, it is instructive to take a look back at the fifty-year history of the world's longest running science-fiction TV show.

Television broadcasting as we know it in the UK commenced at Alexandra Palace in north London on November 2nd 1936 (the year I was born, seventy-seven years ago now) and, except for a break during World War Two, has continued ever since, with the studios at 'Ally Pally' being used for television programme production right up until 1981. The arrival of television changed British people's perception of the world and provided entertainment which previously had been limited to 'live' shows in theatres and films screened in cinemas.

However, television was initially only in black-and-white, and also had to be performed live as videotape recording of television images hadn't yet come into play. I remember as a young actor appearing in a BBC Wednesday Play, transmitted from Studio D at Lime Grove (the studio allotted to *Doctor Who* when it began production in 1963). As the studio was too small to contain the number of sets required, we also had to use a second studio on another floor, separated by stairs. To move from one set to another the actors had to run from floor to floor up and down the stairs, and if they had a costume change it had to be done 'on the run' during the live broadcast. When the plays were repeated later in the week we had to perform exactly the same thing for a second live transmission!

I remember on one particular show I had a very quick costume change and, in my haste, forgot to button the flies on my trousers. I spent an entire scene 'flying half-mast' and wondering why the costume lady was frantically gesticulating about my embarrassing condition! I am happy to say that the 'bird didn't leave the nest', for I believe I was probably too out of breath and nervous to do anything about it anyway! I don't think anyone noticed.

So, to most of us involved, television was simply a way of broadcasting our live performances to audiences who were fortunate enough to have a receiving set. Recording and editing were still a dream in some engineer's eye.

The first television set I saw was a six-inch screen mounted in a large wooden box, but it was an exciting experience by which, from then on, I was fascinated. The pictures were black-and-white, but they moved! I wasn't able to afford a set of my own until much later, at which time I began to realise that this was the way my world of entertainment was going to be changed – and I was to be involved one way or another in that change.

I enjoyed the theatre for its immediacy, its relationship with a live audience, and it wasn't until recording and editing became a part of television production that its true potential really fired me up. I had done a number of films, and the possibility of improving one's performance as it progressed with frequent 'takes' was a great advantage in trying to attain perfection, or at least eliminate mistakes. This is where television fell short and it wasn't until recording and editing became the norm that it gave serious competition to movies.

In 1962, the BBC's Head of Light Entertainment commissioned the Head of the Script Department, Donald Wilson, to prepare a report on the viability of producing a new science-fiction series for television. Around the same time, the Canadian TV executive Sydney Newman was tempted away from ABC to take up the position of Head of Drama at the BBC, officially joining the Corporation at the beginning of 1963.

Taking advantage of the research Wilson's department had completed, Newman, along with Wilson and BBC staff writer C. E. Webber, oversaw the creation of what would prove to Britain's first durable science-fiction television series. After much development work, also involving major contributions from the show's first producer Verity Lambert and script editor David Whitaker, *Doctor Who* was launched on November 23rd 1963 with a story titled 'An Unearthly Child', written by Anthony Coburn.

Sydney Newman's description of the Doctor as a 'hobo in space' was obviously a difficult and vague idea to come to terms with; for hoboes, unlike tramps (who work only when they are forced to) are workers who wander, who travel by choice. I think that Sydney's description was simply undeveloped, too flippant, ignoring the intellectual curiosity of the Doctor which was the driving force of his determination to travel through time and space in an inexorable desire to experience, to observe and to learn. Having stolen the TARDIS, he was like a kid with a new toy; he knew how to wind it up and start it but couldn't control where it would go!

The character of the Doctor was like an onion, with layers peeled off every time it was explored by the creative writers, and with the interpretation by each actor that subsequently played him both revealing and building it a little more each time. The Doctor's origins were initially shrouded in mystery, which was useful since the precise format and construction, let alone the image, had not been determined. All that was known about him in the series' early days was that he was an eccentric alien traveller of great intelligence who battled injustice while exploring time and space. It was eventually revealed that he had been on the run from his own people, the Time Lords of the planet Gallifrey, who were introduced in the final story to feature Patrick Troughton as the Doctor, 'The War Games', which I produced.

The Doctor has the ability to renew his physical body when worn out or dying. This was introduced into the storyline as a way of continuing the series when the writers were faced with the departure of lead actor William Hartnell in 1966, and has continued ever since to be a useful major element of the series, allowing for the recasting of the lead actor when the need arises. The transition from one actor to another is written into the plot of the show as 'regeneration', a life process of the Time Lords, through which the character of the Doctor takes on a new body and a new personality. The initially irascible and slightly sinister Doctor of William Hartnell quickly mellowed into a more compassionate figure when Patrick Troughton took over the character after the first regeneration. Unfortunately, this improvement of the Doctor's personality didn't really progress in the stories, and it was largely left to Patrick to 'unpeel' another layer of the onion and reveal to us more of the character.

The Doctor almost always shares his adventures with companions, who are useful in dramatic terms as they provide a figure with whom the audience can identify and a 'wall' for the Doctor to bounce his ideas and thoughts off. Though not always considered a companion, Brigadier Lethbridge-Stewart, played by the actor Nicholas Courtney, was a recurring character in the series; he and UNIT (my addition to the format of the series which I created in 'The Invasion' to relieve the workload of the Doctor) appeared regularly during the Third Doctor's tenure, and have continued to appear or be mentioned in the revival of the show and its spin-offs. In 'The Wedding of River Song', an episode of the sixth series of the revived show, the Brigadier is said to have died peacefully in his sleep, following Courtney's death earlier in 2011. So my creation of UNIT as an addition to the format was pivotal to its continued success over many years!

Throughout the development of the show in its first year, it suffered the same type of growing pains as all new series that haven't been properly or thoughtfully formatted. To be fair it was, and had to be, a creative journey of discovery; but those in charge of its development had little conclusive idea of exactly what the series was about, least of all the actor playing the lead role. William Hartnell could hardly be blamed for this, for even the creators had little to go on except that it was to be a science-fiction series about a 'hobo in space'! The result was in some ways a confusing and undisciplined mish-mash of everyone's ideas; and it was no surprise, then, that the series at first bemused the audience and came close to cancellation. It was not until the advent of Terry Nation's creation – the Daleks – that *Doctor Who* took off and the audience figures jumped from under six million to over ten million.

When Sydney Newman commissioned the series, he specifically did not want to perpetuate the cliché of the 'bug-eyed monster' of science fiction. However, monsters were popular with audiences and so became a staple of *Doctor Who*. Almost since the beginning, some have become iconic monsters, such as the most popular, the Daleks and the

Cybermen, and many others such as the Ice Warriors and Ogrons, as well as villains such as the Master, the Rani and the Black Guardian.

The Dalek race, which first appeared in the show's second serial in 1963, were *Doctor Who*'s oldest antagonists and arose on the planet Skaro. Later stories revealed that the Daleks were originally humanoid Kaleds, mutated by the scientist Davros and housed in tank-like mechanical armour shells. Their chief role in the plot of the series, as they frequently remark in their instantly recognisable metallic voices, is to 'exterminate' all beings inferior to themselves.

When the original Dalek script was presented to Newman and Wilson it was immediately rejected because of the aforementioned boycott on 'bug-eyed monsters', or BEMs. This caused something of a crisis because Donald Wilson was adamant that the Dalek script (originally titled 'The Mutants') shouldn't be made, but no other alternative scripts were ready. So Terry Nation's serial 'The Daleks', introducing the eponymous aliens who became the series' most popular monsters, and responsible for the BBC's first merchandising boom, had to be made – needs must!

In fact it was the children's fascination with the fantasy nature of the monsters, coupled with the adult audience's intrigue and interest in the science-fiction aspects of the series, that determined its future structure. An odd combination of content, but one which produced the viewing figures that sustained the show.

For me personally the creation of the Daleks as antagonists, although a great and successful story concept, was poorly realised simply because a dustbin on wheels was the most impracticable of villains since the creature could not negotiate stairs! Its aggressive attitude, however, was what appealed to the children, and when the Daleks were reintroduced in a later story they were given the ability to elevate their ungainly dustbin-like bulk.

I wonder how much of the success of these Dalek stories can be attributed to people like designer Ridley Scott, who was on the BBC staff at the time and went on to direct the massively successful science-fiction movies *Alien* and *Blade Runner*; did he have a hand in them? Creative people of this nature do tend to talk and exchange ideas together.

There is no doubt though that all involved in the production of the phenomenal success of the Daleks put their own ideas into the pot. It was a sharp turnaround, and an unforgettable moment for the audience; and one of those strokes of luck for the production, for it triggered the imagination and interest of its audience despite the fact, or maybe because of it, that it scared the pants off the children and sent them hiding behind the sofa in terror!

'The Daleks' was one of *Doctor Who*'s longer serials, running for seven episodes. To my recollection the first four or so episodes played well, but extending it beyond that meant the inclusion of unbelievable plot tricks and padding made necessary because there was nothing else 'ready to go'! However, it created enough interest to build a very sizeable audience, who suffered its inadequacies, to give the series a lease of life and build up a substantial financial return from the merchandise it created.

Unfortunately Raymond Cusick, the designer who created the image of the Daleks and designed the things, unjustly got little fiscal reward, since he was BBC staff and all of the merchandise returns, except those due to Terry Nation as the creator, went back into the BBC coffers, none of it actually reaching the poor beleaguered production team who were obliged to create *Doctor Who* programmes on minimal budgets. The main bulk of this windfall was swallowed up in the general morass and went towards funding other, perhaps less deserving, productions. The BBC management obviously failed to see the possibilities of *Doctor Who*, which would have benefited from a substantially increased budget, and it remained a poor relation – a children's series.

If I remember rightly, the first Dalek designs as described to me were a ludicrous Michelin-Man-type creation resembling a stack of tyres: hardly frightening and really rather comical! Common sense prevailed and Cusick came up trumps, despite the inability of the beasties to do anything but skate around on wheels. In fact, I remember piloting one myself when I took several of the cast to Dublin one Christmas on a *Doctor Who* PR stunt to entertain the patients in a children's hospital; a very uncomfortable experience, and hot as hell. Such was my inability to control the contraption with any accuracy that I spent a large part of the time careening from one hospital bed to another, much to the amusement of the children! That's one Dalek that didn't frighten them!

With the success of the Daleks, and the viewing figures they created, the show's future was assured; and whenever audience numbers started to lapse, the cry went out for the return of the Daleks. However, it wasn't always from the pen of Terry Nation, who presumably was enjoying the fruits of his labour from the merchandising returns which allowed him the luxury of deciding what he wrote thereafter and when. David Whitaker was the script editor during this period, and – if I know anything about script editing *Doctor Who* – then I am sure that David contributed his not insubstantial creative talents to most of Terry Nation's offerings. Dennis Spooner, amongst others, also contributed as a writer of some of the Dalek stories.

So I believe it wasn't the stories themselves or the science-fiction basis of the series that made it such a success, but the terrifying beasties with their appearance and their grating mechanical voices – the very creatures that poor old Sydney Newman wanted to exclude – that attracted the audiences.

On the other hand, it was also the talent of people such as the director Douglas Camfield, designer Barry Newbury and film cameraman Peter Hamilton, who made such things believable (all of whom I was fortunate enough to work with at the BBC), and who contributed in the most difficult circumstances, on minimal budgets that were the backbone of the series; outstanding creative and talented craftsmen. Why is it that those who control the coffers, the accountants or whoever, never understand that success of this nature is down to the creativity and devotion of its participants and nothing to do with their number-crunching?

The Doctor has many characteristics that are similar to those of humans but in essence a human he is not. In fact, if one considers it logically, the Doctor is more akin to most of the monsters invented as his foes because, like them, he is an alien from an obscure planet. In many ways he is distinctly non-human, with two hearts, the ability to regenerate his physical form when necessary and an encyclopaedic scientific knowledge which never seemed to surprise anyone – except those who came up against him. It certainly took me by surprise and I had to constantly read *Scientific American* to keep up!

The only real difference between the Doctor and his foes is that he has no wish to conquer the world and take over the universe – he is the 'good guy'! His affinity with human beings leads us to speculate that somewhere out there, perhaps in another parallel, the Time Lords actually represent the future evolution of human beings and that, as a time traveller, the Doctor has simply stepped back a pace. It would be a useful concept to explore and explain some of the anomalies which have cropped up.

The Doctor is able when necessary to make use of an arsenal of technical equipment, which most famously includes the indispensable (and seemingly endlessly versatile) sonic screwdriver. I am told by my children that I invented this, as an easy way out of inexplicable and difficult small practical scientific problems, and that I made a prototype in my home workshop; I would think it has gone through many upgrades since then!

Far from being a hobo, the Doctor is in fact a genius far beyond our understanding; and may he remain so, for that is his fascination. To attempt to describe him in any other way is pointless, for he develops all the time. However, he is also a renegade, a disenchanted intellectual 'on the run' from what he considers to be the boring and tedious world of organisation; an enchanting oddball in our view, but, to the mighty Time Lords, a naughty truant. He is the embodiment of good, fighting a continual battle against evil and injustice. Children understand this basic concept because it is one which they have to appreciate as they grow towards maturity as adults; often, during the process, experiencing what they see as injustice. Growing up is difficult, even when you *are* grown up, since in many ways even adults still appear to be children!

Chapter Six

Baptism of Fire: The New Boy on *Doctor Who*

It was my term at *Crossroads* that elbowed me into joining the BBC as a trainee script editor, since I was now perceived as a writer and not an actor. Innes Lloyd, the then producer of *Doctor Who*, was about to leave the series, Peter Bryant the story editor was due to take over as producer, and word was out that a new story editor would be required.

I had spent fifteen years as an actor in the worlds of theatre, film and eventually television, then graduating to writing – giving much amusement to producers and story editors, not because of my command of comedic writing but simply because of my frequent and numerous spelling mistakes! I have improved a little, not only because of my determination to avoid such embarrassment but also because I needed people to be able to read my scripts (at least the serious ones) without guffaws of laughter! Nowadays I rely on the computer spell-check.

I wrote everything from Wednesday Plays to episodes of TV series like *Z Cars*, *The Sweeney*, adaptations of novels and even soap operas. I learned the real craft of story writing and TV drama writing the hard way, by contributions to what I consider to be the toughest challenge to any writer: that of creating and writing half-hour dramas for *Thirty-Minute Theatre*. I therefore had a good preparation and experience of writing dramas before joining as trainee story editor of *Doctor Who*.

Shaun Sutton was the Head of Serials and it was he who interviewed me for the job. He asked me if I was a fan of the series and what I thought of the show. My answer was that it obviously had a wide appeal and that the millions of people, young and old, who watched it, fascinated, couldn't be wrong; but quite what its specific attraction was I couldn't say, except that audiences found the 'Everyman' characterisation of the good Doctor appealing. It was also science fiction, which at that time was an unusual platform for TV drama – particularly one orientated to children although children are much more amenable to fantasy ideas.

I thought *Doctor Who* was a great idea for a science-fiction series and with a very interesting and commanding leading character, and Sydney Newman's idea of him as a 'hobo in space' was creatively fascinating, but there was little else to it. The real background of the Doctor as a renegade Time Lord had not yet been developed; in fact this was not revealed until my production of 'The War Games'.

In any event I got the job, and with this appointment began what proved to be a baptism of fire as producer/writer/story editor – my two years with *Doctor Who*. It may not have been the most momentous time in the convoluted development of my career, but it was the period that defined me as a writer, story editor and finally a producer. It coincided with what I consider the most successful period of the show's evolution from a basic idea to a highly popular and financially rewarding series for the BBC, and involved the two most creative lead character actors who were the definitive *Doctor Who* stars: Patrick Troughton and Jon Pertwee.

I joined the series as assistant story editor excited by the possibility of being involved in this new entertainment medium. I was the youngest writer/story editor and eventually producer to work on the series and I had, I believe, a somewhat closer appreciation of what our younger viewers preferred. However, the others on the production team had a definitely adult approach to the stories, and little understanding of the basics of the science fiction which most of the stories and development relied upon. Nobody it seemed could understand the 'hobo in space' concept of the good Doctor; this was left largely to the actor cast in the role to inject his own interpretation.

With my extensive experience in the world of entertainment I was convinced that nothing would happen without the creative input of the writers, as that is where it all begins, and so of necessity I concentrated mainly on the writers' contribution to the *Doctor Who* series. The writing, the stories and the basics of the characters are the building blocks that all other creative elements rely upon: the producers, directors, the actors, the designers and so on all rely on the written word for their inspiration and guidance.

The show was originally intended to appeal to a family audience, a drama with an educational component, using time travel as a means to explore scientific ideas and famous moments in history. This was a big mistake in my opinion. If history is a record of past events then surely logically, in a contemporary drama, it would be nonsense to propose changing them? I refused to consider such stories.

Since it was not possible for me to screen past episodes, as the shows couldn't be recorded, my first six to eight weeks when I joined the *Doctor Who* production team were spent learning the ropes, which meant spending around eighteen hours a day reading back scripts and trying to understand and come to grips with the twists and turns which the various contributing writers proposed, while at the same time attending first rehearsals, read-throughs, final runs before studio recording and the recording days themselves. Every week! This was a terrifying schedule, suffering (as it had done since the show's beginnings) from the lack of prepared and acceptable scripts and storylines which continued to make life difficult for everyone – made worse by the fact that the production team had to make forty-two half-hour shows a year! The weekly rep of television!

Several of the scripts previously commissioned by Peter Bryant and Innes Lloyd were certainly not to my taste, or my professional standards, but as a lowly assistant script editor I had to keep my opinions to myself and my mouth shut – for the time being! When Innes Lloyd eventually left the series as producer and Peter Bryant took over the mantle, I was stepped up to be the official story editor and could therefore have my say to some extent.

The main problem I was confronted with was that not many of the stories developed by Peter as story editor were acceptable, or at least appealed to my taste or ideas on the way the series should develop. It appeared that *Doctor Who* had been seen as a children's serial, whereas it was far too complex in structure and content for that. Neither was it an adult series of stories, although the audience mostly comprised parents who watched it with their children, being fascinated by the science-fiction element. Being neither one thing nor the other I suppose it fell into the bracket of being an amorphous 'family show' and was therefore cursed with having to please both children and adults at one and the same time: a difficult brief for, as Winston Churchill said, 'You can please some of the people some of the time but not all of the people all of the time!'

Sydney Newman had by this time departed the BBC and returned to his native Canada, but his interest in the development of his 'baby' remained and he insisted on receiving video copies of each production for him to comment on – which he did. His comments were not at all complimentary since the series had developed way outside his brief of a 'hobo in space' – not that even Sydney knew exactly what he meant by that!

I therefore had to waste a great deal of valuable time rewriting scripts, to make them at least interesting and in an attempt to make them credible (and acceptable to Patrick Troughton and the directors and eventually the audience), time which could otherwise have been spent encouraging writers to treat the series in a more creative way.

Writers at that time, apart from the few creative stalwarts, treated *Doctor Who* as simply a means to earn easy money, writing what they still perceived as a children's series of serialised stories. They soon learned otherwise under my type of script editorship, and I am afraid I must have ruffled not a few feathers and made several professional enemies and been dubbed with several unprintable names! I'm not sure whether Sydney approved or not, because he had moved back to his native Canada by this time.

The pressure on all concerned was monumental, producing forty-two episodes per year with just two weeks' holiday and the remaining time used for filming exterior location inserts. It was not surprising that so many mistakes were made, from scriptwriting to design, from plots to dialogue and most of all in the studio recording and subsequent lack of any opportunity to rectify such mistakes in editing. Fortunately by the time I joined *Doctor Who* they had at least mastered the ability to record and to carry out a very primitive form of editing (which in those days was a basic 'cut and join' process using a razor blade and sellotape on the two-inch videotapes), otherwise the frequent basic mistakes in recording would have remained and indeed been transmitted! Digital editing did not arrive until a much later date. The studio recording had to be virtually 'as live'; shows and scenes were only halted in recording if really bad mistakes were made, and joined together later with the crude editing facilities available. However, that is the way that all such shows at that time developed.

I understand that one of the frequent problems in the show's early days was William Hartnell's inability to learn the lines he was presented with and his fluffing of such unfamiliar dialogue; a recurrence that, although comic, was a source of embarrassment for all concerned with the production. I do not know if the audiences noticed this or whether it was accepted as deliberate and a part of his character! Certainly his irascible and bad-tempered personality came through as part of his character on screen which continued until the end of his time as the good Doctor. With the change of lead actor from William Hartnell to Patrick Troughton the Doctor's on-screen personality changed and the shows started to develop, as did experimentation in the nature and production of the series giving it a more science-fiction style and content. The arrival of new technology also improved the 'look' of the series and reduced the number of apparent on-screen mistakes.

Nevertheless, and mostly because of the lack of time, the script plotting and characterisation and dialogue still had some way to go to 'grow up' and be acceptable. With my picking up of the responsibility for most the daily script-editing operation from Peter Bryant, as he was preparing to take over the role of producer, I realised that in order to create some space and to ease the pressure I had to try and have a number of prepared scripts ready for production well in advance.

Peter had joined from BBC radio, where he had been producer of the daily radio soap, *Mrs Dale's Diary*. He had little knowledge of writing for TV drama and therefore little understanding of the role of script editing or selection of stories, their construction and execution, and certainly no knowledge or appreciation of any stories that were science-fiction based. Consequently the scripts that I was left with had little merit, and a good deal of my time was involved with restructuring and rewriting to make them acceptable as well as attempting to build up a backlog of stories and scripts: a Herculean task which meant that the eighteen-hour day became the norm and one which sapped my energy and enthusiasm for anything so radical as a change in the format or type of stories.

This was an annoying and frustrating state of affairs and the quality of the scripts, and the dialogue that already-commissioned scripts contained, became a source of irritation not just for me but also for Patrick Troughton who spent a great deal of his rehearsal time complaining about the inadequacies and attempting to rewrite his dialogue – and he was right. Thus I was forced into a never-ending rewriting situation which annoyed both me and the unfortunate writers concerned. I had little or no time to explain to the writers why the rewriting was necessary, for I was forced by the time constraints of the production process to undertake it myself. This also gave me little time to meet with new writers and explore new ideas, let alone confer with the current writers. Time was our enemy always.

The Troughton years from 1966 to 1969 were therefore the height of my 'baptism of fire', for I not only had to spend a great deal of time keeping the current production ship afloat and giving a lot of attention to the current writers, but also, whenever I could, feed in new story ideas, create ideas to develop the series format and introduce new writers. I realised that this process was too much for one over-pressurised person and decided that what we needed was uncontaminated 'new blood'.

I voiced this problem to Betty Willingale, a very knowledgeable and astute lady from the then BBC Script Department. She was the font of all knowledge about writers and the techniques of the craft as far as I was concerned, and we decided that I should create a new post, under her auspices and guidance, to recruit new writers, to educate them in the art of TV scriptwriting and hopefully bring in new blood; her department would pick up the tab! This I did, on the one hand to give new writers some experience of what writing for TV drama production was all about, but also to provide another pair of hands and a new brain as mine was fast collapsing under the pressure.

I therefore asked Terrance Dicks, one of the writers with whom I had worked on *Crossroads*, to join me in my previous capacity as trainee script editor. He, I knew, had a quick-fire and clinical brain from his time working on soap operas – also products of the pressure-cooker world of weekly TV drama – and wouldn't be fazed by the problems and hard work involved in scripting *Doctor Who*.

I also called in another *Crossroads* writing compatriot, Peter Ling, to contribute different ideas for the series. Although he was reluctant to write in this unfamiliar territory of science fiction, I persuaded him just to use his incredibly fertile imagination and his knowledge of children's fiction, and he came up with the fascinating idea of 'The Mind Robber', using many of the fictional characters from children's traditional stories. This was just the kind of 'out of left field' story idea that I was looking for and I immediately commissioned the reluctant Peter to write a four-part story.

Prior to this, however, Peter Bryant had asked Kit Pedler, the creator of the Cybermen, to provide a new set of stories in the belief that the silver-clad semi-robots had further potential as a new and terrifying antagonist for the Doctor. Kit was a delightful man, an ophthalmologist who though not a writer was very knowledgeable about cybernetics; and, working in collaboration with Gerry Davis, who *was* a writer, they had created the Cybermen between them. Kit readily agreed to Peter's request and came up with a half page of an idea, but no real story or plot. However, Gerry Davis was busy elsewhere, and in any case had already had a bellyful of *Doctor Who*. So, we had a credible villain but no story or writer. Peter insisted that the idea was worth developing, but search though I might I could not find a writer capable – nor indeed knowledgeable or willing –enough to take on the Cybermen's rebirth. Peter's answer was: 'Well, you know the series and the script of the previous Cybermen story, so *you* write the episodes!'

As if I wasn't busy enough, this instruction from my producer couldn't have come at a worse time, as I was preparing to take a well-earned rest during a break in production. However, Peter insisted that it was necessary and commissioned me to write the script, and the two weeks I had prepared for the regeneration of my battered brain had to be devoted to creating the story of 'The Invasion' – in eight parts!

It was whilst writing this Cyberman epic that I invented UNIT, the United Nations Intelligence Taskforce, since the Earth's invasion by Cybermen, whose bodies are mechanical but whose brains are neurosurgically treated to remove emotion and pain, required a credible force to combat it. I was fortunate enough to have Douglas Camfield allotted as the director for this epic; he was a very knowledgeable man regarding the Army and helped considerably with the formation of UNIT. As it happened we had met previously because I wrote 'The Invasion' before the production of 'The Web of Fear', the Yeti story, which he also directed.

Around this time we were having big troubles with Patrick Troughton, who was suffering from fatigue and pressure of work, so we had to find some way of reducing the workload for him. As I had already created UNIT for the upcoming Cybermen story, we decided that they should be introduced in 'The Web of Fear'; and so Colonel (as he was then, subsequently to become Brigadier) Lethbridge-Stewart made his debut and became later, with UNIT, a running part of the format. (I am still fighting the BBC over the copyright for my creation some forty-odd years later!)

With this effective introduction of other major lead players, Patrick's workload did indeed become reduced; but by now the damage was done and he was becoming difficult to work with. Maybe he thought it was a criticism of his performance, which it certainly wasn't, but in any event he became almost impossible to reason with. Having inherited a backlog of poorly executed scripts too expensive to discard, and with nothing with which to replace them anyway, we were forced to produce them, which didn't help.

At this point I think it is necessary to spend a little time discussing the problems between script editor and producer.

Peter Bryant was a very engaging and likeable fellow who had come from being an actor in TV soap opera in the early days to being, as already mentioned, producer of a radio soap. He saw everything from the point of view of an actor and judged everything from that position. Television for him had been a live performance, much like the theatre, and he did not appreciate nor understand this 'new' medium or its possibilities, particularly with *Doctor Who*, as a science-fiction based series of stories. Consequently, when I realised this, I had to bone up on the 'new medium' and the technical possibilities with regard to stories and scripts. This meant that I had to take over certain of those areas of production in addition to my role as script editor.

Most of our production meetings with Peter, despite us having adjoining offices, took place in the BBC bar or at lunch over yet another bottle of wine! Peter had a distinct penchant for Teacher's Scotch Whisky and a capacity beyond the norm. Overindulgence, however, did not improve his memory or logical thinking; and therefore repetition, in sober moments, was the order of the day.

Peter, I realised, had taken on the job with *Doctor Who* as a stepping-stone to greater things in his career at the BBC. He had ambitions in adult drama which *Doctor Who*, as a perceived 'family show', couldn't afford him; but he had been preparing another series pilot with another set of writers. He had esablished a relationship with the RAF's PR operation and was planning to make an action series pilot brought to him by two other writers which he asked me to review. I did, but couldn't work up any enthusiasm for it since it was a ludicrous plot and badly written. He asked me to story-edit it, but I felt that my current workload was too crowded and I refused. It was a kind of 'Boy's Own' story and bore no resemblance to reality at all, which as an ex-RAF chap I knew a little about.

Peter finally appreciated my reasoning and asked me to write a completely new story so as not to lose this opportunity of the cooperation and goodwill of the RAF, since making it would involve travelling to the Far East under the RAF's auspices. He asked me to participate, which meant I would have to travel to Hong Kong and Singapore to prepare and research the story and write the new scripts. This was irresistible and I agreed, and I created and wrote two pilot episodes of the series, titled *SPAIR*.

I won't go into this exciting adventure except to say that Peter, apart from being excellent at PR with the RAF, as usual passed all production details to me! This set the scene for our future relationship on *Doctor Who* and I virtually took over as producer to all intents and purposes, as well as commanding the writer and script editor post. Thank God for my foresight in bringing Terrance Dicks on board, which somewhat relieved the pressure of my obligations on *Doctor Who*. Following the production of *SPAIR* we then returned to the 'real world' of *Doctor Who* where, owing to my absence, the script backlog had hardly improved despite Terrance's hard work.

Even as a lowly 'sprog' (I have never understood the derivation of that strange word!) in the RAF I was not susceptible to taking orders, and I was soon upped to the rank of acting sergeant where I was able to pass on orders instead of taking them! Nothing had changed, and I rebelled if I strongly objected to the production decisions that were made in *Doctor Who*, as was my right and duty so to do. It didn't make me any friends though! However, the things I objected to were changes in storyline or dialogue, changes that were made thoughtlessly by actors who wanted only to learn the written lines, not fall over the furniture and take their fee.

I can't stand thoughtless laziness, so recruiting Terrance Dicks, who was as diligent as I was, made life a little easier. In addition, and under the auspices of dear old Betty Willingale, I pulled in another two would-be writers to learn the ropes and to cover most of the unsolicited but possibly useful offerings and report on them in précis form. I'm not sure if it was worth it, but at least it was one way for them to get a taste of what goes on in production and relieved me of countless wasted hours of reading.

The problem still remained, however, since there was no 'Bible' – a basic set of directions about style and content for writers to follow. I had yet to put a firm understanding in place concerning the format of the series and the direction I wanted it to take.

Chapter Seven

FORMAT RECREATION/ADDITION: THE BIRTH OF UNIT

SCRIPT EDITORS PROVIDE A CRITICAL overview of the series or serial, based upon a detailed format and style with running characters within each story, and liaise with the producer. Script editors must have a particular insight into the structure of screenplays, and the effect that different types of narrative have on audiences. Their opinions must be valid within the context of the entire process. They must mediate between the writer's creative desires and impulses, and the commercial and practical imperatives of the marketplace.

Because of the varied nature of their work, script editors often have a keener insight into the structure of screenplays than the writers, and should help them to explore the various possibilities open to them. They usually have proven analytical skills and a comprehensive knowledge of dramatic and screenwriting theories which they can use to help writers to determine suitable storylines and identify and correct any problems within them. They can explain the potential consequences of choices, and help to strengthen and develop storylines to the point whereby they can be seen as a draft construction of the script from which, if acceptable, a full script may be commissioned. It is their job to see that scripts are presented to the producer for his approval and acceptance and finally to the directors and lead actors who have to realise them.

Their first duty is to compile or agree an understandable 'Bible', a guide to the content suitable for inclusion as part of the developing series, with descriptions of running characters and ongoing elements required. The writers will follow the 'Bible' in creating storylines which they offer for discussion; if these are acceptable, the writers will be commissioned thereafter to complete their scripts in the number of designated episodes, joined together, more often than not, if it is an ongoing serialised story, by 'cliffhangers'.

Script editors should have a keen insight into all aspects of screenplay tone, genre, style, structure, character, plot, action and dialogue. They must understand the various development stages, including synopses, treatments and rough drafts. The best script editors provide screenwriters with a different perspective on their story, as well as reminding them of the production company's requirements. They need shrewd interpersonal and negotiation skills, and must be capable of liaising effectively between screenwriters and producers. It requires diplomatic skills!

The script editor will review the first draft scripts produced by the writer, comment on them and make suggestions for further drafts or if acceptable 'sign-off' on them following the producer's approval.

The director, selected by the producer, will be the next port of call for his comments on the scripts and any revisions he might request or observations he might make regarding technical adjustments.

Finally the script editor must, at the rehearsal stage, discuss with the actors or the director any dialogue they might require or suggest to be changed.

These were the guidelines I proposed for my own understanding and that of the producer when I first began work on *Doctor Who*. However, as a new boy, I was taking over an established process of production, however scrappy I considered it to be; and, as trainee story editor, I had to fit in with the establishment! I was told that 'time was our enemy', that we must allow any shortcomings in the scripts to be identified during rehearsals by the actors and the director, and that I would have to rewrite to change or accommodate them. There was no time to consult and instruct the writer to do this: it was my job! My suggestions to overcome this ongoing problem were ignored or brushed aside; I was told that scripts were my responsibility and that I must make the revisions under instruction of Peter Bryant, the actual story editor.

'The Web of Fear' was my first credited story-editing role, although I only took it on after the scripts had been commissioned and written. It was the first time I met the director Douglas Camfield, with whom I struck an immediate rapport. He was a very creative and professional director for whom I had great respect and admiration and with whom I had the pleasure of working several times more. Unfortunately, the script for 'The Web of Fear' was written by two writers who, although professional and creative, were very protective of their work and not prepared to listen to my suggestions as the script editor, since I had not commissioned their work. I had some considerable confrontations with them.

'The Web of Fear' was set largely in the London Underground which we were unable to get permission to shoot in. We therefore had to build the sets for the serial in the Ealing Film Studios. Not an easy task but the designer, David Myerscough-Jones, created his own highly convincing replica. He managed to suggest an apparent labyrinth of tunnels by means of a single large right-angled tunnel which Douglas, shooting imaginatively with a variety of lenses and camera angles, was able to use to represent the entire Underground network!

Indeed a letter of complaint was later received from London Underground alleging that filming had taken place on their property without permission: a true testament to the merits of Myerscough-Jones's designs and Douglas Camfield's direction of Peter Hamilton's camera work.

The dark and gloomy underground tunnels, cobwebs and engulfing mist created the feeling of being hunted by a relentless foe that will kill you when it catches you. These were the stuff of nightmares and were all cleverly exploited by Douglas. *Doctor Who* had, at its best, a quality that makes the viewer accept what he or she is seeing without questioning it.

Unfortunately the same couldn't be said for the monsters, the Yeti, who looked like overgrown and rather tatty teddy bears! The combination of Yeti and web in this story really makes no sense at all. Why should the Yeti have web-guns? – a fact that was simply accepted by the audience because such inexplicable things happened all the time in the series. Transporting the Yeti from the open spaces of the

Himalayas (where the Doctor and his companions had first encountered them in the story 'The Abominable Snowmen') to the familiar yet incongruous environment of the London Underground did, however, increase their menace a hundredfold and plugged into the hidden fears of millions of commuters and train users who have secretly wondered what might be lurking in those dark places, perfectly complemented by the superb dramatic and atmospheric direction of Douglas Camfield.

The serial had one major drawback in that the action had to be somewhat padded out over the six episodes; it would have been better off confined to four or at the most five episodes. 'The Web of Fear' managed to terrify on a basic level while still telling an exciting story; but it suffered, as most stories do in this series, by being padded out and stretched beyond its credible length, as well as from the slightly ridiculous monsters. This was one of the problems with most stories because 'buying time' was necessary in order to comply with the schedule.

However, my observations came too late to be taken note of and certainly too late for rewrites to accommodate them, except to insert the elements of UNIT and the characters involved in place of the ordinary Army contingent that the writers had used.

The basic story synopsis involved Jamie, the Doctor and Victoria experiencing some trouble with the TARDIS before landing in the London Underground. This was a highly complicated and unnecessarily extended plot line which, had I been script editor when the story was in its construction stages, would have been drastically cut, reducing it to a maximum of five episodes. Since the story was already well into the production stage on my taking over the mantle of script editor, however, I could do little about it other than putting my oar in, inserting UNIT earlier than expected and tinkering to make it realistic.

The next epic, 'Fury from the Deep', was another six-parter and equally well into the advanced stages of completion. Victor Pemberton was the commissioned writer and the story concerned the TARDIS landing in the sea off the eastern coast of England, near a beach which seemed to have an improbably large amount of sea foam as well as a major gas pipe marked 'Euro Sea Gas'. Another unnecessarily complicated story but at least one with a credible invading presence.

Fortunately, I didn't have a hand in it, since it would have required a major reconstruction of the storyline, again into a shorter episodic adventure. These two synopses I have noted as representative of the unnecessarily complicated storylines that were created simply to extend the serials and fill screen time.

I also had no option but to pick up 'The Wheel in Space'. The dialogue in this story, another which had been commissioned by Peter Bryant and Innes Lloyd, required a lot of work; and again I considered the story to be unnecessarily padded out to fill the screen time. It did, however, introduce the new girl companion in the Doctor's adventures, Zoe (played by the diminutive and charming Wendy Padbury) and gave me an insight into the Cybermen which I was grateful for.

'The Krotons' and 'The Dominators' (both of which had been commissioned by Peter and Innes and both of which I hated) I gave responsibility to Terrance to edit, since he felt he could improve them and they had been largely paid for and therefore had to be produced, whilst I worked on 'The Mind Robber' with Peter Ling. Bringing Terrance in certainly paid off and we were beginning to make headway in having prepared stories and scripts ready in advance.

'The Mind Robber' needed a suitable transition from the previous story, but unfortunately Peter Ling was unable to stretch his commission to five scripts and we had no budget to commission another writer. I therefore had to write the first episode as a transition from the previous story, 'The Dominators', and an introduction somehow to 'The Mind Robber'.

In defeating the Dominators the Doctor is forced to use the emergency unit to take the TARDIS away from danger and indeed out of reality itself. It lands in the middle of nowhere, a mysterious white void. As the Doctor fixes the TARDIS, Jamie and Zoe are lured outside and are confronted by white robots and curious images and memories of their past.

Being a transition script between two serials I had no budget, no sets other than the running ones and no money for other actors. So I had to work with a plain white backcloth and lots of smoke to create the 'void', and I found some old robot costumes which I had refurbished and used extras to operate them! It worked superbly and created in the audience's imagination a terrifying image as Zoe and Jamie relive their past horrors or memories (using clips from previous episodes). These images, it transpires, have been conjured up by the Master of the Land of Fiction, who is really no Master at all but under the control of the alien Master Brain. The Master has himself been abducted from the 'real' world and obviously wants to escape from his current position by forcing the good Doctor to take his place as the controller of the Land of Fiction.

The Doctor pitches his wits and knowledge against the Master Brain in an effort to release everyone from the fictional world and return to reality. The Doctor and the Master Brain fight it out in a weird battle using the fictional characters of Blackbeard the Pirate, Cyrano de Bergerac, D'Artagnan, Lancelot and so on in fictional improvisation.

This epic was one of the strangest and most creative climaxes in all *Doctor Who* stories up to that time, but it was magical in concept – only hindered by the punitive restrictions of budget! It has since proved to be one of the most popular: not perhaps when set against the popularity of the Daleks, but creatively far superior.

By the time that 'The Web of Fear' was ready to go into production, I had completed writing 'The Invasion', which Peter Bryant was very impressed with, and in the process had created the United Nations Intelligence Taskforce – UNIT. My suggestion that we use UNIT and the new characters of Lethbridge-Stewart and Sergeant Benton in all future stories set on Earth, to take some of the weight off the lead character, was accepted; and it was decided that UNIT should be written into the Yeti story, prior to the production of 'The Invasion'. I gave instructions to the writers to introduce these characters retrospectively, in place of the regular Army characters they had devised, and this was done. However, thereafter these two writers claimed the characters as their creation and subsequently were paid whenever they were used! As you can imagine I was somewhat annoyed to hear this when I came to claim them as part of my UNIT creation some years later! My copyright therefore was and still is being compromised.

My decision to bring *Doctor Who* down to earth was deliberate in order to get away from the seemingly endless parade of incredible and unbelievable monsters. My near neighbour at that time was Nigel Kneale, whose fantastic *Quatermass Experiment* science-fiction story I felt was more the direction that *Doctor Who* should take. I knew that Nigel was far too involved with major movie writing to be at all interested, but the 'feeling', the essence, of *Quatermass* was what I was looking for. Hence the creation of UNIT, which in fact was the forerunner of *The X Files*!

I really felt that I had pulled off the transformation when filming 'The Invasion' outside St Paul's, with Cybermen exiting from the steaming sewers opposite the Cathedral's entrance. Two unsuspecting blue-rinsed American tourists who were passing almost had apoplexy when they were suddenly confronted by the silver monsters! We were lucky that neither of the surprised good ladies had a weak heart, otherwise I don't know what the consequences would have been; in any event I'm sure that our insurance didn't cover us for such eventualities!

With this story, *Doctor Who* was now well and truly 'down to Earth'. The old 'historical epic' school was very much a thing of the past, although I had no doubt that subsequent producers and writers would bring them back since everybody, it seems, likes to think that they can change history!

I had slowly been replacing the previously commissioned stories to make way for the ongoing exploration of the new format. I only kept a watching brief on 'The Krotons', a story which I had given to Terrance Dicks to script-edit. (I have subsequently learned that Terrance hated the idea of bringing *Doctor Who* down to earth!) Although it was created and written by the prolific Robert Holmes, its monster wasn't credible and the story lacked substance: it was flat.

It wasn't long after this time that certain new developments began to appear in the technical departments of the BBC, such as CSO (Colour Separation Overlay) which replaced the previously widespread back-projection, and meant erecting a large green or blue screen onto which a static or moving background was overlaid by electronic means. By standing some three paces in front of the screen, the actors would be superimposed onto the background and appear as though they were actually 'there'. (Nowadays it is simply called 'green screen'.)

Another magical technical innovation was the beginnings of digital editing, which I won't attempt to explain other than to say that gone were the days of the razor blade and sellotape, to be replaced by this new technical electronic wizardry. Since Peter could hardly operate a simple radio, this was not for him; therefore it was down to me to explore!

Having undergone the traumatic experience of moving production to Television Centre, the next big event was the changeover to colour. This was by no means a simple exercise, since in black-and-white it didn't matter what colours we used on the sets or costumes. It now became necessary to consider the colour of everything we put on screen.

Moving everything into colour was an expensive pain and largely a problem for the set and costume designers, whose budgets were already minimal. One of the other big problems was that the TARDIS, one of our main running sets, had to be redesigned. The 'front office', of course, couldn't appreciate what difficulties this meant and our budgets remained the same. Thank God I had the luck (or was it foresight?) to move the setting of the series back to Earth and away from the unbelievable outer reaches of space with expensive and crazy monster designs or sets to cope with!

The change to colour production also necessitated changes to the programme's opening title sequence. Designer Bernard Lodge, who had produced the previous sets of titles used up until 'Spearhead from Space', originally intended to produce a new set using the same 'howlaround' technique that he had employed previously. Tests showed, however, that this method did not produce satisfactory results when used with colour equipment, and so the final set were produced in black and white before being manually tinted. These were completed in August 1969, a month before work began on the serial.

Many of those on the production team were getting less and less able or willing to cope with Patrick's outbursts, but I had a great empathy with his situation for I, too, had suffered over the first year and a half of my tenure from having to deal with poor scripts. The time restraints and minimal budgets finally affected all of us, not least of all Peter Bryant who began to resort to the comfort of his addiction to Mother Teacher's!

Chapter Eight
THE NEW DOCTOR

PATRICK TROUGHTON WAS, THROUGH TIREDNESS, exhaustion, frustration and sheer battle-weariness, resorting to frequent demonstrations of anger, and it was during one of these outbursts on a recording day that he stopped the shooting and he and Peter had a very public row on the studio floor. He finally threatened to resign as the good Doctor; and Peter, equally wound up (and well juiced up following his usual lunchtime indulgence), thoughtlessly accepted. This was a problem we needed like a hole in the head – and just as we were beginning to see the light at the end of the tunnel.

So, we then had to regenerate and recast the lead role of the Doctor; and, after a long and exhausting search, to everyone's surprise we announced that the new Doctor would be Jon Pertwee, more recognised by audiences as a comedian from the radio series *The Navy Lark* than as a serious actor!

It was left to me to engineer the changeover; and I decided to do so at the end of 'The War Games', which I had commissioned Terrance Dicks and Malcolm Hulke to write, since it had the potential to be a long-running serial with 'legs'! The problem with Patrick hit the fan in the middle of the story's development, so I asked the writers to extend it while we worked out who the new Doctor would be and how he would be introduced. Thus 'The War Games' went from being a six-part story to an eight and eventually to a ten while we recast.

The story has the Doctor uncovering a diabolic plot to conquer the universe, with brainwashed soldiers abducted from Earth and forced to fight in simulated environments, reflecting the periods in history whence they were taken. The aliens' aim is to produce a super-army from the survivors; to this end, they have been aided by a renegade from the Doctor's own race, calling himself the War Chief. Joining forces with rebel soldiers, who have broken their conditioning, the Doctor and his companions foil the plan and stop the fighting.

To give the regeneration a new twist, and to give the Doctor a more explicit history, I invented the Time Lords who arrive in the last episode of the serial when the Doctor admits he needs the help of his own people to return the soldiers to their own times – even though in contacting them he risks capture for his own past crimes including the theft of the TARDIS. After sending the message he and his companions attempt to escape, but are caught. Having returned the soldiers to Earth, the Time Lords erase Zoe and Jamie's memories of travelling with the Doctor, and return them to the point in time just before they entered the TARDIS. They then put the Doctor on trial as the renegade they perceive him to be and for stealing the TARDIS and breaking the rule of non-interference.

The Doctor presents a spirited defence, citing his many battles against the evils of the universe, which the Time Lords accept in part mitigation before announcing his punishment: to become an exile to Earth. The details of the operation of the TARDIS are wiped from his memory, and his next regeneration is imposed.

I was in the middle of producing 'The War Games' and planning the introduction of Jon Pertwee when another bombshell exploded. Peter Bryant had been called upon to take over as producer of the *Paul Temple* series, an international co-production based on the stories by Francis Durbridge. He jumped at it. This was another difficult development in my 'baptism of fire': not only was I producing a highly complex *Doctor Who* story, but I now also had to produce the next one which involved the introduction of a new leading man and the transformation of everything to colour.

There were no scripts prepared for this event and so I decided to use a Robert Holmes four-part story, 'Spearhead from Space', which introduced the Autons. As a further complication, the BBC studio staff decided to go on strike! If I couldn't record in the studio, we had no chance of meeting the transmission date; so I decided to rejig the scripts as a film and shoot the whole thing in 16mm.

Owing to budget restraints and to make this reorganisation feasible, we had to contain the whole shoot in one location. The production staff found the ideal situation: a BBC training facility, Wood Norton, previously a large country house, a weird place which (strangely) had alongside it an atomic shelter – a large and virtually characterless concrete space rather like an underground car park, apart from one large corridor-like room with an endless row of unfinished toilets!

We built the sets we required in the atomic shelter, as well as using the grand Victorian country house which had a superb array of rooms and outbuildings which we converted to a hospital set.

I then moved the whole production, lock stock and barrel, out to the location. There could be no objection from the striking studio staff because we were on film!

Jon Pertwee was delighted that we had been forced to revert to filming because the thought of doing our usual recording in the studios 'as live' terrified him as this was his first story as *Doctor Who*. Doing it on film meant that we could retake scenes if they were not acceptable. As it happened, Jon, ever the professional performer, didn't do one retake! He also injected a well-needed element of a more light-hearted attitude into the character – a reflection of his abilities as a comedy actor.

The idea of Autons, the antagonists of these particular stories, I got one day when I was travelling to the BBC Ealing Studio. I saw a shop window full of mannequins, and wondered what the effect would be if they all came to life. I then saw a factory where plastic dolls were being made. Just put the two together with the 'taking over the world' kind of story and there it was: the Autons! These developments I applied to Robert's script and it became one of the 'originals'. Unfortunately my idea for them smashing out of the plate-glass store windows had to be abandoned – the budget just wouldn't stand the cost of the windows' replacement! We had to make do with the sound effect of smashing plate-glass.

One of the great strengths of Robert Holme's writing, as with Nigel Kneale's, is its basis in reality. 'Spearhead from Space' demonstrates this admirably, and to a large extent mirrors his script for an early sci-fi movie, *Invasion*, directed by Alan Bridges in 1965. Just goes to prove that if you get a great idea it can be used again and again! The basic prospect of an invasion from space has been used many times, but in this case it also serves to introduce the new Doctor whilst at the same time telling a terrifying story. It was a joy working on it with Robert.

Jon Pertwee surprised and delighted everyone as the new Doctor. Slightly foppish but a delightful character, and everyone breathed a sigh of relief – and not a tantrum in sight! The Autons, also, turned out to be a spectacular success.

Meanwhile, the large series of stories that was 'The War Games' was shaping up well. It wasn't often that a story could sustain itself for ten episodes, but this one did and it really gave us breathing space, during which Terrance and I had built up a list of stories we wanted to pursue. However, my future with *Doctor Who* was about to be cut short.

Peter Bryant had by this time moved over to the big boys' club at the BBC Drama Series department where, as already mentioned, he was now producing the resurrected *Paul Temple* series, based on Francis Durbridge's original radio stories. The previous producer had decided to keep the stories in their 1930s period, but, with a substantial amount of money at stake, the German co-production company insisted that they be brought up to date.

This seemed like an impossible brief and Peter knew that he hadn't the right qualifications to do this; he therefore asked the Head of Series, Andy Osborn, and the Head of Serials, Shaun Sutton, that I join him as script editor. Given my past experience with Peter, I refused unless I was upgraded to the role of full joint producer. This was a step up in the production world of the BBC; and, as Peter agreed, I had no further excuses to refuse.

So (much to Jon Pertwee's chagrin, for he had really appreciated my help when he took over) I was forced to join Peter again, to rescue the big co-production series and the BBC's face! I was also in two minds as I was just beginning to enjoy working on *Doctor Who*; but the thought of editing and producing twenty-six hours of drama thrillers, with more realistic budgets, travelling all over Europe and liaising with all of the European companies to do so, just couldn't be resisted. I also got on well with the German co-producer, Nils Nilson, who became a good friend and my guide and mentor in Europe. It was Nils who really pushed me into making the move.

Thus it was that I found myself well and truly 'out of the frying pan'! However, with my past experience of working with the impossibly small budgets which the BBC insisted on, I engineered increased budgets and a further input from the co-production partners of an extra £4,000.

Peter Bryant just couldn't cope with these new and even more difficult production pressures and virtually left the whole thing to me, content with approving casting and having chats with the directors.

I meanwhile had to restructure and reformat the series of twenty-six one-hour thrillers to shoot all over Europe and bring it up to date. There were no scripts of any value, and the casting of the two lead actors was not exactly ideal; so I created another joint lead, Sammy, a cockney ex-villain, in order to undertake the more physically active requirements which updating the series required because Paul Temple himself was a more cerebral investigator. I wrote the first story of the new series to set the style and introduce the new character, Sammy, a reformed criminal and a breath of fresh-air reality.

I assumed that recruiting writers for this series of thrillers would be an easier task than I had taken on in *Doctor Who*, but I had to create stories in Germany, Austria, Switzerland, France, Spain, Scandinavia, Belgium, Italy and goodness knows wherever else! I researched stories and took each selected writer to the locations, cast the local actors, with Nils Nilson's assistance, and recruited the foreign staff to participate. We had to make one programme every ten days; so production was even more of a race against time than on *Doctor Who*, for it meant shooting the filmed inserts in each European location, then bringing over the foreign actors and rehearsing and recording each show in the studio – all on a ten-day turnaround!

After a few weeks Peter unfortunately couldn't cope with the pressure and finally gave in to Mother Teacher's, and had to retire from the BBC. I was then asked by the Head of Series, Andrew Osborn, if I could step into the breach as producer; but that was easy, since I had virtually been operating as such since I joined. I was therefore left with the total responsibility; and goodness knows how, but I completed the twenty-six thrillers – but that's another story which I will save for my complete memoirs!

As an aside, something that may be of interest was that, several years later, Jon Pertwee asked me to write a follow-up series for him to capitalise on his reputation from *Doctor Who* and subsequently *Worzel Gummidge* in which he was also successful. I therefore wrote a series based upon a character called 'Tin Harry', a crazy robot who has been asleep awaiting the return of his creator. Jon loved the idea, but before I could get it into production he sadly died in New York – I believe it was at a *Doctor Who* fan gathering! I haven't pursued the 'Tin Harry' series; waiting for the right opportunity and personality following Jon's unfortunate death was difficult, so I have confined this series idea and scripts to my bottom drawer.

The task of completing the production of twenty-six thrillers all over Europe was exhausting, but I wasn't allowed to rest for long. Andrew Osborn, the Head of Drama Series, asked me if I would create a series of thirteen shows for Rupert Davies (the star of *Maigret* which Andy had previously produced) out of the blue. I had evidently somehow acquired the reputation of being able to create things out of thin air!

I pondered on this problem as I took a short break to give some attention to my family. Without any clear idea of how the series was going to be formatted, I tenuously gave it the title *Baker's Dozen*, it being thirteen individual thriller/dramas. To tie them all together I decided that instead of Rupert Davies being a running character, as his depiction of the French detective Maigret had been, it would provide more scope for the writers if he were to simply be the storyteller, topping and tailing each story and only occasionally appearing as his character when necessary. This appeared to please Rupert, and consequently my boss and I promoted the series idea as *Baker's Dozen* within the Drama department with a headed notepaper to give it an identity. Unfortunately this did not appeal to the head of BBC One, Paul Fox, who insisted that no one would understand what a baker's dozen was. Boy, did I have a falling out with him and I almost got fired! However, he got his way: he was after all the boss. The series I duly retitled as *The Man Outside.*

In fact I used the *Man Outside* format for some series idea try-outs or auditions. One of these was a one-hour comedy spoof by the writer

Peter Draper, based upon Welsh village life, which I called *The Perils of Pendragon*. It was hilariously funny and starred Kenneth Griffith and John Clive as an uncle and nephew running the corner general store in an archaic and backward Welsh village. Recognise it? *Open All Hours*? I believe this was a direct 'steal' by the BBC Comedy department; a great comedy series, but I felt sorry for my writer, Peter Draper and the stars of my show. Thank you BBC!

After completing *Perils* I had to take a well-needed rest, and went to a health farm with Jane to rid my body of toxins and my brain of confusion and anger at the BBC management who, because the country was in the midst of an election, decided not to transmit one of the episodes of *Perils* because of its title – 'Marx and Sparks'! How stupid! This ridiculous decision, and the series' basic format apparently being stolen to produce *Open All Hours*, destroyed my faith in the BBC.

I decided that I had been taken advantage of enough and that I was reluctant to 'give' more, even though it had been intimated that I was being considered to take over as Head of Series when Andrew Osborn retired. This didn't appeal to me and I knew that I was neither capable of, nor interested in, the kind of politicking that this would involve me in. Time to leave and set up shop for myself.

Chapter Nine

OUT OF THE FRYING PAN, INTO THE FIRE!

I HAD NO IDEA WHAT the potential problems were and I set up the company with just six hundred pounds of my meagre savings. No one from the television world had done this, and I was in virgin territory. I was convinced, however, that creativity was the be-all and end-all of success. I had ideas, yes, dozens of them; but how was I to finance them, make them and sell them to the closed shop that was the TV world, a club to which I did not belong?

I had taken on board two people I had known at the BBC and who were interested in my independent plans: Martin Hall, an editor I had used at the BBC, and Nicholas Lom from the BBC Drama department. They didn't contribute investment, which was all down to me since it was my company, but worked, as I did, on a wing and a prayer! Dina Lom, Nick's mother and wife of the actor Herbert Lom, assisted in setting up shop; I presume it was my enthusiasm and my success at the BBC that convinced everyone.

A friend of Dina's, a stills photographer, came up with an idea for a series set in a Swiss Alpine resort. He wanted to make it as a documentary series, but I knew this would be difficult to sell and in any case it was nothing but a vague idea. But it was out of left field, and something about it appealed to me; and I started to develop it into a children's adventure show built around the local hotel and a young skier training for the Olympics. From this basic idea I created *Ski-Boy*, a thirteen-part half-hour series for the family audience.

The problem was: who would buy it? What was its market and how would I finance it? I therefore had to research what its commercial value was. The American market was obvious, but hardly anyone had broken directly into this market, let alone a novice like me! One possibility emerged: the American 'Prime Time Access' or early evening slot reserved for family viewing. This fitted, but I had to appeal to American audiences. I decided that I must write it for a young American boy lead, a sidekick American girl – and a dog! The series would have to have stories that would be thrilling and include lots of skiing. I decided on the title, *Ski-Boy*, and created the format with the Swiss Alpine hotel being run by the boy's aunt and uncle as the centre for the stories.

There was no way that I could propose this directly to the US networks, so I had to first make the series and finance it by a pre-sale based upon European potential sales. Now I had to become a salesman and distributor! I went through the figures and they worked out, assuming sales could be made. The budget I created for the entire thirteen shows was a little over £300,000.

I realised that to gain credibility and attract investment finance I would somehow have to 'join the club' to get a network deal in the UK. To this end I made a proposal to media tycoon Lew Grade, without much hope. To my great surprise, having only made my proposal late one Friday night, I received a phone call at the crack of dawn the following Monday morning summoning me to attend at Lew's offices. I didn't believe the call at first, but it proved to be true and I arrived in the mogul's office before his staff!

The meeting was brief – he didn't even have time to smoke his cigar – and I had made him an offer he couldn't refuse: he would get the UK network rights for a measly £40,000 plus the European distribution rights, whilst I retained the North and South American and Canadian rights. I won the deal; and, with my research on predicted potential income from the rest of the world, I approached some small investors and a private City bank to provide the costs.

The bank I chose, through the advice of a friend in the London Stock exchange, was Tom Sloan's bank. I sat for three days in his outer office, nine to five, waiting to make my pitch, until finally his secretary, either because she got sick of seeing my face or because she took pity on me, got me in to see her boss. My pitch obviously convinced him and I walked away with a deal. It's amazing what a well-prepared pitch and enthusiasm will achieve. I had done it: I had created and financed my first independent production; now all I had to do was mount, produce it and sell it.

This was the period of 'hard knocks': the commercial side of the business was tough to assault. I decided to make the *Ski-Boy* series using a combination of staff from the television world and the production management and organisational staff from the feature film world. A very wise decision, as it turned out: for, at fifteen thousand metres up the Swiss Alps, the logistics of having to ferry everything – from basic film stock, equipment and rushes to actors – to and from London on a daily basis were very complicated. On top of this it was during a fuel strike so all fuel had to be imported daily. I also used a very experienced film accountant and transferred cash from the London bank to a Swiss account for convenience. I brought the production in under budget by £15,000, but unfortunately as soon as I completed and delivered the material to Lew Grade's company the private bank of Tom Sloan went bust – into liquidation!

I went with ITC, the distribution company of the Grade Organisation, to the Cannes TV Festival to promote the sales. This was a great experience into the problems of overseas sales, but unfortunately, as I discovered at a later stage, I was cheated in various ways by ITC. They sold the series at low prices to European and other overseas organisations owned by them – in France, Germany and South Africa – who then proceeded to sell them on elsewhere; and ITC, not my production company, pocketed the profits!

I almost succeeded in conquering the American market in Prime Time Access, but to do so I found I needed to double the number of episodes: twenty-six episodes and thirteen repeats for a thirty-nine consecutive weeks sale! Another lesson learned.

However, the series was appreciated and NBC offered to take it on board, appointing me as executive producer with a high salary, a smart office in LA and a pretty secretary – but with no control or contribution on the creative content! Another steal which I turned down because, apart from anything else, I felt I had an obligation to everyone who had suffered in producing it as well as the financiers.

Lew Grade, despite having made substantial profits from the network sale and his crooked distribution deals, declined to take on the role of the bank that had gone bust for a second series of thirteen; he'd obviously realised that I wouldn't fall for the same deal twice! I sold it in Canada and South America; but the US network sale continued to elude me, so the necessary second series couldn't be made.

So, to try to survive as an independent producer it was back to the drawing board. I started a distribution unit to sell other producers' product, based on the experience I had gained at the Cannes TV Festival, determined to do so without screwing the producers. I managed to achieve some big sales, one in particular with Japanese animation which I sold to Saudi Arabia for all Middle Eastern rights which kept the ship more than afloat.

It was around this time that I received a call at my office informing me that my father, who had been working at a local hospital as a temporary porter, had suddenly fallen ill and was committed to hospital. I visited and was very upset when he, knowing that he was dying, pleaded with me to help him. I had spent half my life helping my parents, but this time there was nothing I could do. As already recounted in Chapter Four, my father eventually died of lung cancer, followed a year or so later by my mother. They were both only in their early sixties; I'd had a surfeit of death.

Martin Hall and I created a potentially exciting set of major drama recreations of the 'Berlin Airlift', which we sold in principle to Columbia TV through a co-production arrangement with Quinn Martin productions. Quinn was a great guy and obviously had an 'in' with Columbia from his previous productions. Columbia paid for the script development, and we were to provide the logistical development and production in Berlin. An American producer/writer was chosen and he produced a very credible script. We managed to source the large number of ancient planes required, such as DC4s and DC6s, past their sell-by date but still airworthy, and we secured access to the airfields in and around Berlin.

In order that Quinn appreciated our production work and to prove that we knew what we were doing we arranged for him to visit the UK and meet the network executives here before flying across to Berlin. He had a major reputation and all of the big-name bosses – except Lew Grade – turned up and we began to build momentum for a potential UK co-production.

We then took Quinn off to West Berlin for him to understand exactly what the location and facilities were that we had prepared, and I arranged for us to travel across into Communist East Berlin. This prospect terrified him, but it passed without serious incident other than the fact that I had to persuade him to empty his full pockets of dollars and distribute them amongst us in order for him not to get mugged after we passed through the Brandenburg Gate into the East!

Whilst the script was being written we became great friends with Quinn, even to the extent of him sending over his daughter to stay with my family in Barnes.

The script was very acceptable and Martin and I travelled across to LA yet again to meet with Quinn's production team prior to a meeting with the Columbia executive in charge of the project. I had prepared a full production schedule and budget, again to prove my production expertise.

The meeting at Columbia will be one experience I shall never forget.

We were shown into a plush office suite with a vast empty (unused) desk behind which ostentatiously sat a twenty-five-year-old youth – obviously inexperienced, and probably there simply because he had been elbowed there by one of his Jewish relations or a major shareholder. He was probably more nervous than were.

He pontificated pompously for some moments, and then pronounced that what the script needed was a 'love story, a boy and a dog!' That was his sole observation and contribution to a superb script of an historic event.

Quinn asked me what I thought, and in my inimitable blunt way I told the youth to stuff it! We couldn't possibly work on such a complicated epic with such mentality. In retrospect, I should probably have politely acquiesced, thanked the ignorant executive for his contribution and held my hand out for the money; but that just wasn't me, and in any case I reasoned Columbia would almost certainly want to control the production and this would lead to disaster.

In fact, later at our hotel I came across David Puttnam who was there discussing taking the production helm with the same company, with whom he later had the same experience and walked out of one of the prime jobs in the US film world. No wonder we Brits have got such a stroppy reputation: we are professionals and do not suffer fools gladly – and certainly not just for money!

It was back to the drawing board again as this momentous series of historical drama productions fell apart for lack of finance and executive stupidity. It seemed that all productions were at the mercy of pen-pushing accountants rather than creative visionaries. The Berlin Airlift was a very exciting project and, despite the idiocy of the Columbia juvenile executive, it would have been made as a USA network show and sold worldwide very profitably. I am still pursuing this as a possible product and hope that somebody somewhere sees the sense in my proposals. Unfortunately Quinn will not be there to witness it, since he died soon after this Columbia debacle.

Martin then came up with another series idea: *Boy King*, a children's adventure series set in Iran. This attracted the interest of Nils Nilson, my old friend from my co-production days at the BBC. His company had commercial interests in Iran and saw their involvement as a way in to Iranian TV2. He also liked the project because I suggested that we ran it as a double production unit to allow Iranian TV2 to benefit from Western expertise. This was agreed, and with the backing of the German production company we began the planning and scripting.

Martin and I wrote the pilot scripts, which were approved, and since it was Martin's idea and format it was agreed that he would produce the shows and I would executive-produce with a guiding hand. All seemed to be going well until the revolution in Iran and the fall of the Shah. The Head of TV2 with whom we had a very cordial and friendly relationship suddenly disappeared, to this day we know not where; he has never been heard of since! I was shown out of the country by angry Sten-gun-armed guards! Collapse of yet another great series idea – this time because of politics and not money.

I managed to keep the company afloat by my sales ability in distribution and another production format I created, *Magic Circle* which I managed to finance the independent pilot of. At the same time I had been persuaded to take on management of a family pop group, the Weltons, and negotiated a record contract for them with the Decca record company.

I arranged the co-operation of the Magic Circle organisation to use their London headquarters to mount the pilot in, and convinced Ray Alan, a well-known ventriloquist, to star with a 'character' I had created as his doll – 'Ali Cat' – as a merchandising tool. The pilot was well appreciated and Harlech TV became interested in it as a network show for them. Unfortunately they insisted that it be represented and produced as one of their shows, presumably a necessary political move to give them credibility within the network. I reluctantly agreed; and I was also asked to include the Weltons as the running musical group, and to persuade Decca to invest £1,000 per show for the privilege! This I managed to do, but my doubts about Harlech TV's ability to produce the shows were confirmed; and, despite the success of Ray Alan and Ali Cat and various merchandising deals I set up, the shows were a disaster and a network failure.

This taught me a good lesson as a creative producer, as the dealings with Columbia had: never give your baby away to inexperienced, greedy and unproven professionals – they are sure to drop it!

I did, however, manage to find a good agent for the Weltons and secured them a place in the Royal Command Performance, televised from the London Palladium: a great achievement and one which I was sure would catapult them to fame. They were good professionals, but were governed by the father who insisted on controlling their entire performance, even setting up their on-stage equipment himself. In this very important instance, although the equipment was connected by him, he forgot to switch on the power! The result was a total disaster of a performance without sound. This led to the end of the poor Welton kids' careers and also, I believe, to the sad death of their over-protective father with a heart attack.

At the same time Martin was working on a new and exciting idea with Westward TV to produce a USA network co-production of a drama 'special' about Sir Francis Drake; but, despite several visits to the PBS station in the States, the venture again failed because of finance and the nervousness of the small and ineffectual Westward TV board.

I, meanwhile, had created and pursued a series of four documentary programmes to fill their obligation to the network 'God slot': *Sunday*

Sweet Sunday, conceived as a European co-production which explored, through a kind of vox pop style, the various ways in which the different communities in each country celebrated Sunday. It involved shooting in France, Germany, Italy and England. I appointed another producer friend from my days at the BBC to make the shows since I was busy elsewhere, but after making the first and easiest programme of the series in England he rebelled, I think through lack of experience, to the point whereby I had to sack him and take over the whole production in the three remaining European countries myself. This I did, and the shows were completed, delivered and networked; but audiences were not, as predicted, particularly interested in religious-based TV. It did, however, fill the slot for Westward TV despite an ITV strike, which again I avoided by shooting on film in Europe! The unions and indeed the UK network companies must have been beginning to find me a difficult and persistent character; but 'the show must go on'!

Like all distribution companies I needed programmes to sell, and I got involved in a unique concept based around the 'Circus World Championships' and took on the worldwide sales to both sell and promote it in Europe and in the USA. I took the producer, Adrian Metcalfe, off to meet with my connections in Germany, but for some reason, and despite our offer to do productions there also, they declined. I personally, on the advice of Don Getz, a film distributor friend, went to New York to present the programmes on laser disc. I sold the existing programmes very profitably but couldn't interest them in co-production.

By this time I had attended and taken my distribution company to five or so Cannes TV sales festivals and appointed a good saleswoman to head sales. It was at one such festival that she introduced me to her stepdaughter who was very attractive and what could only be described as a JAP – Jewish American Princess! She set her sights on me and, following several business visits to LA, she decided to travel to London to pursue a career there. I gave her a secretarial job and the relationship blossomed; she had a fairly astute business brain and would be a useful addition to the company. However, this was a foolish mistake in retrospect because our affair, when discovered, ruined my marriage and family, resulting in my leaving home and moving in with the JAP.

Work was scarce, although my distribution company progressed sufficiently well to keep the bank happy. Because of my perceived ability to create something from nothing, Yorkshire TV, through their associated smaller company Tyne Tees TV, asked me to create (overnight!) a children's series format since they were obliged to provide one for the network; another political hiatus which the vast resources of a major TV company could not satisfy.

The same night, bouncing ideas around over a bottle of whisky with Martin in the pub adjacent to our office, I created the idea for *Nobody's House*, about a family moving into a house with only the children being able to see and communicate with the child ghost, 'Nobody'. Just the one set, only five regular running characters and no filmed sequences because of the limited budget! The next day I presented this format to the Head of Drama at Yorkshire (my old boss from the BBC!) and it was snapped up with alacrity and enthusiasm and the seven scripts commissioned.

Martin and I wrote the series and I suggested the directors, but because of the political implications Yorkshire had to produce the network series in Tyne Tees. It was successful, but it could only run for the limited series because Granada had been appointed the rest of the network allocation. Politics again! I was getting fed up with this situation; it seemed that the networks fed off our creativity only when they were in trouble.

Whilst writing and producing a commissioned film for BUPA (about the necessity for preventive medicine), I discovered a visual technique new to the business of film-making, of creating computer-animated graphic images and recording them directly onto colour film. This technique had been pioneered by EMI and a London University, but they had run out of ideas on how to develop it usefully and profitably. I saw its potential and bought the system, equipment and staff lock, stock and barrel for £10,000 and moved the whole operation into my Soho offices. This involved blocking off two adjacent streets, taking out a third-storey window and lifting the heavy PDP-11/60 computer by crane into the building. However, compared with shooting a whole thirteen-part filmed TV series halfway up the Swiss Alps, this was easy!

Chapter Ten

The Creation of Electronic Arts

I managed to refinance the proposed development that I had designed which involved the injection of a further £110,000. I wrote a business plan, presented it successfully to the full board of a tax-shelter City organisation and walked out with cheque in hand!

I had researched the new world of computer-generated graphics and animation as it had developed in the USA, at MIT and elsewhere, which involved a machine called a Dicomed. This was in fact a 35mm camera and computer-controlled recording system, as opposed to a lower quality 16mm machine which we were using. This was the state of the art at the time and would put us right at the forefront of computer-generated slide shows and 35mm animation once we had developed or purchased the animation software.

The company was called Electronic Arts (not to be confused with the American video games company of the same name) and, having upgraded the system and employed new computer designers, the business went from strength to strength.

To promote Electronic Arts, I wrote a two-page spread on computer animation in the trade magazine *Broadcast* as an advertising and PR piece confirming our place in the number one position in CG slide production at less cost than traditional animation. However, that was still too expensive except for the wealthiest of clients like the BBC and other major companies in the world of advertising.

We became the new buzzword in the business and designed and made the new logo for Channel Four, completed several brilliant advertising commissions, won the first prize in the animation awards and designed and made the titles for, I believe, all of the TV network stations and the BBC for that year's Olympics! What a coup!

I tried to spread the word throughout Europe, visiting countries and lecturing on our process; but the main problem was that it took an awful lot of processing time for my designers and operators to construct sequences. Time is money, and I had to spend it as fast as I could make it! That's the problem with 'greenfield' projects that are not adequately funded up front. I soon found that I couldn't sustain our progress despite the obvious success; my tax-shelter partners had a limit to their financial support and now insisted that we fold the company.

After all that effort and the dedication of all involved, money again was to be the enemy of creation and stifled yet another potentially very successful business. A financial professional was brought in, a corporate 'fixer', and the business was eventually picked up in liquidation by a Middle-Eastern entrepreneur who put his own people in to control the board but promised to include me, since I was still MD and had around £21,000 of my own cash involved in the company.

I was warned that this particular outfit had the habit of allowing the company to run for a year whilst they prepared to put their own people in and dump those who had built it and made it a success. I didn't believe that they would be so stupid, since the company had been built by me and it was obviously my creativity and reputation within the industry that was holding it together as the number one animation company. Also, most of the staff were loyal. However, the accountant who had been brought in by the new investors thought he could run the company better than me. He persuaded my software writer, whom he recruited to his ambitions, and together they connived to take over the company for the investors, despite my predictions that, without me, the company and its reputation would collapse within six months.

I was wrong: it collapsed in three months! First my sales person, the JAP, was fired (being Jewish and the financiers being Arabic!) and then shortly afterwards I was fired. To put it another way, I had been right and the money was wrong.

Having moved in with the JAP at the collapse of my marriage, following my divorce settlement I bought a small mews house in South End Green, Hampstead. My new relationship collapsed, as my new business had, as the money ran out.

So, at the ripe old age of fifty, having been diagnosed as having type 2 diabetes (which the financiers used as their excuse for firing me), having had the company I had built stolen, with such savings as I had been able to accrue sadly depleted, divorced from my wife and with my family life destroyed (through my own fault), I was thrown out into the big wide world again. My relationship with the JAP continued for a while but, as a relatively young girl, she insisted on leading what most would call the 'high life'. This involved a new circle of friends, bars, restaurants and parties and indulging in the use of booze and drugs: a nasty habit she had acquired in her native California.

This was the time when I began to live my long-since-past teenage years. It was a destructive period, but I continued working – alone, because the JAP had decided to seek greener pastures elsewhere, as a newspaper executive who could ease her way up the corporate ladder. She was a bright and opportunistic girl and ended up as the European Executive of Universal Pictures' cable operations.

Despite everything being 'in the fan', I needn't have despaired since it soon became known that I was back out there on the market and, as one of the few who had such a thorough command of production expertise in both high class filming and computer animation, within weeks I had been commissioned to produce the substantial 35mm filmed CG animation content and CG graphic slides for a product launch for ICL computers: a £130,000 commission! That would keep the wolf from the door for a time; that, and the long-forgotten thirteen episodes of *Ski-Boy* which I sold to Sky TV for their children's cable channel: rights which Lew Grade and ITC had somehow overlooked! So, I created Production Partners Ltd, of which more anon.

During this period I had the good luck to meet a very talented painter: I can't really pronounce his Polish name, Zeesh for short. He was a superb artist and seemed to have the ability to look into people's souls and see their true selves. Unfortunately, he had macular neuropathy and was going blind: what a terrible thing to happen to an artist. I met Zeesh through the JAP; he had an eye for female beauty and he wanted her to pose for him, but she was reluctant to pose nude which was his speciality.

We met regularly since we both appreciated creativity in our own ways. He was very knowledgeable about people's character which could be clearly seen in his paintings. We spent many a night discussing art and his extraordinary life. He had studied and painted with some of the world's greatest artists in Paris until the outbreak of war when he was forced to flee the Nazis, making his way eventually to England. Zeesh himself was highly regarded as an artist and has some of his work exhibited in the National Gallery.

From my point of view Zeesh insisted that I apply myself to writing and dedicate my life to it with the kind of single-minded enthusiasm that he devoted to his painting. Zeesh, however, had lived a life of near-penury, with his wife Margaret (working as a BBC secretary) providing most of the family income until Zeesh's talents were recognised by a wealthy fur-trader in London, Michael, who became his sponsor and mounted several successful exhibitions which produced income.

Whilst Margaret worked, Zeesh looked after the children and their welfare and continued painting in his studio which was the basement area of their small house in Camden. He both lived and worked in his basement studio, out of bounds to the rest of the family who occupied the upstairs. The studio was where I met with Zeesh and where we drank Zubrowka vodka or red wine and ate his favourite food, pickled herring! These were some of my happiest moments, as Zeesh virtually became my surrogate father and certainly a fund of knowledge and enlightenment.

With Zeesh's eye problems increasing as he aged, I decided to do something about it. I persuaded him to visit the top eye hospital in London, Moorfields, to check his actual vision problems because he was now almost blind, and without his eyes he couldn't paint. He agreed, and I set up the appointment and took him there. Unfortunately his problem was confirmed as being inoperable: he was definitely going blind. I always turned up in a white track suit because then Zeesh could see it more easily and recognise me, and from then on I was known as his White Angel!

Zeesh was undaunted by the hospital's prognosis and decided that, although he may have lost most of his sight, he could still 'see' with his hands; therefore he took up sculpture, and his White Angel was dispatched to find the suitable clay! This resulted in some beautiful sculptures.

A little later he died; I attended his funeral in the Polish community where he was revered, and a suitable wake took place with appropriate, numerous glasses of Zubrowka!

Chapter Eleven
DAVID AND GOLIATH

SINCE A CONSIDERABLE TIME HAD passed and I wanted to tackle the BBC about my copyright of UNIT as tied to my freelance contract, I thought I'd review the progress of *Doctor Who* sales.

The interest in making British TV science fiction seemed to return to broadcasters towards the middle of the 1990s, as companies began to see the possibility of lucrative overseas sales and tie-in products that other genres could not match. In the mid 1990s the BBC screened four seasons of the glossy sci-fi action adventure series *Bugs* (1995–98), made by independent company Carnival, and co-produced the six-part serial *Invasion: Earth* (1998) with the US Sci-Fi Channel.

The twenty-first century has seen a 'live' remake of *The Quatermass Experiment* broadcast on BBC Four on April 2nd 2005, a new time-travel drama *Life on Mars* (BBC 2006–2007), *Eleventh Hour* (ITV 2008–2009), *Primeval* (ITV 2007–present) and in 2009 a new series for *Red Dwarf*, now shown exclusively on digital channel Dave rather than the BBC.

Meanwhile, the revived *Doctor Who* has continued onwards and upwards, ever more popular and wildly profitable, with various series following in the wake of its success including two spin-offs entitled *Torchwood* (2006–2011) and *The Sarah Jane Adventures* (2007–2011).

BBC Worldwide Limited is the commercial subsidiary of the British Broadcasting Corporation, formed out of a restructuring of its predecessor BBC Enterprises in 1995. The company exploits the BBC brand, selling BBC and other British programming for broadcast abroad with the aim of supplementing the income received by the BBC through the licence fee. In this it has been hugely successful; in the year to March 31st 2011, BBC Worldwide's headline profits were up 10.3% to £160.2 million – its highest level ever. The growth helped lift the overall return to the BBC by nearly 9% to £182m.

So why did Enterprises, subsequently known as BBC Worldwide, literally destroy and throw away their assets – their recorded programming? This was typical of the stupidity and lack of foresight of management! They destroyed millions of pounds' worth of finished programming.

I wonder which birdbrain at BBC Enterprises, in conjunction with the engineering department, decided that it was good business to throw away their assets and dump the two-inch master tapes in favour of 16mm film, when not all episodes were converted to film. No one with any commercial sense throws away their masters!

Between approximately 1967 and 1978, large quantities of videotape material were destroyed or wiped. Most *Doctor Who* episodes were made on two-inch videotape for initial broadcast and then transferred onto 16mm film by BBC Enterprises for further commercial exploitation. The 16mm format was used for overseas sales as it was considerably cheaper to buy and easier to transport than videotape. The destruction of the videotape masters in favour of the 16mm film copies (which more often than not were not returned by the buyers) meant that a great number of series were lost forever! Why throw away or destroy the master tapes? It simply didn't make any sense.

BBC Enterprises kept copies of programmes only if they were deemed commercially exploitable. The organisation was a joke at this time, and only became a reasonable, working and profitable exercise once it was revamped as BBC Worldwide and developed into a serious sales organisation – and, yes, made a lot of money.

The first *Doctor Who* master videotapes to be junked were those for the serial 'The Highlanders', which were erased a mere two months after transmission. Further erasing and junking of *Doctor Who* master tapes by the Engineering Department continued into the 1970s. Eventually every single master two-inch videotape of the programme's first two hundred and fifty-three episodes was destroyed or wiped.

Patrick Troughton's Second Doctor was particularly badly affected:

of the fourteen stories comprising his first two seasons, only 'The Tomb of the Cybermen' and 'The Enemy of the World' are complete, and these only exist due to 16mm copies being returned from Hong Kong and Nigeria, respectively – the latter only being discovered as recently as 2013.

The wiping policy officially came to an end in 1978, when the BBC finally realised they had the means to further exploit programmes by taking advantage of the new market in home video cassette recordings. In addition, the attitude became that vintage programmes should, in any case, be preserved for posterity and for historical and cultural reasons: at long last some sense! The BBC Film Library was turned into a combined Film and Videotape Library for the preservation of both media.

Despite this, and despite the continuing search to recover the lost stories, at the time of writing there are still ninety-seven episodes of *Doctor Who* no longer held by the BBC.

So all who had contributed their creative talents lost out because of the stupidity of the so-called marketing arm of the BBC, including the poor viewers who paid their licence fees which could have been reduced – and all in order to save the cost of a few videotapes!

In passing, and on a personal note, perhaps I should mention that my series *The Perils of Pendragon* was also destroyed.

In contacting the BBC legal department to claim my copyright and the residuals associated with it, I fared no better than before. Their excuse was that this was history and that they could not find in their archives the relevant contracts or information with regard to my copyright claim. So much for the efficiency of the BBC archival methods!

They continued, and still do, to refute my claims, though not my copyright of the scripts of 'The Invasion' in which UNIT was created! There had been so many sales of the programmes involving UNIT that retrospective payment of a fee for its use would have been substantial had they conceded, so one can see why they prevaricated. They were inviting me to sue them, a process that would have lasted years and which I was advised by lawyers would have cost me over £40,000. My agent who had negotiated my original freelance contracts obviously didn't want to queer their pitch with Auntie by taking my side, even though they agreed that the copyright in UNIT was clearly mine; that fact alone was a demonstration of the validity of my case. I refused to give up my claim for copyright, but had to accept a small fee to shut up and go away. If I had been in funds I would have pursued the matter, but money was tight and I know how legal battles can leave a gaping hole in one's pocket!

I had started Production Partners Ltd with the prospect of entering the production arena again as an independent, but I realised that this was premature. Although independent production was fast becoming a reality, it had yet to be widely accepted or properly regulated. While the BBC had decided to virtually destroy or redesign their programme production system and farm it out to independent companies, the formation of PACT to represent the interests of independent producers was still some way off, and it was too early to enter this chaotic production world by aligning myself with the greedy finance companies who were taking advantage of the chaos. In any case I had had enough of working with other management bosses; I was a true independent.

I therefore took on joining Terra Firm, a new company specialising in corporate production started by my good friend Clive Graham-Ranger, a journalist who had decided to strike out on his own. It was an interesting job, but hardly satisfying since I was simply applying my experience in writing, producing and directing both stage production and video for such corporate giants as Silk Cut motor racing, and – somewhat outrageously – a sex conference at Brighton for the Ann Summers organisation, involving scantily clad girls whom I had to direct and even select the costumes for! Clive Ranger became a good friend, for we both had a passion for trout fishing. Unfortunately Clive also fell victim to crooked financiers who tried to use his company to filter cash through, I presume to avoid tax or maybe to 'launder' it. His company went into bankruptcy.

Life was still difficult but once again my writing ability saved the bacon and a movie script I had written, *Sugar Daddy*, caught the interest of Central Television who commissioned me to rewrite it as a UK-based six-part comedy serial for a very advantageous fee. They had selected John Nettles, the star of the TV series *Bergerac*, to play the lead and we met at a lunch to discuss it with him. All seemed set to go when Central TV was taken over by a company which had tried (and I had rejected) to take over Electronic Arts: Carlton Communications, for whom the JAP subsequently worked. Carlton dumped all of Central's production plans, and so another of my projects, already paid for, went down the pan!

At the same time I was involved in creating a stand-up comedy series with my American associate Larry O'Daly. I had secured a deal with Central TV for a programme titled *A Different Point of View* which we recorded a pilot of. This was based on a successful American format made by Larry in New York. We also had plans to open a stand-up comedy club in London similar to those in the USA. Stand-up was just beginning to take off here and I found a perfect venue in Camden Town, designed it with the assistance of a professional architectural design company and wrote yet another business plan. It was perfect, and a very profitable proposal with two bars as well as the stand-up club equipped for recording TV shows. I proposed to finance it with the aid of a large brewery company who would have the beer concession.

Once again I learned that my creative ideas were much appreciated by others who had nothing but profit on their minds, and the land owner of the Camden market stole my plans and ideas and, in cahoots with another stand-up producer, built the club from my designs which I believe is still running successfully in Camden Town!

The TV pilot *A Different Point of View* also failed to secure a network commission because the BBC had made a similar series, *Have I Got News For You* (still running today I believe) and Central decided not to run with it. Or again, was it canned because of the takeover by Carlton Communications, a company owned by two Jewish brothers? Is the whole of the entertainment business controlled by Jewish families? Was I being blacklisted by the clan?

My finances being almost exhausted (I was pretty shattered myself too) and with the building society and bank breathing down my neck, I reckoned that enough was enough for the moment. Making what little I could by regretfully selling my delightful mews house in Hampstead, I decided to retire gracefully but temporarily and take a rest.

What had I learned from my experiences so far? A lot! First of all I learned not to trust an upwardly mobile JAP with nothing on her mind except money and self-advancement using her feminine wiles with susceptible powerful men. Second, I learned to trust my own judgment where creativity is concerned in spite of interference from others who have no understanding of the process or appreciation of audiences' needs. Third, I learned not to use my own money to make productions but to attract investors with credible and profitable fully researched and prepared projects, and not to accept investors like the Arab group who had no track record other than profiting through other people's expertise. Fourth, should I change my religion? Above all I learned to continue applying my guiding principles of truth and honesty and to avoid those who didn't practise the same ethics.

I agreed with Jane, my ex-wife, with whom I had retained a friendly relationship, to decamp to the clifftop house in Folkestone which she and her brother had inherited following the death of their parents, and to restore the former Edwardian family home so that she could rent it out as a holiday let. This proved a monumental task as I had to virtually rebuild many of its important features as well as install central heating and build a kitchen, rewire its electrics, rebuild fireplaces and chimney outlets, refurbish the exterior of the house and rip out the damp and dry rot and replace the main and glorious interior staircase.

This refurbishment was one of the biggest construction jobs I had ever undertaken and took almost two years, with the assistance of my son Daniel, but it was ultimately very satisfying. I returned to London to live in my daughter's ex-flat, where my two sons stayed with me on and off, and continued my new business as a builder converting house attics into liveable flat extensions. I continued to write when I had time to do so, but my main source of income was through my building operations.

The 'new world' of independent production at the BBC and elsewhere was still only in its formative stages; but it was already obvious that to participate, to be able to build and develop productions, one had to have a good deal of finance and an established working production company behind one. This I clearly did not have, nor did I have the enthusiasm to start all over again or sell out my experience.

So with Christmas approaching, and not wishing to endure another such festival which I disliked, both my eldest son Sam and I decided to flee the country to warmer climes, something we had done before. It was Sam who came up with the idea. To reduce my depression about the diminishing likelihood of my re-entry into the business of entertainment, and with Christmas looming like yet another grey cloud, he suggested that what was required was a holiday.

Now, my son Sam is an experienced traveller of the backpacker kind. One thing I had learned about getting a little advanced in years was that backpacking was not my idea of heaven, even if it did mean we'd avoid the dreaded Christmas hoo-ha. No, insisted Sam, he meant a real holiday in the sun, such as we'd spent a few years before in the Canary Islands. That had certainly made the Christmas 'drag' easier to live with.

However, destinations that promised sun all year round, in our price range, were few and far between. Where did he consider such a paradise might be?

Chapter Twelve

REST IN PEACE

THAILAND: 'AMAZING THAILAND'. OF COURSE, I should have known. Sam had previously visited this exotic country and its fleshpots and was eager to repeat the experience. However, as I pointed out to him, he was still, relatively, in the first flush of middle age, whereas I was definitely, well… older. Wouldn't I find Thailand a little too rich for my blood?

My previous visits to the Far East had been while making a couple of dramas for the BBC in Hong Kong, when it was still a British colony, and Singapore, before it was sanitised by Lee Kuan Yew. It had intrigued me: another world, another very different culture. However, as I pointed out, that was almost twenty-five years before. Would I still find it as stimulating? Sam was convinced that inside the shell of the old man, a youthful spirit was yearning to escape. In the face of such flattery what could I say? Thailand it was to be.

With economy uppermost in our minds we booked a flight to Bangkok via Vienna with Lauda Airlines. It faintly worried me because it entailed a ten-hour stopover waiting for the connecting flight. With Bangkok some twelve hours' flying time away, this meant an extended journey which I felt might be extremely tiring. I needn't have worried, for Lauda had provided a free hotel room for the stopover. A little nap, a glance at cable TV and a very pleasant dinner and I was more than refreshed for the overnight flight to the Orient.

The airline hostesses were young, jeans-clad, with cheeky baseball-cap headdresses, attractive and very polite without being sugary or condescending. A couple of movies, a very passable meal, five or six hours' comfortable sleep and the vista of our approach to Bangkok spread out before and below us. What a change from BA!

I had prepared for my arrival in the sweltering heat of Bangkok by wearing shorts and T-shirt beneath the comfy running suit necessary for the inclement weather in London and the freezing cold of Vienna. Smart move, I thought, as I stripped off the running suit and stowed it in my overnight bag. Bloody stupid, I thought, as I stood shivering in the refrigerated Bangkok terminal, my aged dangly bits freezing up by the minute.

I was just debating with myself whether or not to don my warm running suit again when Sam returned, having secured a taxi for our next leg of the journey. Thank God I didn't because the temperature outside the terminal was well nigh off the thermometer.

Sam had decided that Pattaya, the Miami Beach of Bangkok, was the ideal spot for me to be initiated into the fraternity of tourists who revelled in the joys of all-night bars and street sex. I, however, had a great fear of being mistaken for a dirty old man, or worse, a paedophile on the rampage! It may have been my natural paranoia but I could have sworn that the officials in Immigration had given me some rather suspect glances. That could, of course, have been attributed to my curious appearance: a grey-haired old fart in shorts and T-shirt, shivering.

Our taxi, an ageing vehicle of suspect parentage and probably a composite of several different vehicles welded together, did nothing to restore my confidence or equanimity. Seated in the front of the vehicle I was convinced that we were travelling in a crab-like manner, the front half of the car having a mind of its own and forcing the rear end to follow reluctantly. The shock absorbers… didn't – they simply emphasised the rutted highway down which we were travelling. This was the underpass beneath the main flyover, which was under construction. (It probably still is.)

Pattaya is something like two hours' drive from Bangkok, but it seemed as though we hadn't left the grotty suburbs of the city before we were in the equally grotty suburbs of Pattaya. The glittering 'jungle' of flashing lights and neon signs became denser and denser as we penetrated the heart of this seaside town. My optimistic son had decided that it was pointless pre-booking a hotel since accommodation was, in his experience, readily available. His plan was to dump me and the luggage at his favourite bar, the name nor the location of which he could not precisely remember, and for him to beetle off to find us a place where I could rest my now very tired old head.

Reaching the seafront of Pattaya, where the bar was apparently located in one of the many side streets, Sam's confidence began to fade. All of the streets off the front looked the same! All were stuffed with girly bars and go-go rip-off clubs. Finally he got lucky and picked the right street; and the confused driver, who was obviously as lost as I felt, deposited us at the bar, together with luggage.

I thankfully flopped into a comfortable chair in the open-fronted bar with a very large iced gin and tonic clasped in my shaking hand. Sam, who had revived somewhat now that he had found the bar and got his bearings, disappeared into the labyrinth of streets to find a hotel for us. Thank God the bar wasn't one serviced by fifteen screaming girls all wanting to get their hands into your pocket – for money only of course. It was relatively quiet. The owner, a lugubrious Glaswegian, sat swigging bottle after bottle of beer as happy as Larry, as though he had never left the Gorbals. The service was provided unobtrusively by two young Thai girls, one of whom had been a girlfriend of Sam's during his previous visit.

Opposite this haven of comparative sanity was a bar whose service was unmistakable: it was crammed full of stunning young girls, all clad in shorts or mini-skirts and little else, who became provocatively animated when anything with long trousers or hairy legs passed their frontage.

I continued to sink one or ten more G&T's and politely refused to respond to the endless array of flesh for sale which passed before my eyes. Taunts of, 'Hello sexy man,' or, 'Papa, you go with me,' and so on were the common come-on. They made it seem as though I was irresistible to them.

Had I reverted to the handsome young buck that I once was who looked good in tights? Sanity returned and I faced reality: no, I was a knackered, black-eyed, silver-haired old gent, jaded from travel, and I concluded that my apparently irresistible attraction was more to do with the alacrity with which I peeled off the thousand-baht notes to pay for my drinks than with my testosterone rating!

Sam rescued me before I became completely legless and we trudged off, luggage and all, to the hotel that, he said, was only a few blocks away. Good old Sam; where would I be without him? Probably seated comfortably in a taxi heading towards the nearest Hilton hotel, a bath and a seat at the air-conditioned bar and thankful oblivion.

Seemingly tireless, Sam deposited me safely in my room at the hotel which, although it wasn't the Hilton, was at least clean and cool, and then disappeared into the madness that was Pattaya at night. I had an ice-cold shower – there is nothing else in such hotels in Thailand – hit my duty-free for a nightcap and retired thankfully to bed. The still-full glass was on my bedside table in the morning, untouched.

Unable the next morning to raise Sam (a sonorous rumbling emanating from his room indicating his state of inebriation and exhaustion), I tottered off to explore the immediate vicinity of the hotel and find some breakfast.

By day the area was even more seedy and grotty than it had seemed to my jaundiced and befuddled brain the night before. Without the perceived glamour and glitz of night-time, the drab, grubby, decaying underbelly became apparent. Girls coming home from their night's work at the bars still tried one last time to arouse my sexual interest. They were sad and rather pathetic by day and it was all I could do to resist digging my hand into my pocket and passing them a few notes; but the consequences of such generosity persuaded me to resist.

I'd done it all, travelled the world, tasted the bittersweet experiences of the London stage as an actor, travelled thousands of miles through America and Canada, had success as a playwright and television producer and eventually as an entrepreneur businessman in the wide, wide world of entertainment. There had been little or no time to 'play' until I was middle-aged; and that, I realised with regret, had been the wrong time to start.

The sex, drugs and rock-and-roll years of the late seventies and early eighties took their toll. The end of a marriage, the financial depression and the downfall of the businesses that I had built up; and, at fifty, the end of life as I'd known it. Each rise and fall had been heralded by my constant battle-cry – 'Next!' Now that I was free of all that desperate and endless hopping from one stepping-stone to another, what *was* 'next?' It certainly wasn't going to be a return to the old life – the 'yoof' rulers had made that abundantly clear for the time being – and anyway, for the moment I'd lost my zest for it.

I explored the seafront and backstreets of Pattaya in brief sorties, stopping every now and again to mop the sweat from my brow and to replenish my liquid intake at a convenient bar. It really was a low-life city. Even in the daytime the sex-in-your-face business flourished. Hardly a minute went by when someone or other didn't proposition me: male, female, teenage tarts and even children.

What was it that made Thailand so vulnerable to the sex trade? After all, prostitution, paedophilia and child sexploitation were all illegal, at least officially. What made the authorities so tolerant? What made them turn a blind eye? Corruption? Perhaps they were right and Western morality wrong? Or was it perhaps the sheer poverty of the mass of the population or the lack of education and opportunity in an emerging nation that made the sex trade so attractive to so many? Easy money but at what price?

Well, I wasn't going to find the answers in Pattaya, and I would only depress myself by trying to do so. In fact, I wasn't going to find anything in Pattaya, except sex and drunkenness. One certainly couldn't bathe in the sea without taking the precaution of inoculation against ten or more insidious diseases that were said to be present. The tourist attractions, such as they were, were without allure, particularly in the sweltering heat.

The short stay in Pattaya had appalled me but at the same time had filled my tired brain with countless story possibilities. Sam, thankfully, after three days of reliving his previous experiences, had also come to the same conclusion. Pattaya was the pits! We'd move on.

The southern mainland coast of Thailand is littered with innumerable tiny islands: some, such as Phuket, developed into full-blown tourist spots, others uninhabited. Gratefully stepping out of the Bangkok Airways aircraft onto Koh Samui soil, after a fairly terrifying landing which had seemed to me to be in excess of the speed of light, I was delighted to see the unique airport terminals with their open buildings, roofed with coconut palm. Even more quaint was the toytown-train-like vehicle that transported the passengers to the arrivals building.

All around us was green; verdant groves of coconut and banana trees. I was soon to learn why it was so green and fresh: it had just been raining and the roads from the airport to Lamai were awash, pitted with deep crevices and soggy with mud. As well as being the beginning of the Christmas holiday period, it was also the season of intermittent rainstorms.

Our slushy journey and arrival into a rain-soaked Lamai, whose main street was more like a tributary of the Mekong River, did nothing to improve my already disenchanted frame of mind. With no luxury hotel waiting to soothe my troubled breast – in fact with no hotel of any kind awaiting us – I took my usual course of action in such circumstances and repaired to the nearest bar. Sam, intrepid as ever, went in search of accommodation, which was, we had been warned, the unattainable.

Mama's bar (that being my choice because it was the nearest one that seemed to be open) was one of a group of twelve or so bars surrounding a Thai boxing ring, off the main road – sorry, river! The owner, Mama, was herself in attendance and welcomed me with generous bonhomie and an equally generous gin and tonic. This was a haven of near civilisation and she a fund of information, none of which was particularly useful in our present homeless situation but amusingly entertaining nonetheless. The rain clouds disappeared and Sam returned. He'd found one bungalow, a basic Thai-style one-roomed hut, with toilet and a shower of sorts. It wasn't exactly luxury on stilts but on stilts nevertheless.

I was not prepared to share my sleeping space with a million and one mosquitoes, rats and God knows what else. I had suffered a serious bout of blood poisoning from mosquito bites before and didn't wish to repeat the experience. My constitution was of a more sensitive nature and required something more akin to a three-star hotel: somewhere at least with clean towels, air-con and a reasonably bug-free atmosphere.

I solved my problem by heading for a sign which read *American Express Welcome*. With great use of the silver tongue and buckets of old English charm, flashing my American Express Gold Card and promising a long stay, I secured a room at the Galaxy Resort. Perfect! An air-con room, large bed, a fan that worked, a shower and toilet and, joy of joys, starched sheets!

The resort boasted its own swimming pool and, I was delighted to find when I explored its well-tended gardens, its own bar and restaurant. This very welcome facility was fringed with gently swaying palms and directly overlooked the beach. An exact replica of the TV advertisements seen before leaving London – even down to the scantily clad Nordic beauties sporting themselves on the beach. Could this after all be paradise?

Sam decided to economise and moved into the 'hell on stilts'. We took our evening stroll after a very passable dinner at the Galaxy restaurant, and I was dismayed to see what I had supposed was a quiet, sleepy, seaside town transformed into a mini Pattaya. Even some of the screaming girls draped over the bars seemed familiar, and their taunting, provocative 'Hello sexy man' cries exactly the same! Did they all take lessons in this kind of unsubtle seduction technique?

Bar after bar, restaurant after restaurant, lined the main street, each festooned with the same gaudy fairy lights and neon strips. It was as if someone had thrown a switch and turned the whole town into a sex circus! Sam was obviously delighted: another playground to explore, albeit touting the same attractions as Pattaya. I headed for my now familiar perch on a stool at Mama's bar, content to survey rather than sample the erotica.

Mama's bar was, by this time, as crowded with young female flesh as every other establishment. How could they all make a living with a strictly limited number of customers available? As the night wore on I realised that the tourists came in waves. Some came before dinner, sightseeing; others instead of dinner, who simply drank their first, second and third courses and retired, tired. By far the most prolific and likely customers for the girls were the all-nighters that arrived fed and fairly well watered. Some of these would go off with the girl of their choice while others simply drank the night away, probably shortening their lives by a day or two with their frenzied assault upon their livers.

Several of Mama's girls tried to tempt me with their seductive techniques until, sensing the pointlessness of their attempts, they turned their attentions to easier prey. Eventually, with my tank full to overflowing and giving Sam up for lost, I found my way back to my hotel, my cold shower and my starched sheets.

The next day was spent on the restaurant terrace, recovering and watching the Nordic beauties soaking up the sun, their bikini-less breasts bared to the bronzing rays and the Thai ladies plying their massage, hair-braiding and beading trades. I was content to be a voyeur, a people watcher; and what a curious bunch they were. Excessively fat Germans, both male and female, displaying rolls of fatty tissue struggling to release itself from their scant bathing costumes. Israeli boys on R&R from the army, posing, strutting and arrogantly insisting that the world take notice of their masculinity. The Swedish contingent, browned and cooked to perfection, intent on soaking up as much of the sun's rays as possible before returning to the half-light of their bleak winter.

The English youths I'd seen at Mama's the previous night, still suffering from the excesses of their debauchery, white-fleshed and burning as the minutes passed, were relentlessly planning to repeat the exercise and boasting of 'the bird I pulled last night...' Were any of them sober enough?

One of the waiters was struggling to write, in English, an invitation to take Christmas dinner at the Galaxy restaurant. I gently corrected his English spelling and he smiled his genuine thanks. 'You come eat turkey dinner for Christmas?' he hopefully asked. I declined, saying that I thought I'd celebrate by singing carols in my shower, to remind myself of what it was probably like in London – noisy, wet and cold! He smiled and nodded enthusiastically, not understanding one word I'd said.

This was another world, with a way of life completely new to me, and it intrigued me and inspired me to write about it; so I began to store away every impression and experience in my memory.

The whole of Lamai was seriously preparing to celebrate this strange foreigners' festival. As Buddhists it meant nothing to them. It was simply something that the crazy Europeans did, the time of year when they were prepared to empty their pockets and get outrageously drunk. All of the bars, restaurants and tourist traps were festooned with the same gaudy decorations for Christmas and the New Year. The self-same madness that we'd left London to escape was here with knobs on! Here in Lamai, at the arse-end of Thailand, in temperatures knocking thirty degrees, the celebrations were in full swing! What had we let ourselves in for? Paradise, yes, but with a distinct touch of Benidorm!

The impending orgy of the celebration put all such daydreaming out of my thoughts. Christmas Eve was the big night for the Germans and the Swedes, and Lamai was hopping that night. Thai lady boxing was the big attraction on Christmas Eve and Mama had persuaded us that this was an event not to be missed. As Mama's bar was our 'local' we felt obliged to attend although, to be honest, the thought of watching pugilistic girls beating hell out of each other did not appeal to me.

Each bar sponsored one of its girls to fight on behalf of her own establishment, and the customers were likewise encouraged to contribute by pinning their donations to a sash around the boxer's neck. Mama's boxer was a tough-looking but small pretty girl whose determined concentration spread across her face. The whole area smelled of a curious pungent mixture of boxing liniment, beer and sweat. The supporters were working themselves up into a frenzy of enthusiasm, bolstered by drink after drink, anticipating the mayhem promised by the pounding, insistent Thai music whose repetitive beat seemed to throb through one's veins.

The first fight set the pattern for the rest. After very elaborate traditional preparations of bowing and scraping, of offering up their entreaties for good luck to Buddha or whoever, the referee eventually brought the girls together to box.

Mama's boxer, An, looked extremely promising in her first round but took a knee to the belly in the second which irrevocably winded and grounded her. For some reason An took a liking to me and, after recovering from her injury, perched herself on the edge of my stool. Here we go again, I thought, prepare to repel boarders. However, she didn't drape herself provocatively around my neck as the others had; she simply used me as a backrest!

Eventually the fights ended and all but the most dedicated drunks left, satiated with lady boxing and booze. Mama had enjoyed a good night and, I cynically supposed, that was what it was all about. Having long ago lost sight of Sam, I paid my bar bill and eased myself off the stool, testing the ground for stability. The horizon stayed relatively well in place and so did An, arm linked through mine, trotting along beside me as I made my way homeward.

Sam found me the next morning in my usual seat at the beachside restaurant. The churlish grin on his face said it all as he watched An tucking into a Thai breakfast of noodles and something disgusting. With Sam came Duang, his companion of several days' standing, and she and An were soon chatting away to each other ten to the dozen – a machine-gun conversation with neither of them seeming to draw breath.

We took in many of the sights that Lamai had to offer, including a snake farm where Sam fell in love with all of the beastly reptiles and ended up with many draped ostentatiously around his neck! I shrank away in horror and revulsion and was never happier to leave a place of entertainment.

Sam and I decided that two or three days in Bangkok before the flight home might be appropriate. By this time we had discussed our private thoughts, which concurred. Could we return to Lamai to find a suitable business in order to make a permanent move possible? The lifestyle appealed to us and seemed to be far more attractive to me than sitting around in London waiting for someone to pick up on one of my scripts.

Were we being stupidly romantic, or was it possible that we could emigrate to 'Amazing Thailand'?

Bangkok we found was dirty, smog-ridden, and hot as hell, noisy and sordid. Even in the tourist spots such as the innumerable temples, palaces and suchlike, the feeling was 'tacky'. Perhaps it was the heat, perhaps the reluctance to return to London, perhaps even my age! Sam enjoyed it and dutifully plodded around most of the sights while I returned to my hotel room, slept or watched TV.

The flight home was depressing and the return to our expensive but very ordinary flat in Putney and the gloom of London even more so.

This made our resolve to return to Thailand even firmer. Five months of hard work lay before us in the building business I had created, saving every penny we could for our return to paradise. Was this what I had been looking for as a relief in my old age from the unpredictable entertainment business in London? I wasn't sure; our previous experiences in Koh Samui certainly made it a tempting possibility, but Zeesh's words of wisdom, 'Dedicate your life to your writing', rang in my ears.

The next four months or so went by remarkably quickly. Our reputation in London as reasonable, inexpensive and efficient builders had spread by word of mouth and work flowed in at an alarming rate. Our success in this business, I am quite convinced, was due solely to the fact that having virtually no overheads we could undercut almost everybody else.

The only real hiccup we had was my annual medical complaint: the discs in the lower part of my back decided to take up residence elsewhere. I was flat on my back on the hard wooden floor of our living room, suffering the excruciating pain of slipped discs once again and, as a consequence, a surfeit of daytime TV. There is nothing more punishing!

Eventually my doctor, a practitioner of the 'old school', prescribed a bottle of Scotch a day and as many Ibuprofen tablets as I could reasonably get down my throat. It worked, and the pain eased sufficiently for me to be able to attend a private hospital to have a scan on some futuristic machine that swallowed me up bodily and scanned the whole of my spine. Such treatment was not, of course, available in the NHS hospitals although they ended up paying for it. This scan proved that my spine was irrevocably damaged and surgery was recommended. There was a minimum wait of one year for the treatment. I had heard so many tales of woe resulting from such surgical invasions that I decided against it, preferring instead the Scotch-and-Ibuprofen remedy. Besides, it would ruin all our plans to return to paradise.

With an alarming amount of Scotch and Ibuprofen and a good deal of sheer determination, I was up off my sickbed (floor) and back to work in a few weeks. I'm sure that the cure also had something to do with the poor quality of daytime TV and the interminable advertisements exhorting me to gracefully settle into my hip-cups and suffer the inevitable senility with good grace. No way! I began to plan 'next' with renewed determination: a pleasant thought but one which I justified by my conviction that Thailand was full of interesting story ideas.

Had I given in to the medical advice instead of bloody-mindedly battling on, I would probably have still been flat on my back. Now, with me back at work and our business going full steam ahead, we would certainly have enough cash in the bank to return to Koh Samui and purchase our first business, a bar. Although the June trip was supposed to be an exploratory visit, both Sam and I knew, in our hearts and minds, that it was to be more definitive than that. We would do it!

All this time I had been in touch with An via the fax machine, through an interpreter by the name of Sue, whose English, although adequate, was delightfully idiosyncratic and amusing. After a while I began to notice that the missives from An, via Sue, contained repetitive phrases which she simply rearranged for each letter. Presumably she had a library of apt phrases which she used for all the girls' letters to their boyfriends. My fears of being conned returned.

Sam, who had not been quite so diligent as I in his communications with Duang, got the shock of his life when she faxed him asking, 'You want to have baby me?' We couldn't quite work out if that was a rhetorical question or a statement of her condition. Very worrying for Sam. Nevertheless, it didn't daunt our determination to return.

Chapter Thirteen

RETURN TO PARADISE

OUR ARRIVAL IN JUNE AT the now familiar toytown airport diminished our fears. We were met by An and Duang bearing smiles and gifts of sweet-smelling orchids. Duang looked far from pregnant, although it was early days yet.

This time, to avoid the expense of a hotel like the Galaxy, I had taken the precaution of asking An to find us two reasonable bungalows. The accommodation she had found seemed perfect, until the resident cockerels began their wake-up calls the next morning, or rather in the middle of the night. Despite innumerable buckets of water and western oaths they refused to budge. I gave up on the second night, conceding victory to the roosters, and we decamped to a small resort nearer the centre of town. Good bungalows, its own restaurant which overlooked the sea – perfect! Not the Galaxy but the nearest equivalent.

We had decided that running a bar would be our first business venture in Thailand, which necessitated visiting those that Lamai had to offer. Not an unpleasant task and one which I, as something of an expert, took to readily and with enthusiasm. Several hangovers later we realised that finding the ideal bar was not going to be easy. The success or failure of a business depended largely upon its location; it had to be in a good catchment area for the tourists, who are notoriously unadventurous in not wandering off the well-trodden paths, and it had to be populated with girls.

Our first choice of location was the group of 'round' bars where Mama's was situated, but these were in such demand that one would grow a long white beard while waiting for one to be available. Our next choice was the Lamai Night Plaza, a rather grand name for a plot of land next to a supermarket which boasted the first group of bars to be built in Lamai some ten years previously. Looking at the dilapidated state of some of them, I could well believe it.

We found one that was up for sale: the Billabong Bar, run by an itinerant Aussie and frequented by ex-pat Australians and Kiwis. The location was by no means ideal as it was situated at the back end of the U-shaped Night Plaza, which was a dark area and one which tended to be shunned by nervous tourists. Nevertheless, it had one advantage over the other bars in that it had a satellite TV dish, which enabled it to pick up live signals from Australia. The Aussie 'footy' matches were a big draw during the season, and they aired during the daytime at weekends. We would therefore have an added daytime trade as well as at night.

There was only one problem, apart from the price and an extension of the lease to be negotiated: the toilet! Every bar had its own toilet and, without exception, they were all 'hell holes' that one would be reluctant to enter even with a gas mask. One would have thought, in a place so geared to making money from selling gallons of beer, that reasonable attention would have been paid to the inevitable results of such guzzling of large quantities of liquid. As a builder, however, I thought that this was a problem I could overcome. I was to fight this toilet for several nose-twitching months!

Over numerous G&T's and a glance at a suspiciously new set of financial books (in Thai), I negotiated a price, handed over a ten-per-cent deposit and set a date for the takeover on September 12th. So, the deed was done. We had committed ourselves, and were rather chuffed that we had managed to do in two weeks what everybody had said would take months. We felt rather proud of ourselves and confident that we could make a success of the venture.

Mama had agreed to be our adviser and agent, although she still persisted in trying to dissuade us against the bar business. She felt that Sam was too young to be throwing his life away running a bar and that I was too old to be throwing my money away.

We knew that just selling booze was not the be-all and end-all of running such a bar. We had to recruit girls for the bar, house them and feed them and referee all the daily arguments, tantrums and squabbles amongst them. Also, as *farangs* (foreigners), we could not work behind the bar legally without a work permit.

The bar licence could not be in our name, so An had to be appointed as the official owner. Hopefully she would also solve most of the problems to do with recruiting and looking after the girls. I was of the opinion that all of these problems could be solved and, as other *farang* owners had overcome them, so too would we. We had achieved our main objective on this visit and were well pleased; and, with hugs and kisses again, we left for London town, with two months to complete our current work and plan our final exit.

Up until this point our friends and relatives in London believed that our intended emigration to paradise was all a flight of fancy. Not so; and, to substantiate our resolve, we booked our tickets for September 2nd. We also refused offers of work that would spread beyond that date, some £70,000 worth. We had so much work on offer that we were tempted to stay a month beyond our planned leaving date. However, as I pointed out to Sam, if we kept putting back the date we'd never get away, and we'd also forfeit our deposit if we didn't take over on schedule.

The eight weeks disappeared at a terrifying speed. We were hard pushed to complete the work on hand and make all the necessary arrangements such as storing our possessions, at least those we thought we wouldn't need or couldn't transport. Of course, some of the stuff we put in storage we later found that we should have taken with us!

Sam's friends and my daughter organised a farewell party, inviting most of our friends, which was a tearjerker if ever there was one. Many were still stunned to realise the enormity of the decision we had taken; we were leaving London, getting out from under nanny's skirts, fleeing the safety of the DSS, the NHS and daytime TV – thank God! It was as though we were leaving on a trip to the moon instead of to a small island paradise off the southern tip of Thailand. But leave we did, on schedule.

Arriving on Samui for the third time was like coming home, we felt that we knew this place so well now. We were somewhat disappointed not to be met by An and Duang again with smiles and orchids. Had our plans run foul of Thai duplicity? Had the girls nabbed the money I'd sent for a house deposit and the purchase of essential furniture? These thoughts passed through our minds, but nothing could wipe the smiles off our faces at this stage.

A few weeks previously I had arranged that Mama should find us a house, with upstairs accommodation for Sam and me and a large area downstairs for the girls, kitchen, toilet and shower. The staff, we hoped, would stay on from the previous bar owners. Mama had done as instructed and rented a house for us similar to hers in the same road.

An finally showed up at Mama's bar; she'd got the dates wrong – typically Thai! She had, however, been organising a bed for us and happily led us to our new home. The house was also typically Thai: unclean, undecorated and with a toilet and shower that defied description. Running along the back of the house was an open drain which was clogged and blocked with old clothes, discarded food, bottles, bricks and anything else the Thais could find to discard. Upstairs was one room, with the rest of the floor open to the world. Obviously this was not suitable for our occupation yet, and we would need to do a considerable amount of work on it to make it even partially civilised.

An and I could stay there, just; at least our room was separate from the rest of the house and had a lockable door – if the landlord could find the key! We booked Sam into the nearby Central House bungalow complex, which he was not unhappy about since it had a good toilet and shower, an effective ceiling fan and TV.

We stayed at the house in very primitive conditions in order that I could organise and be on hand for all the work that had to be done. During the next week I recruited labour to start the building renovations and clear the blocked and stinking drains. I took on a builder recommended by Mama who was supposedly a local odd-job man but was, in fact, a travelling cook! He was more adept at boiling rice than laying tiles and I spent a great deal of my time giving building lessons.

I feel it might be appropriate to spend a little time describing Thai toilets. Without a doubt, they are unique insofar as one doesn't sit on them but squat astride them. Thais are built for squatting; indeed, they spend the majority of their time and do most things in a squatting position at ground level. They cook, eat and rest on their haunches, and find it highly amusing when we 'softie' westerners try to do so to the accompaniment of a cacophony of cracking joints and moans of agony as our limbs refuse to cooperate. Therefore a Thai toilet presents considerable problems and acute embarrassment to us.

Without wishing to be indelicate or offensive, one could liken a Thai toilet exercise to that of a bombardier on a run over a small target: accuracy is essential but achieving it requires considerable practice and expertise. Scatter bombing is no good; one must be accurate, otherwise disaster spells. Well, I think I've made my point as delicately as possible and I will now abandon the subject. The less said about Thai toilets, the better.

We were well pleased with the transformation of our house, and were now ready to receive our contingent of girls for the bar. Despite the Aussie's assurances of, 'Yeah mate, of course the girls'll stay,' in the event only one of them had agreed to stay on after our takeover: Bee, a bright, cheerful and efficient girl who had a smattering of English. I offered her the position of cashier, and looked to An and her to recruit other girls for the bar since I had no idea how to go about this kind of operation. Thus began our problems with bar girls, one which was to stay with us our entire time as bar owners. It was a major headache since neither Sam nor I could work behind the bar and we couldn't really expect An and Bee to shoulder the load. We decided to delay the 'grand opening' to coincide with An's birthday in October, thus giving us time to reorganise the bar, service the dreaded toilet and recruit more staff. An and I built a circular dance platform complete with pole in the centre of the bar and I set about rewiring the place. This, as they say, was a 'shocking' experience: literally, since everything I touched was live! It was a deathtrap and took a great deal of patience and untangling of spaghetti-like cables to solve. The numerous shocks I took probably prolonged my life by several centuries!

We had thought that by applying western logic and management techniques we could solve all of our problems: not so. Most of the problems stemmed from the girls we managed to recruit. Individually they were enchanting, but get them together and they became an unruly, uncooperative flock of cackling, bickering hens! Bee got into an impossible management argument with Sam, got the hump and promptly left for pastures new. We eventually learned that she'd found a well-off German, married him and moved to Germany and had really been looking for an excuse to leave.

An couldn't, nor did she want to, cope with running the bar as cashier. Her resolve and promise to learn English in my absence had evaporated and even writing out a bar bill was almost beyond her, despite our efforts to educate her. Her lack of formal education took its toll. As a temporary measure, Sam and I took to being present at the bar all the time and writing out the bar bills – a necessary function, without which there was no check or control.

Mama came to the rescue once again. She had a young man working for her on her bar who, she said, would be ideal as a cashier. He was pleasant enough and had a little English so we took him on.

The combined opening and birthday party was a great success with An inviting half of Lamai. Mama's own bar cashier, affectionately known as 'A', did the catering and was most impressive. We more than covered the cost with the bar takings and congratulated ourselves on the success. We thought we'd cracked it: that is, until a few weeks later, when our new cashier disappeared with the takings and the float! It was a most disagreeable turn of events and we had to involve the police. If the bar had not been registered in An's name I doubt they would have cooperated; but, she being Thai, they took the case on and found our thieving cashier. We still did not get our money back until after I had personally threatened dire physical consequences and we retrieved some of our losses – less ten per cent for the police fund!

So, we were back to square one, running the bar with only a couple of girls, certainly not enough to attract the hordes of customers expected as soon as the season got under way. However, our Australian 'footy' had proved worthwhile. Only one other venue could receive this popular event, and their satellite always seemed to go on the blink at the wrong time, so we got most of the customers.

With all of the other bars pumping out thumping techno music and sporting bevies of screaming girls, we decided to run a 'quiet' bar: somewhere our customers could sit in peace and have a drink and a chat in English. In the interim before the season this particular ploy worked, and we got several regular customers and even some families who appreciated a comparatively civilised environment where they and their children could have a relatively peaceful time. This meant that either Sam or I had to be in attendance all the time as mine hosts.

All this was becoming too much for me. Sam and I still had to dip into our personal resources to keep the business afloat, and it became increasingly evident that the bar would not support both of us. Mama and An had been right. The bar business was not for us; at least, not for me. I was thoroughly fed up with being virtually a pimp and having to deal with the girls' problems.

We had heard rumours for some time that a bungee jump was to be erected at the end of the Night Plaza on an old tennis-court site, now a disused car-park. We, unlike a lot of the other bar owners, welcomed it. It would bring life to the area and light up what was otherwise a 'black hole' that frightened off the tourists. However, the Phuket company owners were having trouble nailing down their partners who were not, apparently, all they claimed to be.

The entrepreneur with a penny in his pocket smelled an opportunity. I stepped smartly in, offering Sam and I as new partners. What on earth was I doing? Here was I, nearing retirement, negotiating to buy into a bungee business about which I knew nothing and without sufficient capital to do so! Sam thought I was mad, too, but he'd seen me do much more impossible deals before and encouraged me. If I could pull it off, it was certainly a better option than a bar. Nothing ventured...

Chapter Fourteen

Rising from the Ashes

SAM HAD OTHER PROBLEMS OCCUPYING his mind. Duang had indeed been pregnant, and the dates certainly made it possible that Sam might well be the father. The baby was born, but Sam was still not convinced that the child was of his loins. He was dubbed Sam Song – Sam number two! Sam was to struggle with the emotional implications of this new arrival for some time.

Meanwhile, I negotiated a contract for the bungee business and managed to raise enough capital from my own resources to buy a twenty-five per cent share, the right to build and own a bar on the site and an option to purchase a further twenty-five per cent by the year's end. Now we were in business!

On the advice of a friend, and with the assistance of an accountant in Chaweng used to this sort of arrangement, we launched our company. With it came two work permits so Sam and I could now legitimately own, run and work in our chosen businesses. This now gave us commercial credibility. We had the Billabong bar and a bungee business and it was obvious that everyone considered that we had money to burn; in fact, we hardly had two pennies to rub together.

It was somewhere around this time that An, on one of her expeditions to recruit girls for the Billabong, telephoned to say that she had two ladies and should she bring them along? She sounded rather nervous and I couldn't fathom why, until she returned the next night. Instead of two 'ladies' in tow, she had two 'babies'! I had completely misunderstood her words on the telephone, and was now presented with the option of accepting the two children – hers from her former Thai common-law husband – or turning them away.

They were delightful boys: Num, aged ten, and Lyn, aged eight. Big brown eyes, scared, uncertain and pleading but not hopeful. Well, what could I do? They had been living with their father who, being somewhat partial to Thai whisky, was apt to get drunk and beat the hell out of them. An had decided that she'd no option but to remove them from his 'tender' care.

After they had been fed and watered, reassured that their new 'Papa' would not be turning them out but would care for them, they were put to bed in the house. This was obviously not going to be a suitable arrangement for long, since the only place they could lay their heads was in the girls' area downstairs. So, the next day, I set An the task of finding more suitable accommodation.

With Sam now convinced that Sam Song was his son, our joint responsibilities were increasing daily. The bungee had to be made to work. There was no question now of throwing in the towel and returning to London with our tail between our legs. With the cash investment now in, I could go ahead and build the bar and other buildings necessary to house the bungee business, like an office and storage room and clean toilets for the customers. I had little time to do this since the Phuket partners insisted that the bungee should open, at the latest, on December 1st. Just eight days ahead!

I called in Pong, a first-class builder (by Thai standards), who had helped me build the extra room in our house for Sam's privacy. Together we planned the exercise which entailed not only building the bar from scratch but also the office, men's and ladies' toilets, furnishing the bar with a cold store for the beer and other drinks, installing water and electricity and making the area into what it was called: the Jungle Bungee Catapult. Jungle it wasn't, so we had to create the ambience, build an entrance of some seven metres long by five high with an illuminated sign, floodlight the area and service it with bamboo chairs and tables, palm and banana trees and so on and so forth.

I found an enormous entrance sign discarded as junk behind the printer's and sign maker's. Someone had ordered it and then reneged on the deal. It was perfect, though a little large, illuminated from the inside by strip lights. I had the sign maker make us a new sign and he promised to have the whole mounted on metal stilts so that we could erect it at the entrance to the bungee area, and to have it ready and installed in time for the opening party. I have not come across a Thai yet who hasn't promised the earth and only delivered a handful of dust!

Time means little to the Thais. Tomorrow never comes and is never given serious thought. When one sets a time with Thais for something to happen it is very arbitrary. The only thing that seems to happen on time is *ghin cow* – eating. Their stomachs are perhaps their timepieces for without fail they eat every four hours or so, with snacks in between for the half and quarter hours! My sign-maker was no exception. I had to threaten him with non-payment before he eventually turned up with a horde of workers and a lorry bearing the said sign – one hour or so before the grand opening party was due to begin!

Despite similar upsets we opened on schedule with a serviceable but unfinished bar and facilities. In addition to the building work, I'd had to organise the catering for the grand opening and a live rock band to entertain our guests. While I was doing this, Sam had been training as the bungee jump master, learning all the necessary safety measures and tricks of the trade of the actual catapult.

The Grand Opening was indeed grand! The bungee catapult was packed out with guests and tourists alike, and our bar takings reflected this. I MC'd the whole event in a smattering of God-knows-how-many languages and felt like a cross between a circus ringmaster and a stand-up comic. We managed to get the bars from the Night Plaza to sponsor one or more of their girls to jump, so we had a continuous, if hysterical, entertainment of flying, screaming girls going on.

It was at this stage that our Phuket partners realised that, as a showman, I knew what I was doing; and from then on they largely left us alone to run the business. Fortunately we had opened at the beginning of the high season, this being a special one: the celebration of the millennium. We had high hopes of a spectacular turnover.

Opinions about bar girls and their profession vary greatly. Some young men, having come to Thailand for the express purpose of experiencing the fleshpots, were shocked by the openness of the 'sex in your face' trade. The expression, 'I've never paid for it yet and I don't intend to start now,' was often heard coming out of the mouths of ingenuous youths. What on earth did they think they were coming to – a free market where they could demonstrate their masculinity and take their pick of Thailand's finest who'd simply fall over themselves to steal their virginity and jump into bed with them? What did they think they were doing in their home towns by taking a girl out on a date and buying maybe dinner or whatever – *not* 'paying for it'?

Others would come waving wads of notes and, despite beery breath, pimples and a beer-belly, would expect to have success with the ladies. Even girls who are the most dedicated prostitutes have some standards and no amount of money in the world will induce them to take up with some of the European specimens of manhood that turn up. Most girls are not, technically speaking, prostitutes. The young and ingenuous creatures from rural Thailand come to the tourist spots with little or no knowledge of what is expected of them, and have to learn from the other girls.

Certainly the skill of choosing the right kind of *farang* to take up with is only learned by experience, and very often it is the 'Mama Sang' who will wave a warning finger if a girl is about to make a ghastly mistake. Most hope for true romance and a prolonged relationship with a *farang*; if it blossoms into marriage, all the better. Marrying a Thai man does not appeal to most girls as Thai men do not, on the whole, make good husbands.

Many men visiting the bars are past the first flush of youth and look to the experience to reinvigorate their sex life. Some get a kick out of walking around with a young girl on their arm, who may well prefer an older man since these are less trouble and have more disposable income than the young studs. The latter tend to get drunk all the time and demand attention without giving much in return.

When asking a girl to leave the bar a *farang* customer is required to pay the Mama Sang a 'bar fine', payment for depriving her of one of her girls at the bar. He is also required to pay, and will probably negotiate beforehand, a price for the girl's time and attention. This will vary, according to the experience of the particular girl, from five hundred baht to several thousands. The more experienced girls from Pattaya and other prime spots will command, and get, high prices relatively speaking for a night of unmitigated pleasure. Some will stay with their *farang* boyfriends for the entire stay of their holiday and the *farang* will often return again and again to relive the experience. Such is the charm of the Thai ladies.

One girl I heard of had a very nice little business going. She had four boyfriends, all visiting at different times of the year. In their absence they all supported her by sending cash every month. She was raking it in from all four; and, of course, in between their individual visits, working her charms with others. She only came unstuck when one of them decided to visit out of his allotted time and met one of the others she was romancing. Oops!

Recruiting girls to work at the bar was, as we had found out, a particularly difficult task, and very often one had to rely upon recruitment by a Mama Sang to arrange this. She would, of course, charge for this service, and the bar owner would have to pay for the girl's travel. This was a very expensive form of recruitment, and not entirely successful for there was nothing stopping the girls from staying just a few days and then disappearing. We found the answer to this rip-off by holding their identity cards – rather like holding someone's passport as security – for without their ID they couldn't really go anywhere.

Besides the girls, there were also other types of sexual attractions. For instance, homosexuality was well catered for and many of the bar girls were not, in fact, girls but *katoeys* – transsexuals. These lookalike 'girls' sometimes went to great lengths to change their physical appearance. Plastic surgery was common, with nose jobs and boob jobs high on the list of preference. At one time in Lamai there was a nightclub entertainment entirely made up of *katoeys*, in the most extravagant dresses and wigs, miming along to famous pop stars such as Madonna or Marilyn Monroe. They were quite convincing performances, but the *katoeys* always spoiled it by 'camping it up'; they just couldn't resist it, so taken with themselves were they.

These *katoeys* were also quite rough characters and it did not do to pick an argument with them. Many were employed at the bars to keep trouble away. One such that I knew was ex Thai SAS. A more innocent looking 'girl' you couldn't hope to meet, but as tough as an elephant's hide beneath the facade. But definitely homosexual; he died of AIDS a year or so later.

Many of the ex-pats had Thai ladies living in to look after their daily chores such as cleaning, cooking, laundry and so on as well as their sexual needs. Not that most of the ex-pats were too concerned with the latter, since they spent most of their time in one bar or another and simply required a shoulder to lean on at the end of a particularly difficult night! This was how many of the older bar girls ended up, and thought themselves lucky to get such a cushy number.

In addition to their wages of sin many of the girls would try to persuade their boyfriends to buy them a little present. The preference was for a gold something-or-other: a necklace, ring or bracelet. Gold is valued more than paper money since it doesn't lose its intrinsic value. They also see such gaudy baubles as displays of their wealth, and many are heavily adorned.

It was becoming an exhausting exercise for Sam and me to continue running both the Billabong Bar and the bungee business and its bar. I discreetly put the rumour around that the Billabong was up for sale. It was by now the only source of capital we had and I desperately wanted to buy a further twenty-five per cent of the bungee from our partners. As it happened, the grapevine proved to be very effective; Thais love to gossip and it is the surest way of letting the world know your secrets.

Christmas was almost upon us; the big millennium bonanza was about to envelop and bestow untold wealth on us! Everyone was poised for the expected gold rush. As it happened, there was hardly any increase in business; indeed, tourists stayed away in droves, or cancelled. In their greed the resorts and hotels had increased their charges to such an extent that cancellations reduced the visitor numbers by a third. As a consequence, all other tourist-related businesses suffered. However, I did manage to sell the Billabong bar, at a small profit, so solving our liquidity problem.

When Sam and I took over the bungee, we inherited two Thai staff. Sam had trained as bungee master and I knew enough about it by now to muddle through without killing anybody!

The bungee catapult is the exact reverse of the bungee jump. One is catapulted up forty metres into the air by stretched bungee cords; there is no jumping involved. Sam was now the expert at this (to my way of thinking) crazy, mind-boggling 'sport'! He had done three hundred or so 'jumps' himself, demonstrating to potential customers on a daily basis. I, on the other hand, was reserving my maiden flight until my birthday, some months away in April. I had no desire to take this precarious journey into the air until I had to. Chicken? Sure! At my age and with a serious complaint like diabetes, plus a spine that had only just recovered from naughty discs to take into consideration, I wasn't about to take any chances I didn't have to.

I had been a little concerned about coming to the island because of my health problems, but I needn't have been. The local doctor in Lamai was a splendid fellow who spoke almost colloquial English. After a modest physical, checking my blood pressure and suchlike, he sent me off to Chaweng hospital for a blood test to fully diagnose my diabetic status.

In London I underwent this process on a six-monthly monitoring basis entailing a visit to my doctor's surgery, which was somewhat akin to a second-hand furniture store with not one chair in the waiting room that matched and piles of magazines which were so out of date they were interesting! The nurse, after several bungled and painful attempts, found a vein and managed to extract enough of my essential liquid for the necessary tests. A week or so passed before the test results were available, at which point I had to attend the surgery again, with another outrageously long wait, to hear the outcome and get the inevitable lecture on drinking and smoking.

At Chaweng hospital I was greeted courteously by an immaculately dressed nurse/receptionist, asked a few questions and politely asked to wait. I was led to a pristine waiting area where all the furniture matched; there was a TV, and various daily papers and up-to-date periodicals for those who preferred. Before I could even read the headlines of the *Bangkok Post* I was swept away by another polite and smiling nurse who took my blood pressure. Minutes later I was shown into a small consulting area and the diabetic specialist, a female doctor, asked me discreet questions about my lifestyle and so on; not a lecture in sight yet. She took the necessary red liquid for testing with the gentleness of a dove and the accuracy of a watchmaker – I didn't feel a thing.

I waited again in the reception area for only as long as it took for me to sup a cup of tea that had been thoughtfully provided for me. In all it took half an hour from arriving to walking out with the completed results in my hand. I had to pay for this check-up, naturally; but the cost was minimal for the kind of attention and service I had received. Wake up, the NHS!

This was a private hospital, of course, and not equipped for major 'invasive' surgery; but my experience at the state hospital, where I had taken An for treatment on a couple of occasions, was no less impressive. All patients had to pay for was the drugs used in their treatment. More locally, in Lamai, the minor motorbike cuts, bruises and scrapes, of which there were many on a daily basis, were treated locally either by the doctor or by local pharmacies who always had a trained nurse in attendance.

The doctor, unlike my local quack in London, wasn't alarmist about the test results from the hospital and didn't give me any lectures either. Besides, it was obvious to him that I could read the test results as well as he could: long experience in London had given me a good medical education in the field of diabetes. He prescribed virtually what I had been on previously, and produced the Thai version at remarkably low cost. I could provide for my diabetic treatment for under a tenner a month; God knows what it cost the NHS in London. Considerably more than that, I supposed. Anyway, I felt I was in good hands and was reassured about the future of my faithful old body that had served me so well for so many years.

Since neither Sam nor I spoke Thai and our number one Thai man Joe spoke little English, communication was limited to frustrated pidgin and gestures. When An was about there was no problem; but when she was not, we had to rely on the goodwill of Jom, a jolly Thai lady and common-law wife of Scotty, the owner of the Red White & Blue, the nearest bar to the bungee. Jom was a riot: short and fat and almost always laughing – probably due to the fact that she had a penchant for vodka!

Scotty and Jom were two of the original Night Plaza bar-owners and had been there some eight years or so. Having lost all in Chaweng through a crooked lawyer, Scotty had moved to Lamai when the Night Plaza was first constructed. Scotty, confusingly, was not a Scot but had a broad cockney accent and a wicked wit. He came every year for the high season then returned to England in May to resume his job, that of lorry driver on one or other of the road construction enterprises. He was a formidable character, always moaning about the inadequacies of the Thais, or Thai bureaucracy in particular; but beneath his blustering lay a charming and delightful character, a true friend in need. Jom, round, jolly and helpful, had the typical Thai attitude to life; she lived for the moment – tomorrow never comes! They were a well-suited couple whom I took to immediately.

The Christmas and New Year period was a good time for business, although we found that most of our customers tended to come late at night. We initially opened at three in the afternoon, but soon changed this to five. We had to leave some time for those who wanted the bungee experience by day, allowing them to take photographs or videos of their exploits.

However, most of the trade was late-night, which meant extended hours for us, sometimes going on to three or four in the morning. One evening I'd suggested to Sam that he should take a little time off, as it was unlikely that we would be inundated with customers. Wrong! At shortly after midnight the bungee was 'invaded' by ten or so giant Swedes who'd been celebrating at a local bar and restaurant. They were good-humoured but raucous and all, except one, dwarfed me by several disconcerting inches. They all wanted to do the bungee at once and I had the greatest difficulty in controlling this affable but insistent crowd. In the event all went well, but I was exhausted by the end of their visit and only one of them hadn't taken flight. This last was the smallest, and his giant friends bullied him remorselessly until finally he succumbed, was strapped into the harness and flown aloft at great speed.

All seemed fine until he returned to *terra firma* whereupon he collapsed into a faint of delayed terror. He was born away aloft the shoulders of his still noisy and exuberant compatriots! I made a considerable profit that night – the hard way! This became a pattern with groups of men from one country or another, with several Thai ladies tagging along, visiting the bungee to drink and fly, demonstrating their fearless manliness.

The holiday period, particularly in this millennium year, was supposed to break all records. As already mentioned, however, the Thais had succumbed to their natural instinct to make hay while the sun shone and rocketed the prices way up. This had the effect of turning away many people who would have otherwise spent their time in Thailand. Many, put off by the exorbitant price rises, had opted instead for other destinations; and the supposed bonanza quickly turned into a damp squib. A Millennium Bug(ger) indeed!

Our staff were fine for the first couple of months, but it soon became apparent that faithful Joe had his problems with handling money and with the ladies. The other Thai we had inherited from Phuket was a loud-mouthed troublemaker and after several confrontations he instigated a walkout, thinking that Sam and I would have to close up shop. We chose not to capitulate to his outrageous blackmail demands; instead, we demonstrated that we were more than capable of operating the bungee without them and doing their jobs as well as our own. Joe returned the next day, hangdog and recalcitrant, as did the new trainee we'd had the foresight to employ, fearing trouble from the stroppy one. We had experienced a spate of petty thefts from the bar but when we fired the troublemaker these ceased. I say no more!

Having demonstrated our ability to run the bungee we had little further trouble from the Thai staff until one momentous night when Joe disappeared, got outrageously drunk and reappeared and tried to take over operating the bungee. I had to physically remove him; not an easy task as Joe, although small, was as tough as old boots. He had apparently got into debt with the local 'mafia' and also taken a fancy to a Muslim Thai's girlfriend! Double trouble!

An incredible Thai soap opera then ensued which was only sorted out by another Thai we had taken on as staff, in case Joe fell by the wayside or ended up face down in the jungle somewhere. The upshot was that Joe went off with his lady love, back home to Udonthani to get married. The new man, Sompot, spoke reasonable English, had a smattering of German and Italian and could talk the hind legs off a donkey. He was a good salesman and an asset to the business. At last, we thought, one we could communicate with and trust. Wrong!

While none of us would claim to be perfect, we like to think of ourselves as honest and fair with the only allowable lies being those told to the Inland Revenue. Our experiences with our Thai staff indicated that the Thais revelled in weaving complicated webs of lies. They were so transparent they were laughable. 'Saving face' was the excuse, but lying seems to be a national pastime.

Thais are the biggest gossipmongers and blatant liars I have ever encountered. Even the faithful Sompot fell victim to the endemic habit and created an amazing story trying to raise a loan from us. This fell apart at the seams after only a few pertinent questions, and we discovered that he needed the loan to get his wife out of the 'nick'! She'd fallen into the temptation of 'lifting' a gold bracelet and pearl pendant from an unsuspecting tourist who had taken them off to have a massage. Some Thais conveniently call it 'borrowing' but, whatever, it is never returned. They are contrite, apparently, when caught and 'solly, solly' is a phrase to be heard every day as much as '*ghin cow*'.

Gambling is another endemic disease amongst the Thais. Luck is thought to be as tangible and real as a bowl of rice and available to everyone simply by wishful thinking. Although gambling at cards or dominoes is highly illegal, the state runs a lottery that almost every Thai participates in. As an adjunct to the state lottery there are many illegal 'numbers games' which have sprung up locally. Thais will gamble on almost anything, from buffalo and cock fights to, probably, how many grains of rice there are in a kilo! They are mad for it and many get into serious debt; or, worse, lose their house, land and everything else in their quest for lady luck. The lure of the get-rich-quick bug is too tempting for them; and, really, it is understandable when one considers what little they own anyway. They can never understand that nothing is for nothing and there is always a price to pay. Poverty is never a million miles away from their daily lives.

Money – cash money – as legal tender is a necessity but is valued far less by the Thais than gold. Money has a nasty habit of just running through your fingers and leaving one empty-handed all too quickly. Gold, on the other hand, is both a symbol of success and a commodity that can be exchanged for money if the need arises. It rarely loses its value, unlike currency which tends to yo-yo all over the place. However, one never gets as much for gold when sold; one pays a premium when purchasing, because new gold articles carry a manufacturer's or craftsman's cost which cannot be retrieved. Or so the goldsmiths would have you believe: in truth, they pass on the manufacturer's cost over and over again.

I'd bought An a gold bracelet and necklace for her birthday present.

The Thai gold is much more pure, deep-coloured and vibrant than European gold, and looks beautiful against a brown skin. Fortunately An was not addicted to gambling and the gold stayed where it belonged for a while – on her person. She did eventually lose it gambling, but it was nothing to do with cards.

An had found us a two-bedroomed bungalow which, of course, I had to entirely rebuild inside. We had also managed to get the boys into the local Thai school, and everything seemed to be sweetness and light. The main problem was my working hours, the bungee not closing until after one in the morning and sometimes even later. An had become disenchanted with the speed of progress of our relationship, and her constant threat of 'I go Nongkhai' (her home) whenever we'd had a mild confrontation became a reality. She decided to take the boys from the school in Lamai and go home to her village on the Laos border. She gambled that I would go with her. She lost.

To finance this return to the homeland, she sold her gold and a motorbike I had bought and promptly upped sticks, packed her bags and departed with two very sad children. Once in Ban Dongwen, her village, she bought some land for thirty thousand baht (around five hundred pounds) from a man who, it turned out, didn't own it in the first place and promptly disappeared to Singapore. She lost again!

So, without money, without a home and with the children farmed out to stay with another family, she returned to Lamai. 'Solly, solly,' that well used phrase, was all she could say. She did, however, have the grace to laugh at her own stupidity – or was she laughing at mine?

She hadn't lost a great deal of money but it gave me the opportunity to impress upon her that such deals could only be done one way – the right way! I had promised months ago that I would visit her home and family. That she had tried to force forward this promise made me realise just how important this was to her. Family is everything to the Thais. I vowed I would keep my promise and visit, as planned, in February. Her gambling days were over.

Mine, however, were not; but at least they were based upon percentages and a certain amount of calculated business guile. I needed to buy out our Phuket partners who were becoming increasingly obnoxious and bullying, but I had to wait until they wanted the deal. The low season was upon us and income dropped to just about break-even. This downturn, as expected, turned to my advantage. Phuket indicated its willingness to sell. At last my gamble was beginning to pay off. Trouble was, how high were the stakes? The value, on paper, was four hundred thousand baht – which was what I had paid for our fifty-per-cent share. The trick was going to be getting this reduced, hopefully by half! A soft-shoe shuffle was called for, and I let the deal lie fallow while I went up north with An.

I'd got until August to consolidate the deal, the new deadline set by Phuket. It was a good time to let them sweat. That we could survive the downturn in business I had little doubt, but Phuket suffering the same problems was another matter. They would feel the pinch quicker; despite Phuket's bigger tourist industry, their volatile boss was apt to be less patient and liable to make hasty decisions.

While all this activity was going on in my business and personal life, Sam had begun to come to terms with the fact that he was the father of an enchanting baby and Sam Song occupied much of his thoughts. He had, since the beginning, made financial provision for Sam Song, and every day he grew closer and closer to the child. Unfortunately the same could not be said for the mother, Duang. Their relationship, although friendly, did not seem to be developing beyond that.

My relationship with An, however, was going great guns. I'd found a second wind and marriage was on the cards. To be married at the ripe old age of sixty-four to a young woman of thirty-one seemed to be a little unfair on her, but An would have none of it. She was delighted: I was the nearest thing to security that she had ever known. In England I would definitely be considered a relatively poor man, suffering old age on a pension (coming up) that would barely keep body and soul together. In Thailand, however, this pension would make me a reasonably well-off man. That An was marrying for security rather than in a fit of unbridled passion was true, but then I knew that. That she had a great affection and respect for me I also knew. To the boys, I was already Papa.

Chapter Fifteen

HERE WE GO AGAIN!

THIS DEVELOPMENT MEANT GIVING SOME serious thought to leaving Lamai and moving to Ban Dongwen, where the kids were happily in school. What they needed now was a proper home. I would have to relinquish my management of the bungee and hand it over to Sam to run; but, before I had negotiated the total ownership of the business and got shot of our partners, this would be unthinkable and unfair.

There was also the problem that Sam could not physically run the business by himself. It definitely required two Europeans to manage the place; it was too demanding for one for any length of time. The hours were gruelling. This was why we had initially taken on two more partners; but, with one having pulled out and the other propping up a bar somewhere, we were left looking for a replacement candidate for me.

I left this problem to lie fallow as I took the night sleeper with An to Bangkok and thence, the next day, another twelve-hour journey by train to Udonthani. I hadn't realised just how far Nongkhai was from Koh Samui until this point, and any vague thoughts I'd had of trying to commute on a weekly basis were ditched. We arrived in a dilapidated taxi as it was getting dark. The journey through the jungle was an eerie experience.

We arrived at An's sister's bungalow, a concrete-block-and-stucco building built for her by her boyfriend when she was heavily pregnant. It was here, I learned thankfully, that we were to stay during our visit. The thought of having to possibly kip down in one of the Thai peasant huts that dotted the place had filled me with dread. Here, at least, was a relatively civilised dwelling.

Waiting on the porch to greet us, along with the thousands of flies, mosquitoes and assorted moths scudding around the lights, was the reception committee: some ten or twelve Thais who inspected me with considerable awe – and some with open resentment. One old crow, her teeth stained with betel-nut juice, grabbed my hand and began counting my fingers! Was I a freak? I looked around; no, I had the same number of fingers as anyone else there. I was a different colour, yes; I couldn't squat on my haunches and I was a *farang*, but other than that I was normal. She continued to count my fingers over and over again. It wasn't until I smelled her breath that I realised that she was well loaded with a vinous spirit of some sort.

Having been honoured and plonked into a chair in the centre of things, still having my fingers counted, I was introduced to An's mother. I instantly, if somewhat irreverently, dubbed her the 'Betel-Nut Queen' in my mind. Her face was distorted with a gob full of 'chew' and her mouth a viscous streak of betel-nut-juice red. Every now and then she would deposit a well-aimed stream of red spit into a spittoon. This was my future mother-in-law!

An's stepfather (her real father having died from a surfeit of Thai whisky some years before) was a lugubrious fellow who ate with an undying appetite. He also never refused anything: a cigarette, beer, food, whatever. I instantly nicknamed him the 'Phantom Scrounger'. This has since proved to be absolutely on the button since when anything is on offer – a cigarette, bottle of beer, food – he appears like a ghost emerging from the shadows. He also seemed to have a fixed aversion to work, never moving unless he had to and rarely with any purpose other than to perhaps let the blood flow back into his cramped limbs or reach for another tasty morsel or 'freebie'.

The old crone I named the 'Whisky Witch', for she was very witch-looking. By this time she was well out of what represented the remains of her addled brain and retired to have a screaming match with one of her near neighbours. This crazy verbal battle continued until well into the night and after I had, thankfully, retired to my bed.

The following morning An's sister, Goy, prepared breakfast for me. A very passable fried egg, some toast and coffee. I felt mildly civilised and the jungle looked far less threatening in the early morning sunlight. The previous night it was full of alarming sounds and ominous moving shadows, but now it looked like a bit of Kew Gardens transported.

It was blisteringly hot and the vast plains of unending rice-paddy fields were arid now, resting before the next planting after the monsoon rains. The few Thai gardens producing vegetables were surprisingly poorly tended. I thought they would be well looked after and yield good crops, but obviously the Thais either don't have the knack, the expertise or maybe the inclination to raise reasonable crops. As a gardener, whose green fingers could make even a matchstick grow, I would have to investigate this anomaly.

An took me to a plot of land only a few yards from the perimeter of Goy's house on which a peasant home had been planted. At least it looked as though it had been planted, as it was completely surrounded by a jungle of small trees and saplings and a tangle of thorny weeds, which grabbed at one as though they were alive. This was where her mother and the family had lived before being moved to Goy's new house. It was four square walls, concrete blocks, a tin roof and with a small outhouse attached. There was no toilet, no electricity and no water. It was for sale and An obviously wanted to set up home there.

Oh boy! If I took this on it would be a monumental task. I'd have to clear the surrounding jungle, drive a road through for access, install a sewage system and bore down to the water table for a supply. Electricity wasn't a problem, for I had seen a feed cable amongst the jungle branches, which serviced Goy's and the other houses nearby, and I could tap into that. I sat down with pencil and paper and worked out a potential design for a house, using the four square walls of the existing structure as a basis. It would probably work, but what of the price?

We got the landowners to a meeting at the site, and after a great deal of pacing out the boundaries of the land for sale and a lot of Thai yak-yak – they can't do anything unless everyone has their say – we negotiated a price. To my surprise, we got the lot for thirty-one thousand baht – just over five hundred quid! Bearing in mind An's previous deal I refused to part with anything beyond a small deposit until the legal work had been completed and the land registered in An's name.

I had only a few days there and, since An wanted to move in immediately with the boys, I hastily arranged for toilet facilities to be installed, basic electricity supply connected and two vast water vats put in place for drinking and showering facilities. This was, apparently, more than adequate for An and the boys and more than they currently enjoyed where they were. They were delighted to have a home of their own. I deposited some money in An's bank account, enough to pay for the completion of the purchase and for them to live on for a while. That was about all I had time to do during my short stay there as I had to get back to help Sam with the business.

The next day I flew back to Koh Samui via Bangkok. I was determined not to suffer the interminable train trips again, and by flying I could do the entire journey in one brief afternoon. I said my farewells to An and the boys and the Betel-Nut Queen who had come to the airport with us for the ride. I had a mountain or two to climb back in Lamai if I was to return to Ban Dongwen to build our new home: a mountain with what seemed like a couple of impassable crevices looming ahead.

By the time I had returned to Koh Samui from my trip up north, Sam and Sam Song had bonded superbly. Every day, between five and six, Duang brought Sam Song to see Sam to play together at the bungee. Sam Song looked forward to this time of day as much as did the proud father. It was a joy to see this side to Sam, who had previously tolerated other people's babies but showed little or no desire to be involved beyond the 'visiting uncle' stage. This was a revelation and a delight. My son, although now in his late thirties, had begun to mellow, to grow up one more stage; and was altogether another person, and happier.

As he'd had to work the bungee alone during my absence Sam was rather jaded. I suggested that he take a few days off to compensate and renew his batteries while I reciprocated and ran the business. It was a relatively quiet time anyway. To my surprise, Sam readily agreed and announced that he would take both Sam Song and Duang off for a few days to an island only an hour or so from Koh Samui. This would be the test. An hour a day playing with his son was one thing, but could he stand twenty-four hours with a baby who was happy and delightful during his one hour of play time but who, during the remaining twenty-three hours of the day and night, must have at least one tedious tantrum? Sam's three days off spread into four, then five; and he returned even more refreshed and enchanted with his son. His relationship with Duang, it seemed, had also improved.

I'd had a remarkably successful time with the bungee during their absence and had done good business. This turned out to be a freak run of luck and business soon returned to a depressingly slow pace. With the beginning of the lowest part of the season about to descend on us, Sam and I were increasingly like nervous kittens; could we get through the next four months and survive?

Our Phuket partners were becoming fractious. Timing was all; and, since we had not experienced business at this time of the year in Thailand before, we were somewhat in the lap of the gods. August, we thought, would be all right since traditionally the Italians arrived in droves. This was their month.

The reason for this strange 'mini high season' was simple. Fiat, being the largest employer in Italy, had negotiated a package deal with the airlines and hotels as a perk for their workers, and many took advantage of it. The problem was that most of the Italian workers were so low-paid that they had little to spend once they came on holiday. The story persists to this day of four Italian boys arriving at a bar, ordering one Coca-Cola and four straws!

Before August, however, we had to survive what promised to be the worst three months of business in Lamai. We had frequent 'election' holidays to survive, plus the king's designated holidays, during all of which every bar had to close up business. No booze was allowed to be sold, except in restaurants where food was served.

Also we had Song Kran, the Thai water festival holiday, in the first part of April. Many of the girls on the bars went home at this time, and were unlikely to return until October or November – an indication of the downturn in business during these months.

Song Kran is difficult to describe. In essence it is like Mardi Gras in Europe, a cleansing process of the body and soul. The Thais are supposed to clean house, throw out unwanted possessions and cleanse their bodies and minds. In reality it had been corrupted into three or four whole days of sadistic water-fights in the streets where everyone is a potential victim, particularly *farangs*!

My father and mother

In my teens, swimming at Burnham Beeches not only helped to keep me healthy but also brought me into social contact with others of my own age. I'm the handsome thirteen-year-old brat on the far right!

Stepping into the breach to play an Ugly Sister in pantomime in Basingstoke

Me (kneeling, front centre) with fellow members of the High Wycombe Rep company

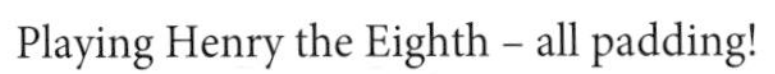

Playing Henry the Eighth – all padding!

Me aged nineteen – oh happy days!

As Nicky Garnet in *The Facts of Life*, a 1960 episode of ITV's *Somerset Maugham Hour*, with Julia Arnall

Me with beard and Diane Cilento in *Cut Yourself a Slice of Throat*, an episode of ITV's *Blackmail* series from 1965

As Jack Chesney (right) in a 1965 BBC production of the play *Charley's Aunt*, with Richard Briers in drag as Lord Fancourt Babberley

My three monsters!

On location in Germany, filming for the *Paul Temple* TV series

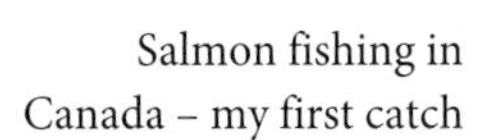

Salmon fishing in
Canada – my first catch

Drunk and entertaining friends on the piano at my sixty-fifth birthday party

My wife, Ingsumon, who kept me alive so that I could write this memoir

Not having the childish undergraduate exuberance I suppose I once had, I endeavoured to avoid this ghastly experience and refused to take part. Sam, on the other hand, took part enthusiastically, and time and again returned to the bungalow (which he had moved into when An had decamped) soaked to the skin and covered in talcum powder. Not my game, I thought, and worked out a route through the backstreets of Lamai to get to the bungee. I succeeded in this crafty scheme right up to the point of reaching the Night Plaza, when I was caught from behind by a particularly sadistic youth who doused me with iced water! So, I was initiated into Song Kran!

Unfortunately, no one from London could visit for my birthday on April 16th. As it came just after Song Kran, I thought I would try to encourage some of the local custom by throwing another of our now legendary parties.

It was also to be the occasion of my maiden flight on the bungee as I'd promised: secretly something I had not been looking forward to. I maintained that such adventurous games were for the foolhardy young; but there was no getting away from it now.

The party was attended by many of our loyal friends and business acquaintances in Lamai, and the running buffet was once again splendidly supplied by 'A', Mama's cashier. I did not, however, employ a live band – the cost was simply prohibitive for such a small party.

My first flight on the powerful bungee was approached with great trepidation but, like the stoic British chap that I am, with gritted teeth and determination. Flying up was a splendid experience and I felt that my previous misgivings were unfounded. When I reached the giddy heights of forty metres, the apex of the flight achieved in a matter of seconds, my stomach seemed to wish to stay there longer than the rest of me until gravity forced it to follow! This experience was repeated four or five times until the bungee cord eventually lost its strength and I was lowered to *terra firma* to great applause, which I felt I thoroughly deserved.

By the time I decided with great bravura to do a second flight, my landlord and I had sunk the best part of a bottle of Famous Grouse, which he had kindly brought along, and I felt no pain. In fact I don't remember the event at all!

There followed a period of desperate uncertainty. Lamai was empty right through the end of April. May looked as though it was going to be just as bleak, but was saved for us by the arrival of four Danes and two old customers from the Billabong bar. All six proceeded to take over the bungee bar and indeed the bungee catapult. They made it their centre of operations, and drank vast quantities of vodka and flew on the bungee until the early hours. They became such good customers that I cooked them special steak dinners and a barbecue lash-up, which they thoroughly appreciated.

May then, rather than the disaster we had expected, turned out to be a break-even month and I hadn't had to touch the cash reserves I'd salted away. June and July saw the arrival of several very good friends from London, a welcome and comforting experience. Some arrived out of the blue, others made sure that we organised their creature comforts in advance. Our friends made the slack business bearable.

With August coming up, the powers that be had decided to run lady boxing again to boost the business of the round bars. At Mama's bar I was introduced to the landowner who sponsored and organised the whole affair. Previously they'd had a *farang* do the commentary for the tourists in English, but he had left. Mama volunteered my services for this doubtful honour. What the hell did I know about Thai boxing? There was, however, no getting out of it, since she had seen me MC the grand opening of the bungee and was convinced that this was no different! After all, when I'd MC'd the bungee opening, what had I known about bungee jumping? She had a point!

I had three days to prepare for an event that lasted approximately four hours and about which I knew zilch! However, as Mama pointed out, it was an obvious opportunity for me to plug the bungee and do some splendid PR with a captive audience. So, I set about the task and wrote a script. The only payment I required for my services was a bottle of Gordon's gin, a supply of tonic and a bottomless jug of ice. This was going to be thirsty work!

The big problem for me was getting all the Thai names right. The sponsors, the organisers, the referee, the judges: they all had unpronounceable Thai names. The girls who were boxing were easy, as they all had simplified names which the *farang* customers used. If I forgot those, I could always refer to them as the 'blue' corner or the 'red' corner. I had no time to worry, however, because the dreadful night arrived in a twinkling. Without a doubt it was one of the most frightening and difficult nights of my life, worse even than a first night in the West End. I needn't have worried; adrenaline inspired me and I was soon imitating the boxing commentators I'd seen on TV in the UK and elsewhere. The only problem we had all night was with a Frenchman who insisted on getting into the ring and performing somersaults everywhere and generally behaving provocatively. I got rid of him by inviting him to demonstrate his skills at the bungee and to try and do the double and triple somersaults that Sam could now do – in the air! That shut him up! In fact he got into a heavy punch-up later and ended up in a Thai nick overnight. What is it about the French that… oh, never mind!

Sam, meanwhile, had made friends with Mark; another disillusioned bar owner who couldn't make ends meet. Being more or less the same age, Sam and Mark clicked immediately. Mark, who'd had one disastrous business experience after another in Thailand and was fast running out of capital and ideas, indicated that he would prefer to sell up his bar and join us in the bungee business.

We had realised early on that the business would only support two management salaries, so this gave me the opportunity to plan the next step in my Thai experience. I would get married to An, hand over the running of the business to Sam and Mark and 'go native' up in the wilds of Ban Dongwen. I would build my house, cash permitting, retire to my desk with quill and ink and write.

Mark joining would provide the necessary capital for me to purchase the Phuket company share, assuming that I could negotiate the price down. Business in these low-season months had not been spectacular, and our partners finally accepted my offer of fifty per cent of their asking price. Leaving them with their tongues hanging out had been a successful ploy.

August was indeed saved by the Italians who, contrary to all of the dire predictions we'd had, turned out to be good customers; and Sompot's Italian served him well.

I set the date for our wedding, almost a year to the day since our arrival in Lamai. This was to be not only a wedding party but also the celebration of Sam Song's first birthday and the birthday of a visiting good friend from London. I was determined therefore to make it a big one!

An arrived back from Ban Dongwen and we arranged for a new wedding dress to be made for her and a pair of new slacks and shirt for me. I also replaced the gold she had foolishly lost. I don't think it was until this stage that An finally believed it was all happening, that we were getting married. Well, officially we weren't: that was a complicated affair that involved the British Embassy in Bangkok, yards of form-filling and bureaucratic bumbling and vast expense. That would have to come later. For the moment it would be an exchange of vows and gold rings at the bungee: a mock ceremony which I would perform but one that would be witnessed by all our friends – a truly common-law marriage.

I organised the live rock band, persuaded 'A' to work his sumptuous miracles again with a buffet and a running barbecue, and drafted in several more girls to help service our guests from the bar. This was a big event and one which I wanted An to enjoy and remember. The last of the big spenders!

Perhaps I was a little unwise to organise such an outdoor event at the beginning of the monsoon period, tempting fate to say the least; and indeed, for the first hour of the party, the gods of the skies showed their displeasure and pissed on us. We rescued most of 'A's splendid spread and got it under cover, not to mention the poor, soggy rock band. With our spirits dampened but not drowned we resumed the celebrations an hour or so later and the ceremony and festivities went on until the early hours of the morning.

I had paid for the band, the catering and a good deal of the drinks at the bar, so all in all it was a successful night, not only for An and our friends, but also for the business. It gave Sam and Mark a reasonable financial leg-up before my departure, and I was sure that their youth and experience could overcome whatever small problems might arise. Having the 'old fart' out of the way would be good for them. This time I had no resentment of the 'yoof' taking over and being innovative! It was time for me to move on to the next stage of this incredible adventure. I was going into unknown territory, into the heart of rural Thailand and to a new and altogether slightly scary culture. Another venture which I was sure would provide many stories for my eager pen!

I was feeling creative withdrawal symptoms.

And so, on September 4th, exactly one year to the day since Sam and I had arrived on Koh Samui to start this adventure, I left with An for Bangkok and thence to Nongkhai and Ban Dongwen. I was going native!

Chapter Sixteen
JUNGLE BOY

LEAVING MY NICE COMFORTABLE BUNGALOW in Lamai, with its cooling fans, well-functioning living quarters, and satellite TV that gave us a taste, whenever we wanted it, of the UK with BBC Worldwide, was going to be a bit of a culture shock. I was going to live on the outskirts of a remote Thai village in the jungle, in a one-roomed shack with a tin roof, a Thai toilet and Thai shower and no running water or kitchen. What I was sure there *would* be was a plethora of bugs and creepy crawlies, and heat – unbearable heat. Lamai had been hot, but at least one could take a cold shower every now and then to cool down; but a Thai shower was a vat of ice-cold water and a pan to douse you with. An said she hoped I would be happy with what she had done to make it a home from home. We-ell…

She had bought us a double mattress, shrouded it with a mosquito net and placed it in the one room next to the boys' beds (also shrouded in a mosquito net), the proximity of which cast serious doubts about any kind of privacy between the sheets. There was the Thai TV I had bought for them, and a straw mat on part of the floor which they squatted on to eat or lounged on to watch TV and which was generally a receptacle for spilt food, dust and the residue from the children's playthings: all a bit alarming.

The toilet had been installed as I'd instructed, but not as I'd planned nor in the right place. Walls had been erected around the outhouse to form the basis of the kitchen and it was in here that they cooked over a charcoal-burner pot stove. Wow! Home from home? To be fair, she had tried her best, and for Thais this was more than adequate; but the dear 'old fart' was going to have to do some quick building if this was going to be anything like habitable in the near future.

It all seemed worthwhile, though, as I watched An and the boys after supper playing cards together. They were happy and obviously looking forwarded to this new life with their new Papa. I spent the first night under the mosquito net listening to all the sounds around me in the dark. That we had rats was a certainty: I could hear them squeaking and fighting and delving into plastic bags. What else there was lurking in the darkness, I dreaded to think.

The cost of the wedding party in Lamai, the gold I had bought An for her wedding present, a gold bracelet for her mother and so on had seriously depleted the hundred thousand or so that I'd set aside for our home-building in Ban Dongwen. We had to have a party for the family to celebrate our wedding: this was expected. An also wanted a contingent of monks to come and bless the proceedings. However, since one had to pay them for these services, not to mention feed them and make a donation for something or other, I persuaded her that it would be better to have the 'holy rollers' bless the house when we'd finished it. I also had to buy presents for the two boys: a bicycle for Lyn and a guitar for Num.

The next morning we hired one of the locals to take us to Nongkhai in his pick-up truck to make some essential purchases. The boys' presents, a fridge, a gas cooker and bottled gas, a water boiler, rice cooker, a toaster, a couple of chairs and a fold-up table for me to write on, a mug for my essential cups of tea, plates, knives, forks, spoons: you name it, I bought it! This was the third home I'd had to furnish since coming to Thailand. It was becoming monotonous. We also paid a visit to the local supermarket, which boasted European fare. Boasted, yes, but… I did manage to buy the essentials like tea, coffee, eggs, bacon, Quaker Oats and bread. Surprisingly they also stocked a very good New Zealand mature cheese.

I'd conceded that we had to have a party for family and friends. My refusal to have the monks bless the proceedings had caused a bit of tension, but love conquers all and I agreed to barbecue a whole pig instead. Upon reflection I think I would have preferred the monks: not barbecued you understand, but instead of the slaughter of the poor beast.

Purchasing the ill-fated animal the night before and transporting it live in the back of a pick-up was an unnerving experience. After I'd chosen the one to get the chop, it was 'hog-tied' and slung in the back of the truck. With thirty-eight kilos of squealing pig protesting at this kind of treatment, and my wallet some couple of thousand baht lighter, we returned home. The animal was tethered in the nearby jungle overnight, and its constant noisy objections filled my slumber with hideous dreams. I didn't know the half of it…

We had decided to have the party in the afternoon, but in reality it started early the next morning with the slaughter of said pig. A whack on the head with a hammer and it succumbed. I then watched with growing horror as a long sharp knife was strategically inserted into its throat, the resultant flow of blood anxiously collected in a jug for use later – for what, I didn't ask!

Under An's guidance I had bought boxes of beer and several bottles of Laos Cal so-called whisky for our guests. By eight-thirty in the morning our guests, butchers and cooks had already consumed a box of beer and a couple of bottles of the lethal spirit. The pig had been shaved, gutted and beheaded. The Thais, with great relish, ate the insides raw with dips of red-hot chilli-flavoured sauces. It was being eaten piece by raw piece from the inside out, leaving the carcass for the barbecue. Nothing was wasted except the tail, which for some curious reason they didn't fancy. Needless to say I refused every tasty morsel that was politely offered and took to sampling my bottle of Scotch very early on in the proceedings.

The carcass was spreadeagled between splits of bamboo and mounted on a crude kind of spit over a charcoal fire. The feast was prepared and the various helpers and guests, already satiated with raw innards and well high on booze, squatted and nibbled at the remaining titbits that kept being produced. The beer and booze kept being consumed and I, not having eaten any breakfast, began to feel the effects of my Scotch; somehow the bottle had become half empty – must've had a hole in it!

The roasting pig carcass was beginning to fill the air with a quite delicious aroma, and come midday I happily scrunched on some crackling and finally a slice or two of the rather more well-done meat from the haunches. The Thais seemed to prefer great globs of fat rather than the lean meat, their faces aglow with pleasure and their chops smeared with fatty residue.

Quite suddenly, and without any warning, a couple of them keeled over and promptly fell into an alcohol-induced slumber. Nobody took the slightest bit of notice, and every now and again as the Laos Cal 'whisky' took its toll another head would loll and finally disappear. They were dropping like flies! Can't take their liquor, the Thais.

Happily I remained relatively sober although my 'medicinal' intake of Scotch had virtually killed the bottle over the period of hours. Quite how the day's festivities ended I do not recall, but I was relieved that I had survived the bloody experience without 'losing my breakfast' – not that I'd had any to lose.

Our desperately hot tin-roofed hut of a home was an ideal place for rodents and other beasties to escape from the relatively cold air of the nights. Wherever there are people there are bound to be rats, and we had our fair share; I quickly uncovered the first nest of four, three of which got away into the jungle with An clobbering the fourth with a broom handle. Knowing that the breeding rate of rats is substantially higher than that of rabbits, I realised that we had only just scratched the surface; that the four escapees would return in a few weeks with an army of family to reclaim their territory. Something drastic had to be done, and I put the word out for a cat.

When we had arrived at the house we found that we had inherited a dog, and also a rather mangy cockerel chick that had seen one too many fights; we named the pathetic beast 'Chuck-Chuck'. For some reason it latched on to me as its protector, and for the first few weeks hardly ever left my side when I ventured outside. The dog I named Black Bugger, for obvious reasons. We had been presented with these two animals by the monk, An's brother (I believe – I was never quite sure), who subsequently arrived again with another dog and a clutch of ducklings which stayed for a few days and were then removed – all very mysterious. The second dog, named Fifty-Fifty (by me again) because he wasn't quite sure if he was male or female, copulation being something he could not quite get the hang of, was the brother of Black Bugger.

Within a matter of days, Chuck-Chuck improved as a result of regular feeding and not being attacked by other chickens. But the unfortunate cockerel was not out of the woods yet.

We were woken one night by a dreadful and terrified squawking, only to find on investigation that Black Bugger had Chuck-Chuck in her jaws, her teeth firmly lodged in the chicken's tail-feathers and up its Khyber Pass. We caught it just in time, and I presented a very passable drop kick up the dog's backside and lobbed her into touch. We dealt with Chuck-Chuck's wounds as best we could and put him safely out of harm's way to roost.

One gets used to the squawking of the ten thousand geckos that inhabit Thai buildings. However, one night as An was making up the bed and I was having my usual dousing of cold water in the 'shower', she let out a yelp of alarm. Leaping naked as a baby from the shower room, I tore into the main room to find An dealing a death blow with my hammer to a snake! The reptile was only about eighteen inches long and no wider than my middle finger, but one bite from the little bugger's fangs was apparently deadly. If one was unfortunate enough to be on the receiving end of this nasty nip a hasty visit to the doctor, within the hour, was highly recommended. The snake, of course, had been curled up on my side of the bed!

There are many more snakes here than one sees, of course; they are shy creatures and tend to slither away at the slightest approach of humans. This one had, however, decided that the relative warmth and comfort of our bungalow was far preferable to the cold jungle night air and had slithered in through a badly fitted back door. The next morning I bricked up the offending doorway.

Again in the middle of one night, we heard a terrible yelping from one of the dogs. This was it, I thought, a marauding tiger had come in from the jungle feeling a little peckish and grabbed one of the dogs. Grabbing my trusty hammer I hit the door at a run with An, having had a fight with the mosquito net, not far behind. Seeing no big beastie we followed the echoing yelps and found that Black Bugger, having tried to get at Chuck-Chuck again by jumping on the water barrel, had dislodged the tin tray covering it and fallen in. A suitable punishment, I thought, for having tried to get at the unfortunate cockerel again; but I gave her another well-placed drop kick to drive the experience home.

So far I hadn't been bitten by anything more deadly than ants and mosquitoes, but I came very close one afternoon while taking my little nap. I was lying on my back on the bed, staring into space before dozing off, when a large millipede dropped onto the netting only some six inches away from my face, its hideously large nippers searching for a victim. This we dispatched rather carefully for, although not deadly (unless, I suspect, one suffers from a weak heart), its bite is extremely painful for some considerable time.

Every day, it seemed to me, something tried to get at me through the mosquito netting. A killer bee, which does exactly what its name implies unless treated very quickly; various spiders, some with equally lethal bites; furry caterpillars, and red ants as big as your thumbnail which sting like the blazes. All seemed intent on making their presence felt and the mosquitoes, I knew, preferred my diabetic sugar-laden blood to anyone else's. In all fairness I must point out that they were also partial to my Thai family, who suffered them with more resignation and grace than I did.

The numerous lakes abound with water snakes and incredibly large leeches. There is also one particularly unwelcome creature lurking in the muddy pools which has a parasitic habit and, once it penetrates the skin, makes a home beneath it and starts its family. The parasites multiply and attack vulnerable and essential organs, ending up inside the brain to consume one's last thoughts before the inevitable happens. I steadfastly refuse to bathe in such stagnant pools and will only take a refreshing dip in running, clear water. Needless to say I never venture into the jungle at night, and only during the day with extreme caution.

The Thais, of course, regard my crazy *farang* caution with some disdain, but then I am alive and many of them are not. Many of these ailments are considered by the Thais to be the result of a visit from the ubiquitous Dracula! They have latched on to Bram Stoker's character and attribute many of the deaths that happen here to him or, as in one case, her, Dracula being seemingly sexless. The 'she' version is said to enter houses at night and eat the insides of all the unmarried males; as a precaution against such a visitation, the Thais create a sort of 'Guy Fawkes' edifice, complete with a protruding penis made up of an old plastic bottle or some such article, and display this grotesque facsimile of a man outside their homes.

A more likely explanation for the death is from some internal problem such as the waterborne parasite. In all probability, the younger men swim in the grotty, muddy waters, either fishing with their 'cast' nets or simply taking a cooling dip, and are invaded by one parasite or another. But the Thais persist in their simplistic superstition that it is all Bram Stoker's creation's fault.

I was woken very rudely one night by a tremendous explosion, and for one moment thought that the previously taciturn Laos extremists had taken up arms and stormed across the 'Friendship Bridge' to attack their Thai neighbours. An got up very hastily, woke the boys and rushed them outside, refusing to answer my urgent questions as to what the hell was happening. Fearing the worst, I pulled on my trousers and shoes and followed them. When I got outside I saw them, all three of them, staring up into the sky. I followed their gaze, expecting at least to see the remains of a space station hurtling towards us, burning up as it hit the atmosphere. The sky looked exactly as I'd remembered it, clear as a bell with innumerable stars dotted across its velvet surface except… It was the Moon. It was an eerie orange colour.

'Frog eat!' said An ominously, and then proceeded to pick up a stick and beat a nearby tree with it. The boys also whacked tin cans or anything else that would make a noise. The whole village seemed to come alive with similar sounds as others took up the noisy game. I asked which frog was going to eat what and why. An pointed to the moon and resumed her banging. There was another enormous explosion as somebody let off a giant cracker nearby.

What we were watching was a partial eclipse of the Moon, and the Thais believe that a giant frog is responsible for this phenomenon. In vain I tried to explain the science behind this event, but they remain convinced that if they don't make a lot of noise to frighten the frog he will eat the Moon and the world will come to an end. I have yet to find out the origin of this superstition, but they are quite serious enough about it to get up in the middle of the night to protect the Moon. Needless to say their efforts saved the Moon and they went happily and contentedly back to bed, satisfied that they had again saved the world from being eaten by the frog. Why a giant frog? Curiouser and curiouser, the Thais!

Water: without it we could not live, yet we *were* without it – there was no mains water, and the only supply we had was in vast water vats or drinking water which we bought in large plastic bottles. I had to find a plentiful source of potable water, which I could plumb into the house. It was also necessary for building. There were wells around which some of the Thais had dug, but I didn't fancy putting the water from one of those in my Scotch! There was only one thing for it: I would have to drop a borehole and find the water table. It couldn't be all that deep as there were man-made ponds nearby that were not more than three metres down. We called in a specialist.

An extraordinary-looking vehicle arrived. It looked like something Heath Robinson would have designed, held together by wire, string and an assortment of cogs, wheels, metal and bamboo struts. This was the local drilling rig! After several disastrous attempts, the three 'engineers' managed to get the contraption across the virgin jungle land, but not before they'd had to dig it out of the soggy, muddy soil into which it had sunk.

The choice of site for drilling was critical insofar as it had to be as far away as possible from the soakaway sewage pit that I'd had dug. The Thais didn't quite understand the logic of this, and I wasn't about to go into a lecture on water purity, so I simply insisted that they drill where I instructed them to and not in the most convenient place that they would have chosen.

After several false starts and much banging and straining they got the drilling contraption vertical and in the correct position. A hole was dug in the clay earth to retain a lubricating water supply for the boring tubes and bit. By this time everyone was covered in a layer of clay mud, sweat and not a few cuts and bruises. The engine of the vehicle was started and the rig engaged. Drive belts and cogs flew everywhere and I retreated to the safety of a nearby wall to avoid being decapitated! The three 'engineers' were unperturbed by this apparently necessary part of the operation and simply put everything back together again with more wire and string and started the motor again. After much whirring and grinding the machine started to turn the drilling rig and we were in business: albeit slowly, but the bit sliced through mud and stone alike with alacrity.

Beer was provided and we sat down to watch the snail-like progress of the boring with heavy sighs of satisfaction. How far down would we have to drill until we struck the water table? My question was greeted with careless shrugs and 'don't knows' – it could be ten, twenty, thirty or more metres. Once it was found, we would then have to put a four-inch plastic 'sleeve' into the bore hole, inside which would be two more plastic tubes of a lesser diameter, one to hold the pumped water and one to 'air' the water table as we extracted water from it. A filter would be attached at the bottom to remove unwanted sediment.

Armed with a wad of one-thousand-baht notes we clambered into a pick-up truck and headed for a town an hour or so away: one which, I was assured, was the place to buy the pump and various plastic plumbing materials. The town of Tabor is an Aladdin's Cave of builder's merchants, with every conceivable tool and piece of equipment to delight a DIY fanatic's dreams. I was in my element, for I was a sucker for such places; but I restrained my urge to buy drills, planes, sanders, saws and so on, and concentrated on the task in hand. We chose a powerful pump called a 'deep well' pump, since we did not know yet how far down we would find water and it wouldn't do any harm to have more pressure than we needed. We also took the opportunity while we were there to visit the very comprehensive food market where I bought a vast selection of strange vegetables to delight my palate, many more than I could possibly eat before they rotted away.

We decided to stop for lunch on the way back and, on the outskirts of Tabor, An directed us to a Thai open-air restaurant. It wasn't in fact Thai food, but Laotian and hot as hell. The workers were convinced I wouldn't be able to eat it, but I did – washed down with copious amounts of beer!

Back once more at the rig we surveyed the progress. How far down had we drilled? Somewhere in the region of twenty-five metres and still no potable water, nor indeed water of any kind except that which we were pouring in to lubricate the machinery. I had a nasty sinking feeling in my stomach that we'd be through the other side of Thailand before we struck water. I should have had more faith in my trusty 'engineers'; at thirty-three metres we plunged into the water table. The plastic tubes were put in place, the pump attached and an electrical feed attached to it. We primed it and switched on and hey presto! Water spurted out!

The 'engineers' attached a length of hose to the pump and directed the stream of water into the nearby jungle to wait for the system to clean itself and provide pure, cool water. They called for more beer which, flushed with the success of the venture, I was happy to provide. The water eventually was crystal clear and as sweet as any I'd tasted. We were in business, and before long I'd connected the flow to the plumbing runs I had planned to two taps in the house and we had running water inside; one of the few buildings in the area to have such a luxury.

With a hose attached to the supply in the shower and toilet room we also had a shower – at least, a stream of ice-cold water from a hosepipe rather than from a suspect vat. This, I was convinced, was a major progressive step forward and well worth the two-hundred-odd pounds that the whole operation had cost – plus the boxes of beer and suchlike that all such operations seem to require!

The first step in the building process was complete. We had water so we could mix mortar for laying foundations and constructing the concrete blocks; it was a beginning. I took a hosepipe shower to celebrate – I needed it!

Now that we were an entity in Ban Dongwen I had to seriously start thinking about how to go about my enterprise of building our house. The landowner had chopped down the trees and sold them but had not taken out the stumps and roots, so the first priority was to clear the land so that I could see what I was dealing with. I hired four Thai labourers who sweated blood digging out the tree stumps and felling the one or two remaining trees.

This done, I had to negotiate for the right to drive a road through from the main road (dirt track) to give access to our house. Unfortunately, the planned road ran through land owned by the Whisky Witch, who was impossible to deal with even if one was unlucky enough to catch her sober. Fortunately, her son-in-law had had the foresight to have all her remaining land put in his wife's name, the Whisky Witch having drunk or been conned out of the vast majority of her land in the past.

Hoon, the son-in-law, was a friendly sort with whom I got on extremely well and we struck a deal for me to acquire, in perpetuity, the right to build an access road through his wife's land. This was duly registered and I called in the bulldozers and landfill 'experts' to lay the road.

One thing I learned about the Thais was that, if a decision was to be made, everyone had to have their say; very democratic, but tedious as hell. Deciding on the site of the road entailed a lengthy discussion between everyone and his dog. If there is one thing a Thai cannot do, it is to recognise a straight line or a level. I let them rattle on for some length of time, then plotted a line with a taut rope between point A and point B; as Frank Sinatra would say, I did it my way.

So the road was laid. Not that it was laid straight, but near enough; and my four swarthy Thai labourers were set to work straightening it to my satisfaction.

My plan was to add to the existing square hut by building a new wing, running along the top end of the square, like the top line of the letter 'T'. This would provide for a bedroom for me and An, another bedroom for the boys, a new toilet and (hot!) shower room, and a kitchen area. When this was completed we could evacuate our original residence and lead a relatively civilised life while I finished work on the rest of the house.

The new wing, however, entailed building from scratch, from the foundations up. Normal Thai buildings are only one skin thick, with air vents to let the heat in and out. Since I insisted on building walls with a cavity, to keep the heat out during the hot season and in during the cold season, I had to go through a considerable re-education process with my workers. I finally managed to convince them of the science behind this simple European structure, and eventually they took to it with great enthusiasm; it would be the only building in the village of such a structure. They approved, not because they saw the sense behind the science, but because it was strong! Ah well, you can't win 'em all!

Getting a group of workers in the first place was an operation as painful as pulling teeth. The normal Thai way of dealing with any building project is for the owner to describe what he wants and for a Thai builder to quote a cost for labour, with the owner supplying the materials. I didn't want such an arrangement. I wanted to employ the labour on a daily basis: one which, as the builder, I could control; if any of the workers turned out to be dud, I could fire them. Even An couldn't understand my logic, the Thai way apparently being set in stone!

I stuck to my bloody-minded way of following European building practices and won in the end. In fact, my workers eventually preferred this arrangement, for they got paid at the end of the week and didn't have to wait until the job was complete; also, they were not penalised in their pockets if the process went over time.

Even with An accompanying me and translating as best she could, a visit to the builder's supply yard was a torturous experience. The Thai words for such things as a 'yard of sand' were completely different. (A yard of sand is a 'Q'!) In the end I resorted to drawing pictures of the various things I wanted, and finally completed my order. All was delivered promptly, but the sand and shingle that I'd ordered was tipped onto my new road without regard for anything else; it looked like a First World War battlefield. My trusty Thai builders, however, cheerfully got to work and made some sort of order out of the chaos – they were used to it!

Digging foundations was a hoot. The Thais normally only put an inch or so of cement mix down before they start laying the concrete blocks of the walls. I insisted on a minimum of twenty centimetres of solid concrete foundation.

The basic structure went up fairly quickly, but came to a dead stop when I had to begin the roof and put the windows and doors in. Timber proved to be extremely expensive. The local supplier was a policeman; they seem to have a monopoly on the trees, and many timber yards are owned and run by them. This particular policeman also gave credit; I suppose that, being a policeman with substantial powers, he was always certain of getting paid! I visited him and gave him my requirements for roof timbers, which he said he would supply. The cost seemed to be the same as anywhere else that I'd investigated, but he said he would supply 'number one wood'.

It wasn't a difficult order to fill, but it took forever for it to arrive. When it eventually did, he delivered it just as it was beginning to get dark. It wasn't until the next morning when my workmen and I inspected it that we saw that, far from being 'number one wood', it was more like third rate, cut in unmatching thicknesses and bent as a corkscrew. I was not a happy bunny; but needs must, and my need to get the roof on was great, so up it went, being bent to fit as we constructed it.

Much to An's annoyance I complained to the policeman and even got him down to inspect his awful wood which, by the time we'd straightened it, didn't look too bad. However, he had to admit from the wastage that 'number one' wasn't really an accurate description. He very generously said he would make it up to me by giving me some free wood in the future. I'm still waiting!

I ran out of money, so I had to call a halt while I worked out how I could finance the next stage of the proceedings. In the meantime I turned my attention to the garden, something I could tackle without labour and the expense of materials: simply my own blood, sweat and tears. I built a Victorian-style vegetable garden as a starter, to see what would grow and what wouldn't.

I had no idea of the seasons, only that it was bloody hot most of the time and very wet for the rest. I dug my garden, planted my seeds and waited. The Thais thought I was out of my mind not doing things the traditional Thai way of creating small raised plots of surface-scraped earth and planting in them. My method of digging the whole plot over, applying a liberal dressing of buffalo manure, digging that in, and planting in straight lines across the whole plot really confused them. But as things started to happen and my seedlings flourished, they changed their tune. Very soon I was supplying them with seedlings to plant out, and in no time at all I was reaping the results of my hard work and harvesting good crops. The crazy *farang* after all was no fool! Perhaps in the next season they would follow my lead. But perhaps not; they are Thai and old habits die hard.

My funds were replenished, and for a short time we went into further building development; but this was short-lived. It was a troublesome period during which I had to come to terms with the Thai way of life. As someone once said to me, 'You can take the girl out of the bar, but you can't take the bar out of the girl.' An apt quote, but one which I was determined to defeat. Most of An's friends were ex bar girls who tended to stick together. They liked to party, and An was out almost every night until I put my foot firmly down. Even then we had to have a blazing row, something that I would normally avoid – particularly as An, who has a volatile temper, came at me with a hammer.

Chapter Seventeen

THE BEGINNING OF THE END

IT ENDED UP WITH ME packing my bags and moving into a hotel in Nongkhai for the night. The next day An, her elder sister and her husband and God knows how many other Thai hangers-on arrived as I was having breakfast. After a little face-saving I agreed to return as my point had been made, unfortunately the hard way. The bar was half out of my girl, but I thought I could see dark clouds still on the horizon; I had won one small battle in what I feared was a substantial war...

My building work continued in fits and starts as money availability allowed. At one point An, bless her heart, sold some of her gold. I knew this was one hell of a sacrifice for her but, being Thai, that's what gold is for. I also hit my Visa card, bought gold in Udonthani and sold it in Nongkhai at a small profit. So we started again, put the roof on, tiled it and finished the basics. However, we still didn't have sufficient funds to complete the work inside. I had done all the plumbing necessary and the installation of new electrical circuits; nevertheless, we came to a grinding halt once we had laid the tiled floor in our bedroom. But at least we had one room habitable, so An and I moved in; we had our own private bedroom at last! I was also able to establish a reasonable environment in which to write, looking out over the newly built road and my flourishing garden.

I had recorded this stop-start operation on film, and it should make an interesting piece for a *Homes and Gardens* feature some time on how to build a bungalow on a wing and a prayer in Thailand!

During this time An's sister, Goy, had her baby but, as a result of not drinking enough water, had to be hospitalised with a severe kidney complaint. None of the Thais really knew what this meant, so I took charge and booked her into the Thai hospital in Nongkhai. I also telephoned Peter, her English husband whom I'd known slightly, brought him up to date and, as best I could, reassured him.

Dehydration is one of the most persistent of Thai problems and yet they don't recognise it. Drinking the local brew produces the most awful consequences and, unless treated, the symptoms eventually lead to kidney or liver failure and results in premature death – all, of course, attributed to poor old Dracula! Death from alcoholic poisoning is rife in Thailand, mostly through ignorance. This wasn't Goy's problem; she'd simply been stupid and not realised that producing milk for the baby would require extra liquid, which she had not taken. Thankfully she survived, and by the time Peter arrived in Ban Dongwen the baby was flourishing.

Having another English-speaking person there did help to relieve some of the frustration of not having anyone to talk to most of the time. He and I would not normally be great friends, but necessity bound us together and we got on well enough.

Up until that time, and apart from An whose English was deteriorating the more she accustomed herself to her village life, I'd had only one other person with whom to hold any kind of intelligent conversation in English. This was a young man named Jackie. He was French, but then he couldn't be blamed for this unfortunate accident of birth. His name wasn't really Jackie either, but since the Thais couldn't possibly pronounce his French name he had assumed one they could.

Jackie had fallen heavily in love with Nee, one of the bar girls from Koh Samui whose family also lived in Ban Dongwen. He had come home with her, trying to convince her to give up her current occupation and marry him. He'd moved in with the family and provided for them, even working alongside them in the rice fields during the harvest: tough enough for Thais, and for a European doubly so. But he persisted and stayed the course, until his money began to run out, at which point Nee's attentions also cooled somewhat; for she then became a target for her family's abuse, her lover not being able to provide the necessary cash to sustain the family.

The crunch was imminent. Nee wanted to return to the bars of Koh Samui and, in an effort to prevent her, Jackie had words with her father. He, however, professed not to know that prostitution was the name of his daughter's game that had provided for the family in the past. It seemed it wasn't just the police who turned a blind eye to the sex trade; the parents, too, prefer not to know the truth, pretending that their daughters' earnings are legitimately come by. In truth, they *are* aware of what working on a lady bar entails, but prefer an ostrich-like attitude: saving face again!

Jackie, however, would have none of it. Determined to overcome the money problem, having exhausted even his Visa card by now, he proposed to buy an illegal substance, run it to Koh Samui, sell it and make a vast profit. I tried to dissuade him from this extreme cause of action. Apart from the morality of the thing, life in a Thai prison if caught was not a picnic; in fact it made European prisons seem like a Butlin's holiday camp.

However, love is a terrible driving force and he persisted. As it happened, he succeeded; but not beyond his wildest dreams because the drugs he'd bought in northern Thailand were not of a high enough quality to satisfy the Koh Samui customers, and his profits were diminished somewhat. Also, Nee got fed up of waiting and really preferred the 'glamorous' life of the bars to the thought of marrying and settling down in Ban Dongwen, so she upped sticks and went back to Koh Samui. She found Jackie, and used his money to party with her friends. He finally departed, smarting from the experience, his pride severely dented, but I think wiser. 'You can take the girl out of the bar but not the bar out of the girl'!

Jackie's mistake, apart from trying to 'buy' Nee's affection, was that he insisted on her changing her ways too quickly. The attitude of 'what's good enough for my father and his father before him is good enough for me' persists in Thailand. There is a great reluctance to have change imposed upon them from the outside; it must be gently implied that an alternative might be better than the status quo, before then allowing the Thai to make up his or her mind to the change as though it was their decision. Saving face once more. Pride and ignorance are a lethal combination.

If there is one thing that Thais like – nay, insist upon – it is that every occasion for a party be taken advantage of – particularly if a *farang* is paying! Apart from their penchant for embroidering the truth, the Thais are really rather enchanting and generous people.

During my early days of building the house it had become expected that I would spring for a beer or ten at the end of the working day. Well, okay, they'd worked hard enough for it, and at three quid a day I felt that they deserved a bit of light relief. Besides, I preferred not to drink alone! If a delicate morsel or two, such as king prawns, a chicken or duck, was provided for them to burn to a frazzle over their charcoal-burner fires then so much the better.

This is a typical beginning to a Thai party, springing from nowhere, often for no particular reason except that it seemed like a good idea at the time. I had been a little reluctant to let this become a habit, thinking that I was being taken for a ride, being the one with the readies. However, more often than not one of the Thais would disappear and return with some tasty morsel or other to contribute to the gathering, and a jolly time would be had by all.

Conversation was of course a bit difficult. My Thai was rather limited, and the Thai's English almost non-existent. I encountered some enthusiasm for me to give English lessons, and if I did there was a good chance that my Thai would improve. But then the old grey cells aren't what they used to be and the short-term memory is only about three seconds now. The enthusiasm of the Thais to learn English was also short-term: they'd forgotten about it the next day!

I had been prone to ignore the more social events and parties since coming to Ban Dongwen. I am easily bored, and I got increasingly angry with myself for being such a 'dumbo' in not being able to speak the lingo. However, An urged me to attend one event for the children's sake. There was to be a retirement party for one of the schoolteachers at the local school. It would be great kudos for the boys and An if I were to attend, it seemed. Full of trepidation, I agreed; and dutifully turned up wearing my newly laundered white shirt and nearly-clean slacks.

I came armed with cigarettes, which I knew was the currency of immediate friendship with the Thais, and donated some American dollars that had been lurking in my wallet for some time to the retirement fund. This foreign currency was received with great joy and An told me that it probably wouldn't be spent but end up framed, hanging on the teacher's wall at home as a treasured trophy.

An firmly seated me at the table of her choice and I was duly paraded as the boys' father and her husband. After a beer or two I looked around the crowded school assembly hall. All eyes, it seemed, were on me. I was the only *farang* present! Not surprising, really, since the other *farangs* who had homes there with their Thai ladies were only visitors for a short time each year; I was living there.

An was delighted and smiled enchantingly, if a little smugly, at her friends. Here was that strange *farang* who had come not to sweep his lady off to foreign parts, as most of them did, but actually to live in Ban Dongwen.

The head teacher, who spoke a little almost-intelligible English, led me off to parade before the other teachers. An, furious that her prize specimen had been stolen away, retrieved me; only just in time, however, because the head, who had been enthusiastically imbibing Thai whisky, suddenly tottered off to his motorbike and tried to mount it. Some of his wiser colleagues persuaded him that a little rest might be in order and promptly spreadeagled him on the ground, and he fell into that now familiar alcoholic-induced sleep that I'd seen so many times before. Curious stuff, this Thai whisky!

The highlight of the evening for me was the troupe of young schoolgirls who performed traditional Thai dancing. They looked for all the world like little grown-ups with their painted faces, hair jobs and tight Thai skirts. They wore jewellery and orchids in their hair, and for one awful moment I had the image of them dancing at the Lamai lady bars and crooning 'hello sexy man'! This, I knew for a fact, was one of the major recruiting grounds for several of the bars in Koh Samui. I hoped that these delicate, innocent little creatures could avoid such a career; but I very much doubted it.

So, my first major social event in the village was an unqualified success. The boys were happy, An was happy and proud. I would have been happy too, had it not been for the recurring thought of those little girls ending up in a sex-in-your-face profession. An had got lucky, if you can call ending up with an old fart like me getting lucky; but even so, I doubted that half those girls would survive the trials and tribulations of the bar girl's life. There was nothing I could do except grieve for them.

Holidays, for the people of Thailand, come with remarkable regularity. Some are designated by the king and the state; others seem to be dictated by the monks, and are often fund-raising events for them. An odd day or two off will come completely out of the blue, normally so that a Buddhist festivity of some sort can be celebrated or, more often than not, indulged in. On such days the general populace 'go with the monks' or visit the temple to, I presume, mutter a few unintelligible prayers, let off fireworks and, of course, *ghin cow* and drink.

On just such a day, my building site became deserted as half my crew decided to 'go with monk'. I couldn't object, of course; I was a *farang* and didn't understand – it was a Buddhist thing. Yeah, right!

It was a sweltering hot day, so I decided that we'd all take a little holiday. An had mentioned a rather pleasant-sounding location an hour or so's drive away, a recreation area with a cooling waterfall. It sounded ideal to me: a picnic, a dip in a shallow pool and something to amuse the kids.

We ordered a pick-up truck and everyone piled in; but, before we knew it, half the village had heard of the expedition and decided to tag along! One only has to cough gently and everyone knows about it, such is the wildfire nature of communication in the village. There is no privacy here. By this time, such a development of communal participation did not surprise me, nor upset me. Sharing one's good fortune with the less fortunate was becoming second nature.

The 'waterfoon', as An called it, was approached along a road I afterwards called Topiary Road. Every few hundred yards or so, at the side of the road, bushes were trained and cut into the shapes of animals. Elephants, kangaroos, buffaloes, giraffes and in one instance two Thai boxers in a ring! There was one particular creation, dictated either by the way the bushes grew or by some curious twist in the topiarist's nature, of two giraffes doing what comes naturally, which rather surprised me; but then, giraffes must do it, mustn't they? Otherwise there'd be no baby giraffes.

Nobody I asked could give any explanation for Topiary Road; nobody seemed to know who the horticultural artist was; it had just always been there, and every now and then another creation would appear.

This road meanders along the Mekong River course on the Laos border. The river itself, even this far up, dwarfs the Thames; and, in flood, as it had been a few weeks previously, is a ferment of frothing, raging torrents sweeping all before it.

Naturally, the waterfalls we were heading for were at the base of some mountainous country, and during the monsoon rains are a sequence of beautiful natural waterfall steps. Now, however, with the rains over and the Mekong returned to its normal level, the waterfall was a series of cooling pools: nonetheless beautiful, and more suitable for the children to bathe in.

This being a blazing hot country, such a natural attraction is ideal for families on a day out. The surrounding area is, not surprisingly, populated with food and drink stalls. Wherever one goes in Thailand, even out there in the wilds, one is never far from the national preoccupation – food and drink! The food, of course, was charred meat or fish, burned beyond any recognition. I chewed on a piece of what I supposed was chicken, but when nobody was looking I discarded this leathery morsel into the bushes. The ants could have a feast.

After a dip in the cool waters and a little frolic with the children to prove that I wasn't entirely senile, we packed up, cleared away the rubbish and headed back along Topiary Road to what I hoped would be a quiet little zizz in the late afternoon. This was not to be. An, in party mood now, had decided otherwise.

The day was not over yet and our driver swung off the road and headed into the splendid market at Tabor. Here, An bought shellfish and stuff for a barbecue, a box of beer, and fireworks for the kids. As these purchases were made, I began to worry about the old coffers which were becoming seriously depleted. An, not the shrewdest guardian of the coin at the best of times, had managed to spend most of the cash I had salted away for the building work. When I remonstrated with her, she lost her cool and a brief row ensued. She still couldn't become accustomed to the fact that money didn't grow on trees or that I wasn't a bloated plutocrat. For her, the party always had priority, and this was party time! And party she did. She disappeared with some of her friends and returned late that night very much the worse for wear.

She'd sold one of her gold rings to finance her indulgence. I feared this wasn't the last of it.

The building crew turned up next day, on schedule, but I was going to have to put off paying them for a week because of the overspend during our holiday day. An was not deterred – this was still the Thai holiday for her and she was determined to enjoy it despite my obvious disapproval. I kept my temper in check; I didn't want another hammer aimed at my aged skull, and I knew from experience that An was protecting her independence, as she saw it. She was going to be a tough nut to crack, and getting the 'bar out of her' was going to be a long struggle.

In the so-called civilised societies of Europe, we have little or no conception of what real poverty is like: there are so many different standards. On the one hand, if a family doesn't have a fridge, a TV, at least one car and take one family holiday a year, they are considered to be poor. They are, more often than not, receiving state aid of one sort or another. The nanny state doesn't allow real poverty, the minimum wage being more than some families have to survive on for a month in some countries.

We do, of course, see TV reports and appeals for starving Ethiopians, Indians squatting on a little bit of high ground during floods watching their possessions float inexorably away, and queuing up for the meagre rations of food aid provided by Western charity organisations. However, like most TV, the impression is only just that: a fleeting moment; and the reality doesn't sink in. Joe Public 'tut-tuts' and throws a few bob towards the relief fund to maybe salve his conscience, and switches channels to something more palatable. Few have experienced real poverty, real desperation and utter depression.

To the Thai peasant it is part of their daily life. Where the next *ghin cow* is coming from is an ever-present preoccupation in Ban Dongwen where the average villager had no regular income, no state aid. He relies upon casual work. Life is hard and when the cupboard is bare, as it often is, he (or more likely she) will go out into the nearby countryside and jungle to forage for food. They will fish for tiddlers no bigger than the average goldfish, shake the trees and collect anything that falls out, collect berries and dig for *man Laos*, a kind of sweet potato. The only thing every family must have is a good supply of the staple food:

rice, the *cow* in '*ghin cow*'. Fortunately this crop is fairly abundant and relatively cheap.

The rice paddies around Ban Dongwen are spectacular spreads of waving greenery with small, raised pathways weaving irregular patterns between them. They are almost all planted and harvested by hand, a backbreaking job but without which the nation would almost certainly starve. If the rice crop failed, the reserves would quickly be used up and, despite Western aid, many people would die of starvation. This is poverty.

At no time were we in danger of getting to that stage; but when my ATM card dried up for a couple of weeks, the old belt certainly had to be tightened a notch or two around the already diminished waistline. The budget for our daily living costs had to be severely reduced. I got some strange and uncertain stares when I cut down my daily glass of Scotch and took to smoking Thai cigarettes – the latter being akin to smoking dried grass gathered from beneath a cowpat!

Since poverty and lack of funds is a state that the Thais are familiar with in their everyday life, my building crew totally understood my predicament and restored my faith in human nature by deciding to a man that they would continue working without pay until my fortunes changed. Change they would, I knew; but it was nonetheless a very touching moment.

An, bless her heart, seemingly over her battle for independence and her party days behind her for the time being, sold the rest of her gold. This was a big decision for her and one that I truly appreciated. We battled on with our construction and eventually, as I knew it would, my ATM functioned again. However, I still stuck with a glass of beer instead of my tipple of Scotch, and the Thai cigarettes had become very palatable; amazing what one can get used to.

An was a great forager, although she had no need to be since we always had enough money to buy food. She simply did it because she liked doing it; it was her contribution. Since I had bought a clapped-out motorbike for her and made her mobile, she would often forage far afield and be gone for hours at a time, returning soaked to the skin or covered in mud clutching her 'catch' of whatever it was that she'd found. One day, early on in our stay in Ban Dongwen, she returned from one of these forays proudly presenting a snake. This wasn't just any snake, but a three-foot-long king cobra. 'Him try eat me so I kill,' she'd said with modesty. Me? I would have run a mile! Of course, she and the boys ate it.

My contribution to these leaner times came from my, by now, flourishing and productive garden. Since I was a young boy I'd had an interest in growing things and my lucky 'green fingers' had stayed with me throughout my life. In Lamai, at the bungee, I had started quite a stunning perimeter of various shrubs and trees, many of which I had grown from fruit stones and purloined cuttings, to justify the name 'Jungle Bungee'.

I had no idea what the seasonal time for planting was, if indeed there was one. I watched the seed shop on my visits to Nongkhai and, when I noticed more activity than usual there, I presumed that the time was right. I planted sweetcorn, carrots, all kinds of salad, onions, okra, and beans of various kinds, and had a harvest to be proud of. I became virtually vegetarian, by necessity more than anything since I didn't fancy the Thai meat at the markets, which was covered in flies, and the way they cooked it (if they bothered to) turned it into a charred, greasy mess which I couldn't get my molars into anyway.

Thus my garden, which had been my pastime, became a necessity. It did surprise me, though, that the family did not eat many vegetables. Thai cooking (or rather Laos cooking, as it tends to be in this region), is largely 'soups' of one kind or another, with 'sticky rice' as the staple. The sticky rice is a special kind of rice found in the region and is steamed, gathered into small lumps, moulded in the hand until a faintly grey colour then dipped in a sauce, meat or fish dish and popped in the mouth. Meat and two veg it is not! Of course, almost everything has lashings of chillies and is devilishly hot. Fish or shellfish and hoy (a kind of snail found in the water or mud) are eaten more than meat, which is considered to be extravagant and is generally reserved for an occasion. Large rats – not the household kind which are shunned but those found in the jungle – are a delicacy and consumed with great relish; never been able to fancy it myself for some curious reason, nor dog! The Thais will eat virtually anything, and when I planted my garden I was exhorted to grow everything 'for eat'. Flowers? 'Good for looking but for eat better.'

The Thai government makes a plea for 'self-sufficiency', but when you don't have a pot to piss in being self-sufficient is rather necessary. The Thais are already self-sufficient anyway, as nobody from the governing bodies seems to help them. The king, the royal family, the prime minister, the army generals, the politicians, police, the local landowners and industrial giants and the local mafia: this is the pecking order in Thailand. Your dear old peasant is at the bottom of the list, and is expected to look after not only himself and his family but also the monks in the local monastery. With virtually no education provided by the state and no professional training of any sort, the peasants are relegated to farm labouring, building labouring and whatever else they can scratch a living at. It is little wonder that they are apathetic and sometimes indolent, and often, when they can afford it, drunk on Laos Cal.

The politicians generally are seen as self-seeking and corrupt, and are only popular at election time when they tour their constituencies 'buying' votes with a fistful of money. There is a constant cry from incoming governments that such corruption will be stamped out, but it persists and even some of the more powerful and wealthy monks have been caught with their hands in the till lately. With these kinds of examples being set by those in power, is it any wonder that the poor old peasant is apathetic? That times will change, there is little doubt; but slowly, slowly, and meanwhile poverty will remain.

An's life had been hard. She had worked on building sites as a child labourer, been taken out of school after only four years of primary education and had to forage for food all her life. She had spent a number of years selling her body in a girly bar, had a Thai thug for a husband and had to provide for her family and her children. She'd taken some hard knocks, so it was not surprising that she was a tough cookie; but underneath that tough skin was a 'heart of gold': she was a pushover for a sob story.

Her soft underbelly became evident when, in the third week of my adoption into Thai society, she returned from one of her visits to 'family' with a new addition to our 'family': Pooie, a puppy. Since we already had Black Bugger, Fifty-Fifty, a rooster and two small boys, I was somewhat dismayed at having yet another hungry mouth to feed. Pooie was, however, irresistible: a little white bundle of fluff, peppered with black patches, one of which was perched over one eye giving her a quizzical, somewhat cheeky look. Very Disney-like. She was an orphan, her mother having died in childbirth before she was weaned. No wonder An couldn't resist her and tucked her into her bicycle basket and brought her home.

Pooie, being the new baby of the family and having to be bottle-fed for the first couple of weeks, was much fussed over. She was given frequent showers by An, even being allowed to stay in the house overnight, something hitherto unheard of: normally, dogs are firmly relegated to outside. Pooie was fed milk and special biscuits, and spoiled rotten in every way.

Fifty-Fifty and Black Bugger took this all philosophically in their stride, although the biscuits did really rather upset them and they stole a mouthful whenever they could. Black Bugger even took to 'mothering' Pooie and generally protected her from the rather rougher treatment meted out by Fifty-Fifty, who simply regarded Pooie as yet another challenger for whatever food was available.

Pooie thrived and was soon romping with the other two dogs and showing great enthusiasm, if little expertise, for the rough-and-tumble games that dogs play. Such was her liking for doggy company that she soon relegated herself to the outside and slept with the other two. She became stronger day by day and was a very popular visitor to the neighbours' houses, the recipient of many a choice titbit I'm sure.

About this time we also acquired Kat. This was the only remedy we could find to combat the rats that, not unreasonably, preferred our house at night to the cold of the jungle and the ever-present threat of the venomous and predatory snakes that relish a choice rat or two for supper. Pooie immediately took a liking to Kat and they became the best of friends, after the initial and not unexpected growling and hissing sessions. Often one would see Kat curled up between a snoring Pooie's paws, content and purring happily. No one threatened Kat when Pooie was around, even the by now aggressive Chuck-Chuck who was not averse to having a punch-up with a dog.

Well, I thought, that's it. Three dogs, one spastic and now aggressive cockerel and Kat – enough of a menagerie for any family. At least Kat was productive: the rats had disappeared. But An had other ideas. She asked if I'd like a hog. A hog? A piglet. All I had to do was to build it a house and... So, I built a pigsty and Piggy was installed. Pooie instantly took to a shine to the new member of the family and, though Piggy was somewhat dubious of this growling, barking, playful bundle of fluff at first, they eventually became firm friends. Pooie seemed to have the ability and the temperament to make friends with almost anyone and anything. Maybe it was this ingenuous ability that led eventually to her downfall.

Pooie frequently disappeared into the outskirts of the village to visit 'friends' and scrounge for titbits. One morning, as I was tending to the early morning chores of feeding the animals, I was surprised to see that Pooie – who was normally at the front of the queue for food – was morosely sitting on a pile of sand, seemingly uninterested in the ritual scramble for rice and the leftover delicacies from the meal the night before. This was very uncharacteristic, and it became clear throughout the day that Pooie was ailing. Her normally cold and wet nose was warm and dry; her tail, which was usually curled over her back wagging vigorously, was limp and lifeless. She could not be tempted to eat or drink anything. Upset tummy, I thought; she'd eaten something that severely disagreed with her.

Throughout the next twenty-four hours she deteriorated rapidly, and even the playful attentions of Kat could not perk her up. I began to suspect that this was more than indigestion. Taking her to a vet was out of the question since there is no such service in Ban Dongwen. The farmers had their own ways and cures and wouldn't, I knew, want to be bothered with a mere dog.

At the end of the second day her hindquarters became incredibly thin. My suspicions turned to conviction: she was seriously ill. There was nothing An nor I could do about it and in her typically Thai matter-of-fact way An said philosophically, 'I think she die.'

And die she did, cradled in my arms the next day, her hindquarters almost wasted away and bleeding. I was determined she should not die alone: nobody should die alone. She shuddered her last few breaths almost thankfully; relieved, I was sure, to be rid of the terrible pain that wracked her body. I was devastated. An was sad, yes, but Thais seem to take death as a matter of course, with little emotion. I, on the other hand, being a soft old Western fart, wept openly. I hacked out a grave for her in the rock-hard ground in the jungle in one of her favourite spots in the shade. We laid her to rest, wrapped in her old blanket, and

I covered the grave with stones in order that marauding rats wouldn't dig her up.

When the boys came home from school, An was away on an errand of some sort, and I broke the news to them in some trepidation, expecting to have to comfort two weeping boys; but, like An, they took it in their stride, calmly and without emotion. There was obviously something I didn't understand about the Thais, some Buddhist attitude or belief that I couldn't grasp that portrayed death as a perfectly normal event: one which, although sad, was not something to openly grieve about.

An returned from her errand. She had not been, as I'd thought, to collect a replacement puppy, but to collect two gold necklaces which we'd bought for the boys to which she had had attached two small-denomination Thai coins.

Num, the eldest boy, announced that it was his birthday. No one knew, not even An, and I found his simple request for a birthday cake and maybe a nice meal cooked specially for him very touching. He had been afraid to ask before because he knew we were short of money. His understanding and acceptance of our relatively poverty-stricken situation touched me deeply and, coming on top of Pooie's death, made my eyes water yet again.

I gave An some money and told her to go and buy food and a birthday cake for Num; to hell with the cost! We'd have a small party. I also told Num that he could buy the football shirt he'd so wanted. His heartfelt 'thank you Papa' got to me again.

I think that day I learned a valuable lesson in humility and about the Thai attitude to living and dying. They accept reality without resentment, without recriminations of any sort. It was nobody's fault that Pooie had died as she did; it was nobody's fault that we hadn't remembered Num's birthday and that we were too poor to celebrate it.

As we sat round in a tight family group watching the candles burn on Num's cake and sang 'Happy Birthday', I felt that an important change had occurred. I felt for the first time that I really was accepted as Papa, that I had been accepted into the family. Thank you, Pooie. Of course, An did replace Pooie a little later – with Pookie! But that's another story.

Chapter Eighteen

THE WAY OF BUDDHISM

LIVING IN THAILAND IT IS impossible not to be influenced by Buddhism and the monks. I am on dangerous ground here, since I am not an expert on Buddhism or the ways of the monks who live in the temples and monasteries; I can only speak from experience and observation.

That the local monks had a profound effect on the villagers of Ban Dongwen there was no mistake. Every day the young monks would venture into the village with their so-called begging bowls and collect their daily ration of food from whoever's turn it was to provide. This is not actually begging, since the justification for it is that the laymen give to the priests in order that their dead ancestors will not want for food, and it is only the priests who can communicate with the spirits. The priests are therefore doing the lay population a favour by affording them the opportunity to 'make merits' by offering them food. The monks do not work; they never lift a finger. We are told that their life is one of devotion, contemplation and prayer.

There are five 'commandments' for the layman. One, they must not kill; two, they must not steal; three, they must not tell a lie; four, they must not commit adultery; and five, they must not take strong drink. I don't know one Thai man who doesn't break at least one of those commandments, particularly the edict about strong drink, at least once a day! By not breaking these commandments the layman can build up his 'brownie points' or merits for when he finally pops his clogs.

This being a male-dominated society, a preference made obvious in the Buddhist lists of do's and don'ts, the women do not seem to feature too much. They cannot become priests or priestesses and cannot be admitted to the order. Some women become nuns and wear white robes, but they are not priestesses and are not considered to belong to the holy sect of Buddhist brotherhood. This is one big 'closed shop'!

Each temple is self-contained, supported by its local community but 'ruled' by the area bishop, some of whom become very wealthy – as witnessed by the Mercedes Benz cars that they drive around in, always chauffeured of course. The priests, however, cannot deal with their own treasures, accumulated over the years by gifts of land, money and buildings. They are not allowed to touch money and must not lay hands on silver or gold. This ticklish problem is overcome by having a government department handle all the big finance, and a lay treasurer is appointed by each temple to handle the filthy lucre at the local end. Where there's a will there's a way!

Some of the more powerful and rich priests do, however, demonstrate a generosity rarely seen in a layman. Recently one such rich priest donated five million dollars or so and over two thousand kilos of gold bars to the state to help bring the coffers back to manageable limits. There's a lot of gold in them there temples!

Every villager, no matter what his circumstances, is expected to support the monks financially. If there is a need for a new building then everyone contributes, either in cash or in labour. There are frequent holidays or festivals that are fund-raisers for the monks. There are markets on the monastery grounds, Thai or Laos dancing, film shows; all of which contribute to the income of the monastery. Nothing, it seems, happens in the village without the monks collecting their dues.

As a *farang* I was of course hit heavily by this 'milking' process, probably at twice the rate for Thai locals. My objections were met by indignant arguments from An of 'but it's for the monks!' That I was not a Buddhist, and didn't give a tinker's tit for the monks, didn't wash. An was so imbued with the traditional way of life that my arguments meant nothing; I could not shake her belief that the monks ruled. She feared them! They do indeed appear to be all-powerful, but it is the power of superstition. These superstitions come mainly from old 'faiths' and beliefs such as the power of the spirits; hence the spirit houses which one sees all over Thailand. They have nothing to do with the actual Buddhist faith, but are simply hangovers of superstitions that are still very much alive in countries like Laos.

It is, of course, the same in Europe. The old ladies who go to Church in England have the same unshakeable faith, or fear of the hereafter, and the priest is regarded with considerable awe. The Germans automatically contribute part of their income to the church or they suffer the consequences. The Italians and French support the Pope as though he were a god!

Religion is a powerful drug and historically has caused more wars and suffering than any political faction. It still persists in this so-called modern world, with wars between the Muslims and the Jews as a prime example.

In Thailand it is no different except that, as yet, there are no wars, only an endemic superstition and a philosophy which in itself is worthy, but in its execution seems to be self-seeking: perpetrated and sustained by its leaders, for profit. It, like Thai society, has become corrupt. What was essentially good has become pervasively distorted. It does, however, persist as the mainstay of Thai rural life. They do not, or do not want to, see the holes in the fabric that is for them a lifeline. Politics are a necessary evil; religion is necessary and, as yet, not seen as evil.

Maybe this is a biased view, since I see all religion as primitive in essence and destructive in fact. I cannot recall one instance in history where religion has played a positive part and had a beneficial result for humanity. Some would cite the ministry of Jesus, his crucifixion and the resulting evangelical spread of Christianity. But was this historical event beneficial? I think the subsequent wars and slaughter in the name of Christianity prove otherwise.

That the Thais are totally subservient to the Buddhist ministry goes without question, and it will remain so far beyond the years I have left to live. Indeed, I don't wish this to change; but I would dearly love for it to reform and clean up its act, for the people must have some beneficial concepts by which to live.

The Thais are delightful, ingenuous people who deserve better of their spiritual and philosophical leaders whom they serve with unquestioning devotion. Such faith requires recognition and reward, not subjugation and punishment. Avarice has got the better of the Buddhist leaders. It would be better if they now recognised their shortcomings and faults and took heed of their own philosophical preaching – simplicity and devotion in life.

Almost nothing is done in the village or the home without the 'blessing' of the monks. This entails their attendance at one function or another, paid for of course, and their ritual feeding. They *ghin cow* like there was no tomorrow, scoffing everything laid before them before the 'switch off' at midday. It is hardly surprising, then, that so many of them sport vast stomachs that would put the most indulgent European scoffers to shame. Well, let's face it, they have no opportunity to 'work it off', since they don't work! The most exercise they get is sitting or rising from a squatting position. No, to be fair, I have seen groups of young monks walking determinedly down the highway; but I have never seen their elder brothers doing so – no, for them it is the chauffeur-driven Mercedes. What is it about physical exertion that is so demeaning that a monk cannot participate? Even the elder monks who take part in the religious processions do not walk: their devoted peasant followers carry them on a bier! I cannot help feeling that the big boys have elevated themselves beyond their reasonable status and that their followers would be more impressed if they walked like all other mortals. Perhaps not: maybe the Thais need a godlike figurehead to look up to?

One hears the monotonous chanting of Buddhist mantras all the time, sometimes starting at three in the morning accompanied by booms on the vast gongs, thumps on drums and clanging of bells. I wonder if there is a reason for this unsociable occurrence or whether it is because this is the coolest time of day? They eat only twice a day, between nine in the morning and midday. After that they fast, rest, meditate, study and pray. Not a life of unbridled joy, but maybe contemplation of the soul or inner self is compensation enough.

Frequently the villagers will 'go with monk', staying for days and going so far as shaving their heads. Both men and women take these types of retreats and sometimes young boys stay at the monasteries to study Buddhism, learning, as they do in school, by rote. If the boys are unfortunate enough to get something wrong then a reprimand is applied – a thwack with a bamboo twig. Good for the soul?

All deaths are the province of the monks. If a family member dies, the monks are called for and they remove and dispose of the body. They also take in stray and unwanted dogs, which are believed to be the reincarnation of monks who fell by the wayside or did bad things. There are many stray dogs in Thailand! Maybe they find them new homes, but as yet I haven't been able to discover what happens to them.

One thing that monks do not appear to do is meddle in politics; they stay aloof from such worldly things and insulated from the problems of government. They own vast tracts of land and their rights are protected. They cannot sell such land for development without a parliamentary change in the law, so a lot of it lies fallow when it could be put to good use.

Many people bequeath land to the monks, thereby adding to their burden of ownership, and build temples and monuments – as if there weren't enough of those already. Idolatrous edifices to the Lord Buddha abound, mostly sitting cross-legged with a stunningly fat belly and a beaming, benign grin on his golden face.

One wonders if Buddha used drums, cymbals and bells? He certainly didn't have a Mercedes, and he gave up all his worldly wealth in order to devote his life to a simplistic regime of contemplation and purification of the soul. Where then did all this mumbo-jumbo and ritual come from? Buddhism grew out of the philosophy of life of one man some two-and-a-half thousand years ago in India, or to be more precise Nepal, and entered Thailand around the thirteenth century. It can only be assumed that the original philosophy was influenced in the intervening period by a number of kings, astrologers, Buddhist priests from Ceylon and India, soothsayers and purveyors of superstition who used cant and idolatry to give credence to their preaching. No doubt some of these influences were assimilated and grew into what is today known in Thailand as Buddhism. Possibly some changes were engendered by the Thais themselves, who were in fact from the south of China. They entered what is now known as Thailand and conquered the Khmers and the Mons before settling down. Who knows? In any event, Buddha didn't travel around exhorting people to follow him in his chosen way of life with gongs, drums and so on. He would certainly have needed a Mercedes to do so if he had!

There are some priests or monks who are said to be endowed with powers to cure illness. These were the so-called priests of the forest who lived a hermit-like existence, not in a temple. Nowadays they do not live the life of a hermit or yogi, but they still exist, and many of their claimed cures are said to have been achieved simply by meditation and not by some miracle herbal concoction. There are many such accounts of cures even today; one particularly of a European man whose doctors had given him little time to live owing to the growth of an insidious cancer inside him. A priest was asked to help, and meditated and ordered several herbs to be given to the man who was miraculously cured. This case is authenticated. Not all bad chaps.

Chapter Nineteen
LIFE IN THAILAND

WHILE TENDING MY GARDEN AND waiting for money to arrive in order that I could continue building our home, I had a great deal of time on my hands: time enough to reflect upon the way this particular 'clock' called Thailand ticked. It is certainly nothing like I had encountered before.

The current king is said to be the best ruler since Rama V. He is totally adored, as are the rest of the royal family. Every night on television a goodly portion of the evening news programmes is devoted to royal PR, and their good works are lauded continuously on both TV and in the press. Certainly the king seems to be very active in supporting many innovative and worthwhile projects around the country, many of which are financed or certainly sponsored by him. It is a pity, therefore, that he is just a figurehead, that he doesn't actually govern, because I think he'd be rather good.

By and large, however, the country is run by a curious kind of feudalism of the rich and powerful, with each province having its own local laws and peculiarities. The federal laws are nonetheless upheld throughout; punishment for breaking these laws is swift and hard. It is sometimes seen as unjust, as in the case of the peasants who have inhabited the forests all their lives and rely upon them for survival being turned off their land because the Forestry Commission suddenly had the power to do so. There is no argument against such fascist heavy-handedness.

Some say that the Western multi-national corporations actually control the country because of their financial grip and aid packages. As ever, oil plays a large part in the financial structure of Thailand; the price rises worldwide hit every part of the economy, even the price of a modest ride in a 'tuk-tuk'! America is, of course, blamed for a lot of this with its exploitative methods of doing business: colonisation without occupation or responsibility.

The Japanese also come in for a fair amount of stick as the problems with the yen were blamed for most of the ups and downs of the whole Far Eastern economy. Since the slump in the value of the Thai baht the Thai economy has made steady progress and recovery; and, apart from hiccups such as government elections, will continue to do so – but not without the continued support of the Americans and the Japanese.

However, the future probably lies with the Chinese, that massive nation of beavering workers who seem to have discovered capitalism and taken to it like a duck to water. They have begun to dominate a lot of trade in the Asian area and are said to be so powerful that in a few years' time they will out-trade the West.

Not that such a development will necessarily affect Thailand. It will probably hardly change at all. What little natural resources it has, such as rice and coconuts, are controlled by the landowners, the feudal lords, who in turn are controlled by the politicians, and they by… and so on and so on.

One of the most profitable industries in Thailand is the trade in replicas: fakes. Everything from watches to designer-label T-shirts, high-class luggage and so on are made at a fraction of the cost of the real and self-same product in Europe. Of course, they are not necessarily of the same quality and may fall apart in a couple of months or so; but you wouldn't know it to look at them, so cunning is the fakery. This is such a big 'black' industry that it is doubtful that a value can be put on it since it is largely undeclared, for obvious reasons. Many of the goods being 'exported' are bought by tourists, some of the most frequent travellers actually funding their entire trip by stuffing their suitcase full of this illicit produce. Designer-label T-shirts bought for a pittance can turn a tidy profit back home in the pubs or sold at a 'boot sale' market stall.

In starting up business in Lamai we encountered several of the lower stages of Thailand's insidious feudalism. In places as small and as touristically 'active' as Koh Samui the landowners wield great power, owning vast tracts of valuable land, hotels, supermarkets, bars and so on. Land prices near the sea soared as tourism increased. Landowners built bars by the dozen and sold the leases on them before they were even completed. Money poured in. And so the process continues and presumably will do so until the 'bubble bursts' – probably when the landowners price Thailand out of the market and make it less attractive because of price hikes to travel half way round the world for what was previously seen as a 'cheap' holiday.

In places such as Chaweng, Pattaya and Phuket, that have developed more rapidly than others, a 'sub-strata' of control and power exists: groups of the so-called Thai mafia, mini thugs who try to rule with fear and violence to extract money from the restaurants, bars and other small traders. This doesn't cut much ice with the *farang* owners; all one has to do is smile benignly and say, 'Sorry, no speak Thai,' and they go away, preferring easier prey. It is pointless complaining to the police, some of whom are directly complicit and in the pay of some of the mafia. In fact, the police collect their own 'protection money', approximately one hundred baht per month per bar. Quite what protection they provide we have yet to discover.

It is not surprising that some of the police, particularly those on the lower scales of pay, are corrupt. Their jobs may be secure but their rate of remuneration is pitifully low, although being government officers they do get the perk of a pension. Most of the bureaucracy is in the same boat although those who reach the higher ranks certainly do get the pick of the perks. Petty corruption and payola is rife throughout the state bureaucracy. If one needs something done sooner than next year, one has to pay for the 'service'. But that's the system in Thailand: no money, no honey – again! Much the same as the Western world where 'money rules'!

Being confined to a hermit-like existence in the jungle, in a small Thai-speaking village, one must of necessity have relief from isolation, and contact with other mortals of the same tongue, otherwise therein lies madness. Every week therefore I took the bone-shattering journey by tuk-tuk into Nongkhai, a reasonably sized town that contained a small population of ex-pat *farangs*. Owing to its proximity to the border, where it is necessary to go if one wishes to cross into Laos or renew one's visa, it is visited by many itinerants on a casual basis.

My usual routine was to visit the bank to raid my ATM card for the coming week's necessities, the few shops for essential supplies, and the email service for my mail, invariably ending up at the Danish Baker, a European-style café that served drinkable coffee and reasonable food. I could sit there for as long as I liked, reading yesterday's paper (as the daily doesn't arrive until midday), and swap a few English-language books if any tourist had been thoughtful enough to leave any there. A welcome oasis of relative civilisation.

Communication with other beings is essential, but my choice was limited. At the Danish Baker one was, however, more or less certain to come across someone who spoke one's mother tongue; albeit with an accent you could cut with a knife, but intelligible nonetheless. There were several ex-pats who frequented the place, although the majority were travellers passing through. One such was an Irishman, Paddy (!) who had, like me, just been across the border to renew his visa.

Paddy was married to a Thai lady and had fathered children with her. They lived halfway to Bangkok and this was the nearest border that Paddy could reach to do the visa 'run'. Paddy was as unlikely an ex-pat as I could expect to meet. My first thoughts were that he was in the building trade in London, but his knowledge in that area was limited as became obvious when he started asking me basic questions about his house-building.

He didn't volunteer any information about his profession other than to say he only returned to London when a 'contract' came up. What on earth was he? A 'hit' man… a gun runner… a dealer in narcotics? That his profession was somewhat dubious I had no doubt, and he was such a flamboyant and enigmatic character that he inspired a short story for my ever-hungry pen. He was probably the leader in one of the Irish folk groups who toured the country or did seasons at one or other of the Irish pubs on the Kilburn High Road. Who knows? I hope I never do: I prefer my imaginative choice.

On Christmas Eve An and I, Goy and her husband Peter decided we really ought to make some effort to celebrate; at least, Peter and I did – the girls were always up for a night out. So, we put on our best bib and tucker, the girls dolled themselves up and we hired a car to take us into Nongkhai and the Danish Baker. Christmas Eve was, of course, the big night of celebration for most of the Europeans, we cussed Brits sticking to Christmas Day. The place was therefore packed with Danes, Germans and the odd one or two from the UK.

We had a splendid Danish dinner of roast pork, roast potatoes, and a peculiar kind of white Danish gravy and pickled red cabbage. The wine, unfortunately, was undrinkable. The whole evening turned faintly riotous after dinner, with middle-aged men cavorting around like two-year-olds, dancing to Thai music. It is curious how ex-pats behave when out of their homeland environment. Schoolboys, every one of them – naughty ones at that! We got out of the increasingly drunken atmosphere and headed back to Ban Dongwen.

On the way home we decided to stop for a nightcap at one of the many karaoke bars. For some reason the Thais love these singalong places. Karaoke arrived and departed in Europe in almost the same breath: it just didn't catch on. In Thailand it has become the ultimate entertainment, apart from the ever-present opiate of the people: free TV. Even in the middle of the jungle, people who may have no basic services in their houses, such as water or sanitation, have TV – and welcome they are to it! It is a hideous facsimile of the worst TV in Europe with game shows, soap operas, dubbed TV dramas some ten to fifteen years old and 'sponsor' advertising by the yard.

However, even TV takes second place to a good old evening at a karaoke bar. Give the Thais a microphone, a backing track and a computerised tape of the lyrics and they sing along to their heart's content. They just love to 'show off' and wallow in the perceived glory of the pop stars.

Karaoke bars are more than that, though. They are largely a male province; that is, of course, with the exception of the girls who 'hostess' them. For karaoke bar, read boozer and brothel. Vast quantities of liquid refreshment are required to 'oil the wheels' of the Thai karaoke customer, and represent the main source of income for the owners of the bars. They are almost exclusively owned by Thais, and indeed largely populated by Thai men out on the razzle.

Thai whisky or Sang Som is the main tipple as the effect is fairly immediate, lowering the inhibitions to zero in as many seconds as it takes to say 'Ah…!' Assuming the imbiber doesn't pass out within the first glass or three, there are many would-be Frank Sinatras waiting to 'do it their way'. When the places are in full swing they vibrate and heave with thundering bass and squawking microphone. The performers, high as a kite more often than not, screech into the mike somewhere near the right note and undulate to the beat of the music which, if it is Thai, is always the same. If they run out of steam or need an invigorating 'massage' they will disappear into a back room or up rickety stairs to indulge their more suspect sexual appetites.

The girls who work in the karaoke bars are local and use it more or less as a training ground for the more lucrative jobs in the tourist areas. Once they have 'graduated', most girls, by now sixteen or seventeen and well experienced in the delights of the flesh, will be recruited by the Mama Sangs from down south. From then on, there's no stopping them. Bright lights, booze, *farangs* galore with money and no sense: a veritable gold mine if a girl can only get lucky! Or perhaps she'll get *un*lucky and end up with one or other of the venereal diseases or, if she's very unlucky, AIDS; if none of these, then quite possibly pregnant or hooked on booze or drugs with a liver the size of a ripe melon. Perhaps nobody tells them the truth about their chosen profession; or perhaps they just don't want to hear it, preferring to believe that it couldn't happen to them.

Entertainment is not exactly plentiful in rural Thailand. There are no cinemas, except in the larger cities and the film shows which the monks arrange, more often than not as a 'come on' for some sponsor or other. There are Thai or Laos dancing nights that the Thai youths, heavy with drink, use as fighting arenas: not to be recommended to the *farangs* as they often become the targets of disapproving Thai thugs.

Apart from that there are the lean-to shacks which represent the local bars, and little else. Leisure time, which the Thais have too much of, is hardly catered for and it isn't any wonder that Thais drink as much as they do: there is little else to do, except watch TV which even the square-eyed Thais get tired of sometimes.

Nobody reads, mostly because they can't and probably couldn't afford to buy a book even if they could. The Thai newspapers are about the only printed matter that the average Thai manages to read, although there is no shop that sells them in Ban Dongwen. In any case, there are only comic books available outside the one library in Nongkhai, while the odd bookshop seems to sell nothing else other than religious books, books on 'how to' this and 'how to' that and a smattering of erudite tomes that I doubt many even bother to look at. Literature is not a priority in Thai rural life.

In Bangkok there are numerous bookshops but the prices are outrageous, particularly for books in the English language. My quest for discarded books in English was therefore a constant preoccupation; even trash was considered to be a gift from the gods!

The Thais seem to rely upon 'yak-yak' as their pastime; in fact it is an essential part of rural life. Chatter for chatter's sake, without saying a great deal of consequence; simply gossip. If An didn't get her hour or so of yak-yak every morning she would be unliveable with. Yak-yak precedes and also accompanies the preparation of the day's first *ghin cow* and continues after the rice and whatever has been consumed, aiding digestion and expending time.

It was not only the women, I discovered, who indulged in this ritual. My building crew suffered from the same preoccupation. The day's work had to be preceded by a good old chinwag which did not cease once the work had begun, every task having to be discussed in committee before being performed. I think their language, however, did not contain as many expletives as the average English labourer's did!

There are often special buildings for gathering for yak-yak: not so much buildings as covered areas with raised platforms upon which the participating yak-yakkers squat or lounge, or even doze off if the conversation isn't to their liking or their first *ghin cow* takes its toll.

Yak-yak is often indulged in over great distances, the strident fishwife-like voices between two or more women being heard ricocheting round the village. Somehow they seemed to understand one another, although to my *farang* ear it sounded like so many chickens clucking away together. Maybe it didn't matter what was being said precisely? With Thai being such a monosyllabic language, aggressive and confrontational in sound, it appeared on such occasions that there were several staccato-like verbal battles going on at the same time. In fact, they were probably discussing the merits or otherwise of each other's *ghin cow* of the day, since the word cropped up so often in their machine-gun conversations.

With life being such a daily battle for survival, the whereabouts of a particular beetle or mouth-watering underground bug was obviously of great importance. Word consequently spread rapidly, and soon afterward there often followed an exodus of women, bearing the correct implement for the task of capturing the unfortunate quarry. Success or failure of such expeditions was spread again via the yak-yak method of broadcasting.

The 'over the garden fence' conversations of European women bear a great similarity, except with discussion being about the availability of this or that at whatever supermarket rather than what could be found lurking in the undergrowth. The Thai housewives are, however, without doubt the reigning champions, having perfected the art of such gossipy gatherings over many generations. Ultimately it was this gossip-mongering that was to be partly responsible for the final split in my relationship with An and my exodus from Ban Dongwen.

With the sun cooking everything in sight for nine hours a day, my garden was now a limp rag of leaves gasping for water. Inside the comparative shade of the house we were somewhat protected; but despite my cavity walls, which seemed to keep the heat in as well as out, life come March was unbearably exhausting.

My finances were at an-all time low and it was becoming increasingly difficult to keep the ship afloat. My pension – my lifesaver – wouldn't kick in until mid-May (one month in arrears, of course), and meanwhile we survived on two small personal pensions and my equally small retainer remittance from the bungee when it could afford it.

Would I have to return to the smoke to hit the building site again, or could I last out? By this time I couldn't even afford the fare home even if I wanted to return. In addition, my Visa card had also refused to cooperate!

A friend in London came to the rescue and whisked a few quid into the bank account, so saving the day. My ex-wife had said that she thought I had bitten off more than I could chew and that I should 'get real'. Well, maybe she was right; but, even if it was only a handful of rice a day, I was still chewing and determined to continue doing so. If that isn't getting 'real' then I don't know what is! So there! Another friend also made enough cash available for me to return to London if it became necessary. Well, hell, what are friends for?

It was about this time that my daughter, Kate, decided that she would make the trip out to Thailand and visit. Sam was to meet her in Bangkok, and together they would travel to Duang's village to pick up her and Sam Song and all gather round the 'old fart' in Nongkhai for a reunion and joint birthday knees-up. She would then return to Koh Samui for a well-earned holiday by the sea. Kate is a professional camerawoman for one of the London TV news channels and earned good money for this gruelling task.

I booked them all into the Pantawee hotel in Nongkhai and decided to stay one night myself for a good old chinwag and for the inevitable piss-up with my kids. This was really something to look forward to, and after the trials and tribulations of the last month or so a very welcome relief. As it happened I stayed for three nights, my daughter insisting on picking up the accommodation bill.

I hadn't seen Sam Song for six months. He had grown, both physically and emotionally; and, despite a time away from Sam (Duang for some reason having taken her son home to her village), Sam Song was still deeply attached to his father, as of course Sam was to his son.

Kate fussed over all of us like a mother hen and, fortunately, also took to An and the kids, although An was behaving a little strangely. This was their first meeting, and I was somewhat nervous about introducing my new wife. An was younger than my daughter; but then Kate had been introduced to numerous of my amours, all of whom had been younger than her, and she hadn't turned a hair. She was used to her father's taste for younger lovers although she had never met one quite as exotic as An nor one with two grown boys.

We had a good joint birthday party for me and Sam at the Danish Baker. The staff produced a stunningly attractive but very creamy birthday cake. An, who had been burning the candle at both ends recently at various parties in Ban Dongwen, had to depart early. Quite what was wrong with her I couldn't fathom. However, the sturdy Brit revellers went on to a riverside venue I'd seen previously, which boasted Western music. We ordered up jugs of beer and proceeded to take over the sparsely populated bar with Sam and Kate insisting on punishing everybody by attempting to 'entertain' us all with the dreaded karaoke machine.

My children cannot sing nor hold a note and the result was hysterically funny. In punishment for my unbridled laughter I was hauled to the karaoke microphone and ordered to perform. Singing was not something I would normally choose to do, other than in the bath or shower; but such were the derisory comments that, as an old actor who had trodden the boards for many years, the challenge was too much. Unlike my children's, my voice is trained and, though somewhat crackly now in my dotage, still a fine baritone. That I can pitch the right note, in the right key, phrase properly and sustain notes came as somewhat of a surprise to Sam and Kate, and my ending with a powerful rendering of 'My Way' (changed to include some of my own lyrics) brought appreciative applause from my audience. I retired with dignity and a certain satisfaction.

We did shopping, we did a trip on the Mekong River and Kate, dear sweet generous child, decided to buy me a second-hand computer as a birthday present. Writing in longhand is extremely laborious and this development would give me renewed enthusiasm and much relief from the pain in my fingers!

I took Sam and Kate on the tedious and uncomfortable tuk-tuk ride to Ban Dongwen to see my house and the village we lived in. On the way the tuk-tuk suddenly lurched to the left as a tyre burst, and Sam and I spent the next hour assisting the driver to replace it by using brute strength, instead of a jack, to hoist the machine off the ground. We continued on our way to Ban Dongwen.

To my surprise they were both impressed by my unfinished dwelling, and adored the village. My local pub, Mr Mun's, received our crowd with great alacrity and Kate scored a definite triumph with Mr Mun by rolling him a cigarette of Western tobacco, complete with filter tip. We drank gallons of beer again, were entertained by some of the locals who helped us refresh ourselves, and took our leave of Ban Dongwen in our tuk-tuk and headed back to the delights of town with, would you believe it, yet another burst tyre as we entered Nongkhai!

After an unusually filthy meal at a German restaurant, which I had noticed earlier in the day, we retired thankfully to the hotel, exhausted. All that is except Kate, who spent a couple of hours with two Polish sailors on their way home to see their girlfriends who insisted on buying Kate beer after beer. Quite what two Polish sailors were doing in the middle of Thailand, on the border with Laos and a million miles from the sea, I do not know and I didn't ask.

The visiting party was due to leave the next day, Sam and Kate to Koh Samui and Duang back to her village with Sam Song. Sam suggested that his relationship with Duang had improved and that a more permanent arrangement might be on the cards. I left them all mid-morning with fond farewells, my condolences to Kate for her hangover and returned to Ban Dongwen, much pleased by the visit and Sam's news.

Chapter Twenty
THE REAL END

THIS REALLY WAS THE END of the beginning. We had struggled through hell and high water to establish ourselves and start building our house. I had anticipated that it would be difficult - hard work on both the back and the emotions - but we had survived the worst and, hopefully, we could take the rest in our stride without tripping ourselves up by overstepping our finances. Besides, I now had my new computer to occupy my time and energy and a mountain of handwritten pages to transfer to the beast.

Once my pension kicked in and finance started to trickle in once more I could start the building process again, slowly, since we now lived in relatively civilised conditions. A return to the smoke was now looking less necessary than a month previously, thank God. I was happy in Ban Dongwen, content with the simple things in life: to write, redesign my garden, and continue the building of the house as finance allowed and to teach the boys English. The latter would prove the biggest task of all!

Education in the local Thai schools is traditional. They teach by rote and therefore the children's brains do not become accustomed to logic, to problem solving. For instance, the school said it taught English, but all the children had learned was a kind of singsong recitation of the alphabet; they couldn't recognise each individual letter.

I started off my efforts at teaching by scrawling the entire alphabet on one of my unfinished walls with a lump of charcoal. When the boys had learned it both forwards and backwards I went on to explain, as best I could, what vowels and verbs were. After that we began to construct simple sentences, but every lesson entailed going back to the beginning of the process, starting with the alphabet. It was a tedious task, but slowly the boys' brains began to take in logical progression and their difficulties in recognising the individual letters of the alphabet slowly lessened as familiarity took hold.

One of the main problems was pronunciation. That the Thais cannot pronounce their 'R's is common knowledge, but there are other sounds, essential to clarity in the English language, which are equally difficult for them to get their tongues around. The Thais are accustomed to speaking through their nasal cavity; therefore the use of the tongue, in pronouncing 'th' for instance, was anathema to them. Consonants also tend to get lost but this, as in English children, was largely due to laziness.

The Thai school curriculum was a mystery to me. Each day started with a 'regimental' assembly, accompanied by a dictatorial lecture on good behaviour, cleanliness and so on. This was followed by a rendition of the Thai national anthem – at least, a token since only the first phrase was sung by one or other of the pupils into the public address system. This was, thankfully, brief since few of the children's squeaky voices could actually hit the note. There would then be a short Buddhist prayer of some sort before the assembly broke up and the children went off with their teachers to their classrooms. That was unless their guide and mentor took it into his or her head to curtail the proceedings for the day for some curious reason, which they seemed to do with remarkable regularity.

They seemed to concentrate very little on the three 'R's and spent a great deal of their time on practical 'play', making various things thought up by the teachers. While this was probably beneficial for the younger members, it did little to educate those brains that needed developing. Num was clearly a bright receptive lad who, with the right kind of educative nurturing, could be exceptional; but for an eleven-year-old he was way behind his European equivalent.

Every age group has a curriculum, a book printed and issued by the state authority, which is followed religiously. Sporadic homework seemed to entail copying out from one book to another: again the rote principle. The use of the bamboo twig was common if the unfortunate pupils do not assimilate the lesson. The dreaded cane was also used to encourage the boy pupils to get a haircut! The regulation Thai schoolboy haircut, short back and sides, was religiously adhered to and any deviation severely punished. The result was that they all looked like mini-convicts.

European and American private schools are proliferating; the value of such informed, tried and tested methods involving teaching the three 'R's was being recognised, and there were moves afoot to alter the curriculum and style of teaching in all Thai state schools. First of all, however, they will have to educate the teachers! It became obvious to me that this was not the most lucrative of occupations, rather on a par with a post-office worker, and that recruiting suitable teachers would also be a question of reviewing their rates of pay. It seemed I'd heard that somewhere before in my previous life.

So, if the children were going to get half a chance of a good education it would be down to me. I would have to get them up to a standard of English reading and writing that would make transition into one of the more enlightened colleges feasible at a later stage.

I began trying seriously to teach Num and Lyn the English language, but I was hampered by the drill of teaching by rote that they were used to in their school. Having managed to teach them the alphabet and the frequency with which vowels were used in the English language, I then tried to progress, in a logical way, to construction. This was a big stumbling block; and Lyn, whose undeveloped brain could only cope with the most elementary of problems, began to rebel.

An, who would sometimes join in these sessions, became very protective and aggressive when I tried to discipline Lyn's brain into some form of logical activity. She was perfectly capable of learning herself, and her English had improved remarkably simply by picking up words from me. However, she became a protective 'mother hen' as far as Lyn was concerned and even went so far as to refuse to let him attend the classes. Num was a different story: he was a bright, keen and eager student and a delight to teach.

After a short time, other children in the village began to take an interest and I soon had a class of nine or ten pupils crowding into our bedroom for their daily lessons. My 'children' ranged in age from eight to twenty-one; it became a pleasure to teach them and I think both they and I looked forward to the sessions.

It was around this time that An took to staying out late to party with her friends. Almost every night, it seemed, one of her friends would be celebrating a birthday party. Her return home became later and later until eventually she would arrive with the sun and shatter the peace of the early morning as she urged her ancient motorbike up to the house. I was left to look after the boys, get their meals and generally speaking babysit them as soon as they came home from school. An took to staying away most of the day as well as half the night, and when at last I became impatient with this behaviour she flew into a terrible rage and stormed off.

One early evening I was taking my usual end-of-the-day repast of a couple of beers at the local bar when An arrived, much the worse for wear and obviously wanting to pick a fight. She started to slug back a beer and glared at me, and when I asked if she had drunk all of the five hundred baht that I'd given her she flew into a rage. I knew her temper: she had already come at me with a hammer and a knife, and I had warned her that such behaviour would not be tolerated. I decided that confrontation at this moment would not be wise, so I paid my bill and began to leave. She swigged back the rest of her drink and came after me, brandishing the empty beer bottle threateningly. That was it – I snapped.

I confronted her and said that if she wanted a fight she should come and get it, and waved her on. She staggered out into the road following me, and aimed the bottle at my head. I, being relatively sober, took her head on, swung her about face, pinned her in a nelson grip and took the bottle from her. Having disarmed her I pushed her away. She was furious at having been thwarted in her attempt to brain me and rushed into the bar, picked up a knife and came back again. Fortunately the bar owner, Mr Mun, stepped in and grabbed her and, with the assistance of two other customers, took the knife from her. Mr Mun said he thought it would be wise if I were to leave. With my temper now under control and my dignity intact, I said I would do just that – leave.

Chapter Twenty-One

THE RELUCTANT GOODBYE

I WENT BACK TO THE house, called for a car and packed my clothes and bits and pieces. I had plenty of sympathetic willing hands to help and soon everything, including my computer, was packed into the back of a pick-up and, together with four or five of my friends, I headed towards Nongkhai.

I checked into the Pantawee Hotel and my small 'army' helped me transfer my belongings to one of the rooms. We were a curious sight and we must have caused many a raised eyebrow as we trudged through the hotel lobby with suitcases, hastily packed boxes, clothes and my computer, table and all the other paraphernalia, but nobody blinked. I was obviously in a state and best left alone.

I slept like a log that night and woke in the morning feeling… free, there was no other word for it. I realised that the events of the last weeks had exhausted me, both mentally and emotionally, but after a good night's sleep I felt capable of rational thought. I was certainly not going back to Ban Dongwen to suffer An's outrageous behaviour any more; I'd had enough of that and the humiliation that went with it.

I was enjoying a good breakfast of bacon and eggs and ruminating on what I should do next when my visitors arrived. An's elder sister and a friend of the family sheepishly asked me what I was going to do. I truthfully told them that at this stage I really didn't know. I thought they had been sent by An to urge me to return, but quite the reverse! They said I should stay in Nongkhai. An had apparently taken a Thai boyfriend, Pong, which accounted for the late nights and general revelling. This was a revelation that hit me right between the legs. An had obviously got fed up with the 'old fart' and wanted a 'stud'. That I certainly was not; I had, however, tried to be a good husband, but that apparently wasn't enough – I was no fun! My aged bits and pieces were still functioning, but not with what one could call a great deal of enthusiasm.

My feelings of inadequacy were somewhat sidelined by the realisation that I was in a financially diminished state. My pension wasn't due to arrive for two weeks, and hotel bills in Thailand had to be paid 'up front'. I also had to eat! I managed to front it out at the hotel, and existed on rice soup for the latter part of the experience.

With the help of my friends at the Danish Baker, I managed to locate a furnished condominium. It was a very pleasant building that overlooked the Mekong River and had a balcony, air conditioning and the means for me to cook my early-morning porridge and brew the odd cuppa. The only problem was securing it. The owners required a month's rent in advance and a month's deposit. This, together with my hotel bill, would 'skin' me virtually for another month until the next wad came from Her Majesty's Government.

Much against the grain I had to appeal to my friends in England, none of whom were particularly well off themselves but many of whom came through with the odd quid or two to tide me over. My daughter, bless her heart, contributed a loan; and I still had a small income from the bungee business. Somehow I survived, and when the next pension payment came through I could budget realistically and breathed a sigh of relief.

My new home, my bachelor pad in the sky, was peaceful and sublime. I spent a great deal of time writing, and relieved my boredom with my own company by taking a daily walkabout which ended at the Danish Baker for a couple of beers and a passable European-style meal.

I settled into a tranquil routine which nurtured the kind of quietude that my battered brain sorely needed after the past few months. I was concerned about the boys; but the thought of returning to Ban Dongwen, a dirty house and a recalcitrant An filled me with horror. No: I had found peace of mind in placid old Nongkhai, and some new friends at the Danish, many of whom had suffered the same kind of treatment and humiliation at the hands of their 'wives' and some even worse. The tales of stupid old *farangs* like me being taken for a ride by unscrupulous Thai girls, having built a house for them and had their ATM cards caned to the point of drawing blood, was a common one that I heard time and time again.

One such story amused me greatly. A German man who thought that he had found true love lost a fortune. He had built a house, married his girlfriend and moved into it with her. He bought a car, and a ton of gold with which his newly beloved adorned herself until she could hardly stand for the weight of it; and, when his coffers ran low, she berated him mercilessly and told him to get out of the house. When he protested, quite naturally, that he had bought the land and built the house, she ruthlessly pointed out that the land and the car and everything else that he had bought was in her name, and there was nothing he could do about it – a point that was backed up by her particularly tough brothers who had also been living off his largesse for many months.

He consulted a lawyer who confirmed his worst fears. The land and everything else was certainly hers; that was Thai law. However, the lawyer said that if he could prove that he had paid for the house-building it would, in law, belong to him. Being a fastidious German gentleman, he had in fact kept every single bill involved in building his house. So, the house belonged to him! Yes, agreed the lawyer; but without the land rights, the house was useless.

My German friend pondered this problem for some time until eventually he came up with a unique solution. He hired a bulldozer, proceeded to the village and took the house apart, brick by useless brick. The astonished villagers watched helplessly as he demolished the entire structure, leaving a pile of rubble in its place! He might have been a few hundred thousand baht lighter in his pocket, but his heart was full of satisfaction at a just end to his problem!

I nurtured thoughts of copying my German friend's tactics, but realised that such an action, although satisfying, would leave the boys with no place to live. I resigned myself to sit it out.

Eventually, after about four weeks in my new home overlooking the Mekong, An turned up. She wasn't particularly sorry, and in fact gave the impression that she felt that I was to blame for the whole incident that led to the split. She asked for money without turning a hair. I gave her a little to feed the boys, but she obviously wasn't either grateful or satisfied and stomped off back to Ban Dongwen. She returned a couple of days later saying that she had put the land and house papers up as a guarantee against a loan. She had also sold everything I had bought including, it seemed, even the precious pump I had installed to raise water from the well. She was going to use the proceeds to take a holiday in Bangkok!

Needless to say I was speechless and furious. I told her that her actions only proved what a stupid, selfish, thoughtless person she was, and that I was appalled that she had such little consideration for her children. It was like water off a duck's back, and she flounced off in a huff. I had thought of returning to Ban Dongwen to pick up where I'd left off, but this encounter drove all such thoughts from my head. I determined to stay in Nongkhai and pick up the pieces of my life.

So, I was back in comparative civilisation once more: no more filthy red dust everywhere, no more neighbours soused in Laos Cal and grinning betel-nut-juice grins at me, no more creepy crawlies emerging from the jungle to plague my life; but then, no more of what I had become accustomed to call 'my new family'.

I had a great sense of relief, but at the same time a greater sense of loss. I hadn't realised just how accustomed I had become to life in Ban Dongwen. Having 'gone native', it was a difficult and heart-rending experience to lose what I had come to love and indeed need. I would probably have gone back to the village and patched up my differences with An, had it not been for the fact that she had sold everything to finance her new venture of disappearing to Bangkok on a 'spree', a holiday as she called it – probably, also, financing her Thai lover to accompany her.

However, my newfound friends at the Danish helped me over the worst of these anxieties. Kai, the owner of the Danish, had just begun to set up the Danish Baker internet website; and since writing was not only my business but also my passion, I agreed to take on the task of writing for the site. This I started to do more as occupational therapy in the first instance but, once I had begun work on it, it became not so much therapy as a joy. It was such a big 'canvas' that, the more I explored the possibilities, the more fascinating it became. It also brought me closer to the problems of retirees, like myself, who were contemplating transplanting their lives to Thailand, and in particular Nongkhai.

The American magazine *Modern Maturity* had surveyed the world to find the most attractive places where retirees were likely to find what they were looking for in their latter years. Nongkhai had been listed as seventh behind such places as Spain's Costa Del Sol, France's Provence and the Grenadine Islands. Nongkhai is indeed a very quiet, friendly and clean town, but it lacks the facilities that most of us have become accustomed to and which have become second nature to our Western lifestyles. If Nongkhai was to attract retirees to the town, it had to face up to these shortcomings.

I therefore set about the task of exploring the town, the culture, the housing, health facilities, the legal visa regulations and the like that retirees might need to know before travelling halfway round the world to pay an exploratory visit.

Prior to this time I'd only had contact with the rural community of Ban Dongwen. Most of these simple people had only the most minimal education, and their lives were ruled by the need simply to survive. Small-scale farming of the rice fields was their main preoccupation, for without the annual rice harvest they were doomed to starvation. Over the years apathy had developed into lethargy: do the minimal amount of work necessary to produce the rice, and if the opportunity came along to earn money by any other means, grab at it. Some of the more enterprising individuals actively sought work, but this was mainly labouring on the odd building site; or, perhaps, the more adventurous would go to Saudi Arabia, Singapore or whichever country was looking to recruit cheap labour.

The girls of the family were often encouraged to travel south, to the tourist hotspots such as Bangkok, Pattaya, Phuket, Koh Samui and so on, to work in the bars, karaoke bars, go-go bars and other more sinister sexploitation venues. The lucky ones would earn enough money to send home to support the family. The really lucky ones would 'snare' a *farang*, declare undying love and bring him home to the village to meet the family with the prospect of getting married and moving to Europe, thus securing a steady income to support the family back home. Or, as I'd found was more often the case, screw as much out of the poor sop's ATM card as they possibly could before ditching him.

Sadly, many of the girls would fall victim to disease, drugs or booze and end up worse than they started, leaving the family to look after the children they'd given birth to in their teens before starting off on their adventures into the profligate south.

However, once in Nongkhai and transplanted into a more educated society, I met up with more of the well-educated middle-class Thais who were the 'movers and shakers' of the area. Of this elite group the most impressive was Khun Prasit, the head of the administration for the whole of the province of Nongkhai. Here was a man who spoke good conversational English, who had completed his education at Leeds University in England and whose heart seemed to be in the right place. While everyone else in Nongkhai seemed to be preoccupied in acquiring as much money as they could, Khun Prasit seemed to be intent on working for the good of the people of Nongkhai.

He invited Kai and me to attend a seminar that he had organised to meet other Thai notables from nearby villages and to talk about what we felt was needed to make the town of Nongkhai, and the province as a whole, more attractive to tourists and retirees alike. Since he and I spoke a common language, I did most of the talking with Khun Prasit interpreting into Thai.

Following the main part of the seminar, we were wined and dined as honoured guests and met some very interesting people from the surrounding villages. In all it was a most interesting and exhilarating experience and one which made me realise, with considerable humility, that what I knew about Thailand and the Thai culture was, at best, primitive. I had a lot to learn.

In confusion, I started to review my experiences in Thailand and, in particular, my relationship with An, her family and my friends in the village of Ban Dongwen. Had I been ill informed, hasty in my conclusions about their avarice and dishonesty? Should I have been more tolerant and less 'European' in my judgements? Probably; but then, with only a modest grasp of the Thai language and customs, my understanding would remain minimal. My ignorance would continue and would be a constant source of frustration; for, try as I might, I could not master the language, which to me seemed primitive, naive and monosyllabic. I am quite sure that I was wrong for, although complicated in structure, Thai is probably as sophisticated in its true form as any Western language. However, Isan – the dialect spoken in the north-eastern region of which Nongkhai is a part – is almost an entirely different language to Bangkok Thai and is more akin to Lao, so much so that the people of Isan find it hard to make themselves understood when travelling south.

I buried myself in work, writing story after story, block after block of information for tourists and retirees to Nongkhai for the Danish website. In no time at all the number of visitors to the site climbed and climbed, and I was answering question after question from potential retirees about Nongkhai, and also from tourists wishing to visit, or people wanting visas and so on! It seemed that I had become the central source of information, since the Thailand Tourist Authority's website was so bad and non-specific. It became a time-consuming 'hobby' and it meant a daily, sometimes twice daily visit to the Danish to keep up with it. I was also running out of space in my tiny condo.

In the meantime, Sam had decided that he had really had a bellyful of the bungee jump; and Mark, our other partner, had indicated that he might like to take it over, having found a serious investor who might buy out our interest. Since the business was now only just making money, I thought this a good idea and I planned a visit to my old haunt.

I hadn't been there since I'd taken off for the jungle and my new life, so I looked forward to it. With my daughter due a visit to Koh Samui in August, I thought I could kill two birds with one stone: complete the sale, and see my daughter. I would also have to close up my house there as Sam was planning to move to Bangkok to study a TEFL course in order to teach English. I arranged to visit for a week, make all the necessary arrangements for selling our interest in the business, sell my furniture and close the lease on the house. The end of another era.

I flew down and spent the first few days enjoying my revisit to the old haunts while Mark got his business interests together. These, however, did not go according to plan; his investment partner fell through, but a new arrangement was made and a price agreed on. As Mark couldn't come up with the entire purchase price, I took a small portion in a barter deal: a portable computer!

It was good seeing my daughter and Sam again, but before long I had to return to Nongkhai; other business was waiting.

Within a week of returning to Nongkhai I had received the cash portion of the sale and I was relatively rich again. I determined that I should find somewhere else to live, a small house with enough accommodation for the family should An come to her senses. Kai knew of a place that a mutual friend of ours had rented but which was about to become vacant. It was fully furnished! A rare find in Nongkhai.

My new abode, although small, was similar to my small mews house in Hampstead, London. Although the roof leaked and it was dirty and uncared for, it was at least fully furnished and owned by a Swedish friend of Kai's. It was also a fair distance from the centre of town, so I recruited a local tuk-tuk driver I had become acquainted with to help get the house straight and also to provide me with transport.

In no time at all we had the house clean, the holes in the roof plugged and the kitchen in reasonable order. It became quite a home from home; and, if An decided to return and resume a civilised life, there was a second bedroom to accommodate the boys and move them out of the grotty village of Ban Dongwen.

Once again I was on my own, but this time I had the activity at the Danish Baker to occupy my time. I set about writing more material for the website. I started a monthly 'News' column, comprehensive information on Nongkhai, a 'Property Page' and so on. As Christmas approached we were clocking up something like one hundred hits on the website every day.

I had created a page on the site that dealt solely with real estate, having travelled miles around the town and its environs to find suitable houses and apartments to rent and for sale. For sale was easy: there are many good houses available, most with all of the required amenities, except European-style kitchens. However, furnished properties for rent were few and far between. Europeans when renting accommodation expect it to come furnished but this is almost impossible in Nongkhai. This is not surprising when you think about it, for the average Thai family prefers to live at ground level, squatting or lounging on rush matting. For beds they normally put the mattress directly on the concrete or tiled floor; it is cooler. Cooking is usually done on a small charcoal-burner or a two-plate gas stove. Ovens are rarely used.

I now try not to get involved in renting accommodation; it is far too time-consuming and soul-destroying. I will help and advise, and if I know a suitable condo or something I will try to arrange this for a visitor; but most do not stay long enough to be bothered with trying to persuade the Thai landlords to put in furniture. For those staying for a month or so, the hotels or guesthouses are cheap enough.

Having settled into my new lifestyle in Nongkhai, I was somewhat disconcerted when An arrived on the scene again. Her 'holiday' in Bangkok over, she was broke once more, and naturally she had come to me for money. I had virtually written her off, thinking that she was now living with her Thai man, Pong. However, Pong it seemed didn't want An unless she was providing the readies through me! Typical.

I told An that she must choose. If she truly loved this Pong then she should go and live with him; she couldn't have her cake and eat mine! She said she wasn't sure, so I said I would provide enough money for the boys but no more. She said she still had a 'good heart' for me but didn't know what she would do. I told her to go away and think about it, and she returned to Ban Dongwen and the boys, our future still undecided.

She continued to return every week when she had run out of money until finally, somewhat understandably, I gave her an ultimatum and said that if she would come to live in the house in Nongkhai with the boys then, if it would make her feel more secure, we would get married officially.

This seemed to persuade her which way to jump. We would go off to Bangkok to do the dirty deed officially. Had we been able to do this in Nongkhai it would have saved a great deal of money; but I had been advised that, owing to the British Embassy permissions that were required, the translation of official documentation and so on, we would be better off doing this exercise in Bangkok.

As An had never flown before, I decided that we should do this in style and fly from Udonthani to Bangkok as it might shake her out of the strange mood she was in. She seemed to thoroughly enjoy the experience of flying, and I hoped that this new development would somehow cement our relationship.

So we arrived in dirty, smelly, noisy, expensive Bangkok. We booked into the same hotel that we had stayed in before when Sam and I had first visited; the prices had gone up and the service down. I employed an agency to cover all the paperwork and make all of the necessary arrangements, and we did our best to enjoy a city I despised as much as I did London.

Our relationship still did not noticeably improve; we passed the four days there equably enough, but I somehow sensed that there was no warmth. It was a dreary, unemotional ceremony at the registrar's, and as soon as it was over we got out of there. We had intended to come back to Nongkhai by train on the overnight sleeper, but it was booked solid. I worked out that it would cost less to fly back rather than stay another night in an expensive hotel and eat one more meal at an expensive restaurant. Anyway, I'd had a bellyful of Bangkok and couldn't wait to get back to Nongkhai and relative civilisation, and start life as a family.

This, however, was not to be. The boys were still in school in Ban Dongwen and, we discovered, could not be moved to Nongkhai to continue their education because their family name was not registered there. Despite all efforts it appeared that this was so; damned Thai government administration! We didn't have the right papers: neither Num nor Lyn were on the 'family book' – an official record of Thai families. This was held by An's mother, but the boys were on their father's family book, way down south. An said that the only way she could solve this problem was to visit him and ask him to give his permission to change this. We had thus not been back more than a couple of days before she left again, ostensibly to persuade the boys' father to sign the necessary papers for us to educate them in Nongkhai.

Meanwhile, the two boys had moved in and seemed perfectly happy with their new situation and soon made friends with the local kids; amazing how children can do this as a matter of course. I bought them each a new bicycle, and at the same time bought one for myself. This meant that we could go on local fishing trips together, something I knew the boys particularly enjoyed. However, I suffered considerably since I had not ridden a bicycle for twenty-odd years and my backside and ancient legs suffered badly.

An kept in touch by mobile phone and it soon became obvious that her ex 'husband' would not cooperate unless bribed. I refused, and An went off to see the local boss of the village to get him to intervene; it was, after all, better for the children. She returned to Nongkhai without the necessary paperwork but having spent a considerable amount of money. I reluctantly used my influence with Khun Prasit, the Nai Amphur (district administrator), to put his weight behind our case. We signed more paperwork which was sent off by post for action, and had to be content to wait for the result by return.

Time was not on our side and An and the boys had to go back to Ban Dongwen for the boys to return to the village school. This was against my wishes, but there seemed to be no alternative. I bought An a motorbike on an instalment plan in order that she could commute between Ban Dongwen and Nongkhai.

Finally the permission came through; but the boys could not register with the school in Nongkhai until the end of term! Nobody seemed to know when this would be. So An lived with the boys with her friend in Ban Dongwen, while I remained in the house in Nongkhai. Not the ideal situation, and certainly not one to nurture our fragile relationship. An visited only once every two or three days, and then only stayed long enough to collect enough money for living expenses for the boys and her. This was going to be a long haul with an uncertain outcome.

An old couple from Korea, a university professor and his wife, got in touch with me to see if I could aid them in their search for a place for them to retire to. They had heard that Nongkhai had a pretty equable climate and had decided to come and see for themselves. Unfortunately he was in poor health, and required a reasonably accessible hospital should he have problems. This I found for him, and even nursing attention around the clock should it be necessary. They stayed in a first-class hotel for a few days while I showed them Nongkhai and several of the houses we had available to buy. I then had to find them somewhere suitable for them to rent for three months – furnished! Well, I finally sorted the problem through a Thai friend, although it wasn't ideal by any means.

The Prof and his wife enjoyed their stay in Nongkhai, and indeed his health did improve. Time will tell if they decide to come back when they retire. I hope so; they were a delightful couple, with whom I became great friends.

Christmas and New Year celebrations were outrageous; it seemed that half of Denmark had turned up to frolic in Nongkhai. Barrels of Carlsberg and numerous bottles of vodka were consumed.

I only saw An and the boys briefly over this period, to give them Christmas presents to buck their spirits up. An was beginning to realise that changing her life and moving into Nongkhai to set up a proper home and education for the boys was maybe for the best. Perhaps there was light at the end of this particular tunnel.

On New Year's Eve there was, of course, a big party and feast. I got a little inebriated, and come the early hours of the morning was taken home in my friendly tuk-tuk and safely tucked up in my bed by one of the Danish Baker's ladies. She was still curled up in my bed the next morning but I don't remember a thing about it! It took me several days to fully recover and return to a semblance of normality.

Maybe it's the season, but Christmas seemed to be the period for romance amongst the Danes. A double marriage was arranged between two Danes and their recently acquired Thai girlfriends, with a celebration 'in style' at the Danish Baker. At the party, which of course I attended, I saw a beautiful Thai woman whom I had seen around the area several times. Her name was Nong. She was intelligent, spoke a little English and was altogether delightful, but she was unavailable. She was the *mia noi* (the second wife or, as we would say, the mistress) of the local bank manager. Filled full of 'Scottish courage' I asked her to dance – the dance floor was the middle of the road! We got on superbly well and danced several more times but that, I supposed, was that: a pleasant experience at a party – nothing more. I was married, albeit precariously.

An came to see me a few weeks later and found me at the Danish Baker; she was obviously very unhappy and ashamed. After some persuasion I finally got to the root of the matter. She was pregnant! I knew this couldn't be my child, for I had established, irrevocably, years before that I was unable to give children. She admitted that it had to be her Thai lover's, and that it had been conceived before we had gone to Bangkok to get married!

There was also a problem with the pregnancy: there were two foetuses, one in her womb and the other in her fallopian tubes. This was, of course, very dangerous and a condition that needed to be dealt with immediately, by an abortion. So, why was she telling me and not her Thai man? He, apparently, would have nothing to do with this and refused to help. Most Thai men do not make ideal husbands and the one An had chosen as her paramour was no exception; he was obviously quite young and relished his freedom still, and had no taste for taking on a wife who already had two grown children. He arrogantly also refused to help her abort his children, even though carrying them was dangerous for An. Being a stud with a woman who could provide the necessary dosh for them to party all the time was more his style.

Once again I was put on the spot. I paid for her medical treatment which she insisted must be done in a village where others of her family could tend to her needs traditionally! Was this another of her wild lies to get me to cough up more money for her illicit nightlife? I was not happy about this, but there was little I could do about it. If it was true, then she was obviously in some danger. So An went away, and stayed away for over a month to recuperate. I could only hope that I had done the right thing and that she would recover. In retrospect, I think this was another con of the kind-hearted Englishman, and the money was almost certainly spent on yet another party.

The bureaucracy of Thailand once again ruined my plans when I discovered that the boys could not change schools until Song Kran, April, another three months or more away. An also threw a spanner in the works once again by declaring that she had been offered a job in the capital; she'd arranged for the boys to be looked after in Ban Dongwen and was off to Bangkok. I couldn't see the sense in this, and told her so; but she was determined that she would earn 'big money' and return after Song Kran. When she gets an idea into her head it is impossible to move it.

So, off to Bangkok she went, with me left to look after the boys in the village; by 'look after' she meant support financially. I was immediately suspicious and asked what had become of her motor bike, feeling that she was quite likely to have sold it to provide herself with sufficient finance for this new madness. She made a lame excuse that she had rented it out for the three months she would be away, but I didn't believe her since she refused to tell me which 'friend' she had rented it to and where.

It wasn't long before she was on the telephone from Bangkok asking for money. Her friend who was to have given her the job had been on holiday when she arrived and she couldn't find any other work. I insisted that she give up this mad adventure and return to Nongkhai, the boys and me. She claimed not to have sufficient money to do so and I forwarded her enough for her return trip. The next phone call I got was from Hat Yai, right in the southern part of Thailand on the Malaysian border. She'd moved down there and had a well-paid job, so she said, as a hostess on an airline bus which ran a service between Hat Yai and Bangkok!

Here we go again, I thought; and indeed, here we did go again! I began to seriously review my situation with An and the family. It was a fairly negative and depressing period, and my suspicions about An's motives and behaviour began to grow and grow. My faith in her was dented even more when she did not return from Hat Yai. Her determination to 'earn big money' only compounded my worries. There was only one way for someone with An's limited education to earn such money.

Again she called me and asked for money, since she wouldn't get paid until the end of the month. I sent a small amount, cautiously, and warned her to return to Nongkhai and her children. The next thing I heard was that she had taken herself off to Singapore! This confirmed my suspicions about her determination to get rich quick. There was definitely only one way she could earn money in Singapore: on her back!

Unscrupulous 'agents' (for this read pimps) promised gullible and naive Thai girls to get them to Singapore and find them work. For this they charge a hundred thousand baht which the girls have to pay off from their earnings. Once hooked, the unfortunate girls are forced into working in bars, 'go-go' establishments or other such venues which are 'fronts' for the illicit sex trade; although, curiously, prostitution in Singapore is not illegal. However, working in Singapore as a Thai national without a permit is.

An rang and gave me several sob stories, including one about having been arrested at the border for smuggling drugs and thrown into the 'monkey house' (the Thai euphemism for prison). She finally rang me and said she wanted to come home and needed money to pay off debts before she would be allowed to leave. For her children's sake, I transferred money to her bank account; against my better judgement, but in the vain hope that this would get her out of whatever situation she had gotten herself into and reunite her with her children.

Meanwhile, I was working hard on the Danish Baker website, and towards the end of the first year of its life the number of people who had visited the site hit thirty thousand: a very impressive start. Also, I was getting many requests by email for advice and guidance, both from visitors to Nongkhai and from potential retirees.

The Thai celebration of Song Kran, the water festival, was looming and so too was my sixty-sixth birthday. For the last month or so I had been becoming more and more friendly with Nong, who frequented the orange-juice bar opposite the Danish. We'd had several very equable and enjoyable conversations, and I'd begun to give her tentative English lessons. She was a fast learner.

Chapter Twenty-Two

WILL I NEVER LEARN? HOPE NOT!

NONG WAS SHOWING SIGNS OF more than normal friendship; and, as my birthday approached, Nong and Apple (the owner of the orange-juice stall) said they would like to cook for me on my birthday, at my house. Delighted, I declared a party for which I would supply the venue and the booze and they would provide the food.

I bought flowers as gifts for all of the girls who would be attending and a bunch of roses for Nong. Everyone duly arrived and Apple immediately set about cooking some special Thai food in my kitchen. Copious amounts of booze began to flow, and in no time at all the party was in full swing. Nong had bought me an expensive wallet as a birthday present and Apple had bought a pen. I was both surprised and delighted. The food was delicious, and towards the end Nong became very affectionate and my hopes rose for a new beginning. But I suspected these hopes would be in vain, for Nong was still with her bank manager and I was still, legally, married to An.

As luck would have it the money I had transferred to An's Bangkok bank account was not accessible to her in Singapore. There was indeed a Bangkok bank branch there, but with no ATM machine! Again a plaintive call from An. Not only could she not get at the money I had put into her account, but she found she needed more to get out of Singapore and back to Nongkhai. In fact she needed double! What a con, I thought; but for one last chance at getting her back home to look after her boys I complied, and found a way to send her the money she said she needed to get home. Sucker!

Sure enough my suspicions were confirmed when An called again after about a month and told another cock-and-bull story: someone had stolen her tickets home, and would I send more money? I told her that I had visited the boys every two weeks and paid for their accommodation. The family she had 'parked' them with were unsuitable, to say the least, and had apparently been promised a great deal of money to look after them. I had agreed only to pay for their subsistence and schooling needs, but within a few weeks the family demanded the money that An had promised them. I blew my lid and decided to remove the boys from their 'tender care'! I called a family conference with An's mother, Yai, the head of the family, and managed to persuade them that this wasn't my problem but a family problem. Finally the boys moved in with An's sister – and she didn't want money to persuade her to have them! I, however, said I would continue to look after the boys' needs.

At this point I told An what I thought of her motherly attentions! I refused to send her any more money, and said that I considered her behaviour, both towards me and to her boys, disgraceful; I would sue for divorce. It didn't faze her at all! It was almost as if she expected this reaction, and was possibly surprised that her luck had held out this far. Wow!

My relationship with Nong, meanwhile, was improving no end. She told me that, come what may, she would leave her bank manager at the end of October when he was due to retire. We had grown really close as the friendship blossomed, but there was nothing of a sexual nature to it. In Nong's mind this could never be until she had finished with her current boyfriend. I said this was fair enough; and, as I intended to divorce An, I suggested that we might consider marriage. This delighted Nong for this was what she really wanted – more to please her father than anything else! He had never really approved of her relationship with the bank manager, and the only thing that would really satisfy him was marriage and respectability for his daughter. I wasn't so sure; marriage to a man who was literally as old as him? I would have to meet him first and discuss it.

During one of my numerous visits to Vientiane to renew my Thai visa, I sat down at my favourite restaurant, a French café that served excellent wine and superb steaks and suchlike, and thought about this very serious next move. Was I really going to marry a woman half my age, again; and was there any real prospect of such a union succeeding? Well, I thought, there was only one way to find out. Nothing ventured, nothing gained!

Nong and I discussed the timing of this new development. It was not going to be easy for her because, as yet, her bank manager did not suspect that there was anything going on. Indeed, there wasn't really, and there couldn't be until Nong left him. This was easier said than done. The move had to be at the right time, and it had to be a clean break. I also had to start proceedings for a divorce: not an easy thing to do in Thailand as I discovered.

I employed the services of a female lawyer who dealt with a lot of *farangs*' problems. I had previously discussed with her the problems of foreigners purchasing land, and had come up with a scheme that she said was clever and indeed legal under Thai law. So, we vaguely knew each other on a professional basis, and when I approached her with my marital problem she quizzed me mercilessly. Finally, she said she thought I had a case; but it would cost ten thousand baht and take at least two months to get a court date. I immediately agreed because the timescale was critical to my plans. We set the wheels in motion and within a week I'd got a court date for two months' time.

To complicate matters, I had been approached to write a document for the owner of the Pantawee Hotel. Nopporn was a curious character who at one time had been a 'him', but who had fled to London and emerged a 'her'. She had gone to Germany, studied at Hamburg University, got married and subsequently divorced. She had returned to Nongkhai at her ailing mother's request to run the business. Her mother eventually died and Nopporn had run the business ever since. She wanted to buy out the rest of the family in order that she might have freedom of management. They were, in any case, simply using the business as a cash cow and draining it. I was set the task of working up a document to attract financial partners. Back again in the hazardous jungle of corporate business that I thought I'd left behind in my exodus from London!

The timescale of my divorce was the pivotal date around which everything else revolved, Nong's flight from the bank manager included. A date was set, and I borrowed a car from the Pantawee and effected the move, and duly deposited her and the few personal belongings she wanted to take with her at her sister's house. She would not take anything that the bank manager had bought for her, but her dog, Gangana, was an essential passenger. So, the deed was done.

Through my contacts in Udon I managed to find a condo apartment on the outskirts of the town but within easy striking distance of the centre. This was important, because I'd insisted that Nong take the opportunity of this available time to study English. Nong liked the apartment, and the following weekend I moved her and Gangana again. That was the first weekend we'd spent together, and although we slept in the same bed there was no hanky-panky. It did, however, give us the feeling of a sense of freedom.

The only contact the bank manager had now was through her mobile phone; and he used it, mercilessly. He cried, he threatened, he cajoled – every trick in the book; but she patiently fended him off, appealing to me to be patient and let her work this out her way.

I had my work cut out at the Pantawee for, apart from the financial documents, I had now been asked to rewrite the entire English website. This was a task and a half so Nopporn, who now trusted me implicitly, employed me on a permanent basis. I had moved in to the Pantawee at her invitation, been given a free room and board and a free hand in running the English-language side of communications and business. It was, at this stage, a full-time job; and I was glad I had this to occupy my time while I waited for my divorce case to come up.

I got the odd telephone call from An in Singapore, pleading for money again with different stories as the excuse. I was pretty sure by now that she had a new man in her life, maybe even her pimp. Her calls to me were simply to try and squeeze some more money out of the stupid old *farang*. I told her of the impending divorce, but again it didn't seem to faze her. I refused to send her any more money.

The lawyer, Rayrai, said that I would need witnesses to lend credence to my story, so I took her off to Ban Dongwen to meet some and test the water. An's eldest sister, to whom I was still paying subsistence for the boys, said she would bear out my sorry tale. So too did the bar owner, Mr Mun. So, we ostensibly had two witnesses.

Nong and I set a date for the wedding and planned a visit to her village to meet her father and get his approval. It was a curious experience but I need not have worried; he had married a younger wife himself and we sat chatting together over a bottle of Scotch and several packs of cigarettes which I had had the foresight to bring with me. We set the date for September 1st.

Once back in Udonthani, Nong and I began to budget for the ceremony, a traditional affair with a massive party for virtually everyone within the village. We would have to hire wedding clothes, traditional ones. Three dresses for Nong, two outfits for me. There would also be official studio photographs of the happy couple, wedding invitations specially printed, gifts for the guests, gold for Nong and a fifty-thousand-baht dowry for her father… and so on. In the end the figure came to about two hundred thousand baht! Could I do this? I figured it out; yes, I could, but not in the time allowed. Ironically, the pension people in England owed me almost this much from my marriage to An. They had taken so long over processing my documents that I had almost a year's back pay coming. So, my marriage to An was to pay for my marriage to Nong! We moved the date of the wedding to September 28th, enough time for me to gather in the funds.

My traditional costume was hilarious: a kind of loose-fitting nappy of a violent dark blue colour, wound around my body with the loose end passed between my legs and tucked in at the back. On top of this I was to wear a traditional high-collared Thai jacket. Thank God none of my friends would be there to see me! In the evening, after the ceremony, I would be allowed to take my nappy off and wear ordinary white trousers for the party part of the event.

Monday, August 19th came up: my day in court. The day before, we had visited Ban Dongwen to make sure the witnesses knew what they had to say. As I had feared, An's sister reneged on her promise and dropped out of the case; she probably wanted payment! Mr Mun, however, was as determined as ever, although I feared that there might be a mishap. As we arrived at his bar he and some of his friends were preparing to roast a suckling pig in celebration of something or other. There was also a bottle of the dreaded Laos Cal being imbibed, and I feared for the state of Mr Mun's head the next day. Nevertheless he swore he would be there.

The next morning we arrived early as arranged at the court to make our final preparations. Come the appointed time, Mr Mun did not appear. The judge arrived and we prepared for me to plead my case without witnesses.

At the eleventh hour Mr Mun, prodded into action by his wife, arrived by tuk-tuk. As I feared he had been in no fit state to drive when he woke up. Could he speak, we asked? Well, to cut a long story short, he made it into court and gave a reasonable, if somewhat muted, performance. He got some of his testimony wrong, but was prompted in the right direction by the stalwart RayRai. All we had to do now was wait for the judgement. Wait? Again? Apparently the judge, who looked no more than sixteen and was constantly recording all the events and questioning on a portable tape recorder, was busy and he would have to review the cases of the day at home. I would have thought that my case was open and shut; but then, this is Thailand.

I was knee-deep in work, gathering as much information as I could about Nongkhai Province and the various festivals and attractions in order to write lucid and correct information for tourists. I had also had to explore the hotel, its finances, management structure, staffing and service and God knows what else in order to write a coherent document for investors. The ownership was a complicated affair because it was all bound up with the mother's wishes as expressed in the will and concerned the whole family. However, when dealing with the land documents, we discovered that two members of the family had been guilty of a little fraud. This gave us leverage when discussing the settlement, but it also caused Nopporn considerable angst as she didn't want to harm the family members involved.

The protracted negotiations dragged on and on and any hopes I had of attracting a large corporation to take an interest were dashed. This would have to be done the hard way, and so I started to prepare another scheme that involved bank loans. My aim was to negotiate the family out of the business as equitably as possible, persuade Nopporn to turn the business into a limited company and then work towards a public company launch. It was going to be a long haul of audits and legal matters: wranglings that were sure to go on for some time. It would need patience and vigilance to bring it off, reminiscent of Nong's situation and my divorce. I had to constantly tell myself to hold my tongue and my horses.

Finally my week of waiting for the court was up: the judge had decided, and my official legal divorce was granted! Great! But it was not quite over yet, for I had to visit the Amphur offices, the local administration, to apply for my divorce certificate. As it happened it was a relatively painless operation, and I walked out of the offices of the Amphur in one hour with my precious divorce certificate.

That weekend I presented Nong with a copy of the official document, and I think for the first time she really believed that it was all going to happen. She was still getting wild phone calls from the bank manager, alternately pleading, crying, threatening and declaring undying love. Someone had apparently seen Nong and me having lunch together on the previous Saturday and reported to him. He was furious and vowed to find her and physically take her back. However, the whereabouts of my condo, which we'd been careful to keep secret, prevented his attempts to locate her.

I was getting more and more pissed off with a man who couldn't take no for an answer! Nong, however, persisted with her quiet refusals to his overtures and offers of vast sums of money, houses, cars and whatnot. The threats, I am sure, were real; and, if he had been free to wield his power – if he'd discovered the whereabouts of our little hideaway – he would have almost certainly sent in the cavalry. It would all change after we were married, Nong assured me. I wasn't so sure.

We paid yet another visit to her village to make arrangements for the wedding party, the ceremony and somewhere for us to stay during the event. Nong owned two houses and vast tracts of farming land, but neither house was suitable for us to stay in.

Everyone seemed to be Nong's friend in the village, long-term friends from her schooldays and such. One in particular, Neng, offered her house for us to stay in and the grounds for us to hold the party; a splendid lady, very pretty but with a sad history of a failed Thai marriage dragging her down.

During this trip everyone from the village seemed to visit the house to meet the *farang* whom Nong was marrying. It was a big local interest story and I seemed to spend my time giving English lessons to all and sundry! We had to visit all the suppliers of the goods needed to service the party, and I drove four chattering females around the pitted roads in what seemed to me to be ever-increasing circles to the various locations. Like Ban Dongwen, the spider's web of roads connecting the various small communities was totally confusing. The only thing they had in common was that they all had craters about a foot deep in them which made navigation considerably hazardous.

Our weekend of visiting and organising ended, we took a circuitous route back to Nongkhai. We had decided that Nong should stay with me at the Pantawee and spend a few days trying to find us a house where we could live after the happy event and start a small business of some sort. Nong was dead keen to work after spending nine years 'imprisoned' by her bank manager. I also needed to get away from the Pantawee: my small cell of a room was becoming far too claustrophobic.

With the divorce finalised I no longer felt responsible for An nor the boys, so I stopped my financial support. I'd said I would do this once the divorce was final, in a last ditch attempt to make An aware of her responsibilities. I needn't have bothered: she couldn't have cared less.

Finally her mother took the situation in hand, and I learned that she had put the younger boy into the temple with the monks. They would look after him and educate him. My opinion of the activities of the monks has changed: they really are a responsible community body who will help out in critical circumstances. The elder boy remains at school, as far as I can tell; and neither blames me for the attitude I have towards their recalcitrant mother.

I sweated blood waiting for the rest of my cash to come together, but I made it. I had been passing some twenty-odd thousand baht to Nong every week or so to assure her that all was well. We had bought her necessary gold for the occasion and she had enough now to pay for the ceremony and party, the photographs, flowers and so on. All I had to do was get together the last commitment, the fifty grand dowry for her father. This I managed to do but Nong wasn't happy: the notes were all there but they were old, dirty and used. Nong was determined that everything should be new, including her father's dosh! So, off we trudged to the government building and exchanged the old cash for neat, crisp bundles of hundred-baht notes – it looked rich that way!

The weekends I had spent with Nong in Udon in the condo

apartment were delightful and, as our wedding date approached, very much more intimate. Nong had what is called in Thailand a 'good heart'; and she was honest, a rare trait amongst Thai ladies. However, most of the ladies I had known in Thailand were bar girls and these are notorious for their talents for fabrication. Nong was from a different part of society, educated and morally responsible despite her nine years or so as a mistress to the bank manager.

To be a *mia noi* was somehow considered to be fairly acceptable and respectable; a second wife was common enough amongst the wealthy. Even the official wives and their families accepted it. Indeed, Nong was good friends with the bank manager's son and daughter. The wife liked the arrangement because it kept her husband happy; he was away from Bangkok most of the time anyway, and made no demands on her other than that she remained faithful (!) and looked after the family interests. He was very much the spoiled 'little boy' by the sound of it: a true male chauvinist! Most Thai men are, it seems; their women are treated very much as their property and are there to serve. Things are changing, however, and women are beginning to assert themselves and are seeking much more independence. With education comes logic; with logic comes enlightenment and a need for freedom of the mind.

Nong felt that her life had been wasted: that her nine years with the bank manager, although secure up to a point, had been so restrictive that she had no 'self'. She had been brought up to work, and she had been denied this fundamental right for too long. She wanted freedom and, with me, she saw a new future, for I certainly wasn't rich enough to support her in the way to which she had become accustomed. I had enough money for us to live reasonably comfortably from my pension and the small job I had at the Pantawee. The little I had left over, plus a small amount that Nong earned from commission on selling a health product, was enough for us to consider starting a small business. So we began to plan for this.

We had first of all to determine what we could afford to do and what product or service wasn't available in Nongkhai. I could capitalise on the small reputation I had acquired as a knowledgeable dealer in property for sale to *farangs*. It seemed that this knowledge was in some demand by the rich Thais who wanted to build houses for sale to *farangs*. However, this wouldn't achieve the object of the exercise, and my time was pretty well taken up with work at the Pantawee. We had reached our first objective at the hotel by easing the family out of the business with a bank loan. The next exercise was to make it into a limited company, and then attract investors in order to begin the development plans we had. A heavy demand on my time that was, in any case, fairly fully occupied writing for the websites; so what could we do that would occupy Nong's time and at the same time make a bob or two?

When the orange-juice stall had opened up opposite the Danish Baker, I had noticed the steady build-up of trade in this simple commodity. I spent a few hours sitting sipping a beer at the Danish and counting the number of people who stopped and bought fresh orange juice. I was staggered by the numbers. Apple, the owner of the juice stall, was taking between five hundred and a thousand baht a day; about fifteen grand a month, roughly half of which was profit! Not a bad little business; and one that, a month or so from its small start, had doubled. Nong was a good friend of Apple and spent much of the time each day talking to her friend (and me). Consequently she knew what little there was to know about the orange-juice stall. This was obviously one area to consider exploiting.

But we wanted something a little bigger and better than that; and the idea grew that we would start a small café, specialising in the kind of European food that wasn't available in the town. Pies, roasts, good solid English breakfasts and so on. This would obviously take up some of my time, for I would have to teach Nong and whoever we employed how to cook the European way. So, it was settled: we would open a small café/bar, in addition to selling orange juice, milk and fruit shakes and so on from a specially constructed stall that I designed.

We therefore occupied the short period of time before the fateful day with searching for the right property to rent in the right location. This kind of property was at a premium and therefore I would have to find somewhere that, with the aid of my design and building talents, I could convert – and somewhere that was within my price range. Not an easy task, and almost everything we looked at that seemed at all hopeful fell apart in our hands. Such is the Thai way of doing business. As the big weekend approached we were no nearer finding our home and business premises than we were when we first conceived the idea.

It would have to take a back seat until the main business was over.

I had already tried on my clobber: my 'nappy' sarong, high-collared Thai white jacket and traditional sash worn over one shoulder. What I hadn't bargained for was the variety of clothes I would have to wear at the portrait session that was to take place on the Saturday morning of our wedding day. This was something that Nong insisted upon: the official photographic session, in a well-lit studio, with two cameras clacking away at us in a variety of poses. The wedding photographic organiser, a jolly, smiling girl who insisted that we strike poses as she instructed, pushed and shoved us into a number of equally awkward positions and directed the whole session as though she were directing a movie. I had three 'costume' changes, as did Nong, and she had had to attend a make-up and hairdressing appointment beforehand. I declined to wear make-up since I wanted to look reasonably natural and not like a pancaked dummy. They were somewhat put out, but this was one thing I insisted on; I wanted every wrinkle to show!

The wedding ceremony was to be at five o'clock in the afternoon of that Saturday, which meant a very early morning start to fit in the make-up session, pick up the hired ceremonial costumes, do the photo session and finally travel the eighty-odd kilometres to Nong's village. The photo session was never-ending; it took two hours of climbing in and out of various costumes, striking innumerable unlikely poses, forcing smiles and wiping away sweat before we could get on our way.

We had managed to grab some croissants before we set out on the journey so we ate lunch on the run. We had meant to have a nice quiet buffet lunch at the four-star hotel we frequented every Saturday, but our photographic director had run into overtime! The journey itself was quiet and subdued, but we were both a little nervous and perhaps just knackered by the interminable preparations.

When we finally arrived in the village at the house where the ceremony was to take place, I was literally floored by what I saw. The whole of the grounds of the house had been transformed into a colourful, flower-decorated party area with tables and chairs for at least two to three hundred people. In one corner of the garden a stage had been erected, likewise decorated with garlands of flowers; and a bridal arch was built alongside it, again smothered in beautiful orchids and yellow chrysanthemums. A polystyrene cut-out was placed across the back of the stage spelling out, in Thai, 'Nong LOVE Derrick'. It was all so like a fairytale set that even my cynical old heart missed a beat or two.

A massive array of sound equipment was mounted to one side of the stage and a million people were rushing about making last-minute adjustments. The cooks were stirring vast cauldrons of food, and every second someone else arrived with more goodies. All of this had been arranged by Nong and her friends and relations; it was a tremendous effort.

Inside the house, an area had been set aside for the ceremony itself, in the centre of which were two *pacquan*, tree-like structures made out of crafted banana leaves and decorated with candles and yellow flowers. On the low tables covered with beautiful lace-like cloths lay a plucked chicken and an egg! Highly symbolic, I'm sure; but, despite high hopes of progeny from the coming union, unlikely to come to fruition given that I have been sterile since day one.

Also nearby were two ornate silver platters that we had purchased in the market in Nongkhai. I now understood what they were for. They were to hold the offerings of the groom to the bride and to her father. Nong's gold that we had purchased was placed in one, while the other contained the piles of pristine hundred-baht bank notes that we had received in exchange for the grotty ones that I had gathered together. It looked for all the world as though we had just committed a bank robbery! Everyone was duly impressed.

Nong and I changed from our street clothes into our ceremonial gear. Nong looked very beautiful, having taken care to preserve the expensive hairstyle and make-up that she had been adorned with early that morning. I felt I looked like an overdressed, embarrassed Englishman in the middle of a tiny Thai village in the heart of the jungle.

Downstairs, everything and everyone was beginning to hum with expectation as we descended – me being particularly careful not to let my droopy nappy trip me up. Everyone was sitting cross-legged on the floor, grouped around the *pacquan* tableau. I, being a *farang*, could not manage the cross-legged bit, and so two low chairs had been placed for Nong and me. Opposite us was the local headman and his assistant, chanting away at some Buddhist mantra. This didn't seem to deter the rest of the gathering who chatted away as though they were having their early-morning gossip.

Nong's father sat to one side with his friend, next to the goodies on the silver plates. He was grinning like a Cheshire cat and was obviously happy that his daughter had finally got lucky and was marrying. I was obviously acceptable, since I had come up with fine goodies; and, although I couldn't squat like everyone else, I had made the effort to conform to their customs.

I couldn't understand a word of what was said but this didn't matter a bit; I just did what I was told and followed Nong. At some point someone picked up the egg, cracked it and began to shell it. We were then passed half an egg each and had to eat it. I had no difficulty, but Nong almost choked on her half. The headman then proceeded to anoint us, copiously, with what seemed to me like pure whisky; I reeked like an old bar mat for the rest of the night.

We exchanged gold rings which we placed on the appropriate fingers. Everyone, it seemed, joined in the next stage: that of tying small lengths of cotton (*pokan*) around both our wrists for good luck and best wishes. I ended up with so many *pokan* on my wrists that I felt like a shaggy doll.

So, more photographs, handshaking and so on, and that was that. Nong and I were married. No signing of documents or priest's blessings, no giving the bride away, best man, bridesmaids: nothing in common with the Western tradition except the exchange of rings. The official registration would have to be done later at the Nongkhai Amphur offices before we were issued with an official marriage certificate. However, such niceties are rarely indulged in amongst the Thais; the witness of the village is enough it seems. However, if I wasn't satisfied with my bride in any way, I could come back within six months and tell her father and he would reimburse me fifty per cent of the dowry and that would be that. I would be un-married the Thai way!

Nong and I were then escorted upstairs to our bedroom where we were to change into our party clothes. On the way up I had a slight accident: my nappy finally gave up trying to cling to my hips and dropped unceremoniously around my ankles. Very embarrassing, but I carried it off with true British aplomb, gathered it up into my arms and, in my striped shorts, followed the girls upstairs.

Once in our bedroom Nong's girlfriends began to anoint the bed with rose petals and stood back admiringly, giggling at us. For a moment my heart skipped a beat; surely they weren't expecting to witness the consummation of our marriage? Thankfully it was all just part of the ceremony – although I feel sure that, historically, it did involve witnessing the 'you know what'!

So, to the party, the part all of the guests had been waiting for: *ghin cow*! Well, it is Thailand, and celebration meant nosh! I had provided for a certain amount of beer and soft drinks, but no Thai whisky; I had seen before what effect that had on the Thais. Nevertheless, they all seemed to be perfectly happy and gnashed their way through a pretty substantial amount of food.

All the while Thai music blared from the numerous loudspeakers meaning that the guests had to shout at each other to be heard. This was nothing unusual, since shouting seems to be the accepted form of communication anyway. Nong and I had to troll around the tables doling out trinket-style gifts to all of our guests, thanking them for their good wishes. One old *yai* (a grandmother) took a fancy to me and we had quite a good old chinwag together – in two different languages!

Then came the speeches, most of which I didn't understand; but I could guess what was said. When I spoke, I was surprised how many obviously understood what I was jabbering about; and my friend, the *yai*, applauded almost every word I uttered.

More photographs under the bridal arch with almost every relative and then, almost thankfully, a respite as the music started for the jolly Thai dancing. I managed to push the cork into a bottle of French wine I'd had the foresight to bring along and glugged down several glasses in succession. Nobody seemed to be dancing, so I donned my MC guise and jollied everyone along onto the dance floor. By this time I was truly knackered and, after half an hour or so of urging the party into some sort of frenzied momentum, I flopped thankfully into a plastic chair and watched the party. A Thai country wedding is a very colourful and exciting event and everyone, all three hundred of our guests, were happy; and I seriously felt that I had been accepted into this large Thai family.

By ten o'clock people started to drift away to their beds. Most of our guests were farmers and a dawn rise was the norm, so for them to be still up and kicking after sundown was very unusual. A group of young men were still hammering the remains of the beer and the children were wrecking the flower arrangements as I wearily took my leave, left my bride and made my way up the wooden hill. I was now happily starting out on a new journey full of joy, hope and promise.

Chapter Twenty-Three

A NEW 'NEW LIFE'

WE TRAVELLED BACK TO NONGKHAI, decamping from our condo to live at the Pantawee to plan for our future. I would still have to work at the Pantawee, but we decided that we had to move out once we had found a suitable place of our own. As luck would have it we did so almost immediately: a small Chinese townhouse with a large living area downstairs leading to a bathroom and kitchen, with two bedrooms and a box room upstairs and another toilet/shower room. Also downstairs was a small area suitable for half a dozen tables, a bar and a lounge area – ideal.

The rent for this establishment was about what we would pay for a private house anyway, so we would be quids in. We started to plan and prepare, buying as much as my limited resources would run to. I decided that I wouldn't open for business until we were completely ready; besides, the new investor at the Pantawee was taking up a great deal of my time. However, we managed to put in two English toilets, a hot shower, fix the air-conditioning unit in the bedroom and do some basic work in the kitchen: enough to make the place comfortably habitable as a home with some preparation work for the business.

So, we finished 'camping out' at the hotel and instead camped out in our own home. It might take another six months, maybe even a year before we would be ready for business, but in the meantime we were happy. What is time after all? Just days going by; if one can be happy with those days, that is all that really matters. I was deliriously happy; I had a beautiful new wife, a comfortable home, a job and a business –

nearly.

Designing the bar/restaurant was no problem for me, since I had started and built a similar small business before. The problem was the small amount of capital that I had from my monthly OAP income. I had only a few pennies left over following the expenditure on our wedding, and my salary from the Pantawee added but a few pennies more. So I had to continue every day to ride my bicycle to the hotel and apply my knowledge of management to the hotel business. Not easy with a Thai ladyboy boss who was convinced she knew it all!

On planning for the Pantawee business as a limited company, I had to persuade Nopporn to adopt a Western style of management. This proved to be impossible, and ended up in an argument: one which, fighting against a dyed-in-the-wool Thai, was impossible for me to win. I eventually had to give in and resign, thereby losing the extra income so necessary for us to survive and build our own business. However, survive we did; and I built an orange-juice bar to mount outside the restaurant which flourished. In the meantime I applied my talents as a builder and carpenter to build a splendid bar and a workable kitchen for the restaurant.

Next was the task of teaching my Thai wife to cook Western-style food to attract the Western retirees to our restaurant for the 'comfort food' they craved from their homeland: food such as steak pie, fish and chips and full English breakfast with the special addition of American-style fried shredded potatoes (hash browns). We also offered a wide range of Thai meals. In all about forty-two dishes – very attractive and cheap!

Initially, of course, I had to do most of the work in the kitchen as chef, until such time as Nong learned the rudiments of Western-style cooking. My efforts to provide a typical Sunday lunch were disastrous at first, because buying beef in Thailand is an impossibility. I eventually discovered a Thai/French butcher's which provided almost edible meat. Nong soon learned, and now cooks better than me – which is not that difficult! The main problem with running a business based upon Western-style cooking is that, in Nongkhai, customers who prefer this kind of cuisine are mainly limited to Western tourists and ex-pats; although the good steaks I eventually found were relished by the Chinese!

We had decided to install a massive air-conditioning unit in the main part of the restaurant which proved to be very beneficial for our customers. It cost a fortune to install and also to run, but it was one of the few establishments that boasted such a luxury.

The name I had chosen for the restaurant had been based upon our first venture of installing the orange-juice bar – OJ Bar & Café. We became known as 'OJ' for short, and I became referred to as Mr OJ or Papa!

The new business attracted many of the seventy-odd local retirees and I met some very interesting characters with individual stories. One of these was Sydney, an old rogue but charming with it. Through him, I was introduced to a broker in Australia with whom I have worked ever since – an honest broker and one of the few who has become a true friend.

Sydney was a throwback to days gone by: immaculately turned out with immaculately polished shoes, polite in his manners to the point of being obsequious, and generous to a fault. Everyone liked Sydney – except those who had been caught by his claims as an ex-banker, having fallen foul of his ability to make money and lost their shirts! He latched onto me and used my writing abilities by promising me a portion of the rewards from his 'investment' expertise. He always seemed to fall foul of failed investments which some unsuspecting investors had participated in. I did, however, learn some interesting insights into certain banking operations which, if he had observed the rules and respected the investments, instead of using them as his own funds, would have proved useful for him. But he didn't. Sydney had been expelled for similar misdemeanours in Laos before setting up shop in the Thai Laos Hotel in Nongkhai where, in the final analysis, he succumbed to a cancer in his scalp and eventually had to be transported to his native homeland, Australia, to die.

At the same time I decided to try and boost Nongkhai's attractiveness to tourists by making use of its proximity to the mighty Mekong River. I had been impressed by the success of the London Eye and could envisage a Thai equivalent on the Mekong: not a wheel, but a tall observation tower, a river cruise on a hovercraft, a water park and several other attractive venues which I was convinced tourists would travel to north-east Thailand to take advantage of, and also cross into

Laos on the Friendship Bridge which spans the Mekong at this point.

I developed a full business plan and conducted a great deal of research into the business side, and also approached the then governor of the province for support. He was one of the few business-enlightened Thais that I had come across, and we were soon confronting the conclave of businessmen to pursue the project. I also met with and got the agreement of the British Chamber of Commerce and the Thai Tourist Board.

All seemed to be going well when the Thai government, as is their natural wont, decided to do their normal musical chairs and change the governor! That put an end to around a year's worth of intense effort, for it meant starting again right back at the beginning with no pick-up by the new governor. This is the norm for the way government is run in Thailand and, I am sure, why many such attractive projects bite the dust.

Having got the bug for adventurous business projects once again, I decided to look at my own area of expertise: the movie and TV business. I had heard and read of the new and burgeoning movie business in New Zealand, largely nurtured by the American companies keen to capitalise on the availability of financial breaks and the superb locations.

I investigated, and decided to set up a production company there; for I had written a new movie set in Thailand, which could be serviced by and from New Zealand. There was no money in Thailand, but services at an affordable rate; and I had been promised a large amount of finance from an American company. I encountered a producer with good skills in computer animation, and we struck up a rapport and decided to set up shop. All was going well and I had written several scripts and a TV series for production with the new company, when the banking crisis occurred and the financing vanished!

Taweesilp, my doctor friend who was an orthopaedic surgeon, convinced me to tend to the problems of my aged body, specifically an old wound from two misplaced vertebra in my spine. He flew the king's surgeon up from Bangkok to perform the operation on my spine, which doctors in the UK had said was impossible. It worked, and – despite having to spend some time trussed up like a Victorian chorus girl in a corset – is now fully recovered.

The restaurant business, by this time, was beginning to show signs of fatigue owing to the fall-off in tourist numbers. When the rent was hiked up to almost double, my clever wife was persuaded to look for an alternative property for the OJ Bar. She found it: a run-down Chinese shop/house. I was depressed – not again! But Nong herself took the project on, arranging to hire a gang from one of the major building projects that were going on. The old bar was removed, including the bar I had built (albeit with the possibility of dismantling it in the future); and this, along with the rest of the moveable materials apart from the massive air-conditioner and the glass windows and doors which I had installed at the front of the bar, we loaded onto a truck with the assistance of half a dozen sturdy Thais and moved to the new premises.

Sam visited during that time and assisted me in reconstructing the bar and so forth, for I was still trussed up like a turkey in my corset. Nong had also had the foresight to build me a proper office, for in the old restaurant I had hidden behind the bar area. My new office was faced one side with glass, with a sliding door, in order that I could view the comings and goings in the restaurant. After a while I did begin to feel like a fish in a bowl, but it did allow me a certain privacy.

But that was to be the beginning of my poor old body's problems. At the age of seventy or so I had forgotten that age, as one gets older, takes its toll and the body, like an old car, begins to lose certain mechanical functions. I had come to realise that, by now, I lacked the exuberance of my youth for sexual gratification; but I never dreamed that the old machine that had served me so well without major mishap for so long would suddenly give up.

It was at this stage that I was made aware that I was no longer a youngster, as I succumbed to something I had developed fifteen years before from my overindulgent life in London: diabetes. The problem started with a small and almost insignificant cut between two toes on my left foot which the doctors at the big private hospital in the local city of Udonthani couldn't diagnose; even, after at least three visits, continuing to claim that it was gout! However, on a visit to another doctor recommended by my friend in Nongkhai, it was diagnosed as a diabetic wound which, through neglect, had developed into a gangrenous and badly bacterial infection. He continued to treat it until it got too bad and he declared that I would have to enter the hospital for proper attention.

The long and the short of it was that it got worse and worse and I had to have my left big toe removed; but they couldn't treat the underlying problem of the gangrene or the bacteria because they just didn't have the facilities. Their normal treatment was to cut and cut until not only the gangrene was removed, but everything right up to the hip. Then…?

Nong, who by this time was getting worried about my actual survival because they were shoving more and more morphine into me and I was hardly alive and in a dream world of pain, called her aunt who was a state registered nurse. She insisted on joining us and telephoning around to her contacts to find the best treatment. She found it: a specialist hospital in Bangkok which dealt only with diabetic wounds and thyroid problems.

I was admitted after a torturous journey by plane, about which I remember very little; in fact all events after that were as vague as any nightmare because of the pain and the morphine combined. I seem to remember a curiously circular sci-fi type of operating room with numerous operating tables in it, which – when I achieved any form of semi-consciousness – made me think I had been transported into an alien spaceship like something out of *Doctor Who*.

After that, and apparently despite (according to Nong) much raving on my behalf when I was on the operating table, and agonised screams and demands for more pain-relieving morphine, I remember nothing until I finally woke up in a hospital bed. My dreams of being elsewhere continued for about another week, with doctors and nurses pouring various treatments into me intravenously via a complicated dispenser to which I was attached. The problem, I later discovered, was the bacteria with which I was infected, and a new antibiotic had to be developed before it had the desired effect. Nong stayed with me the whole time, sleeping as best she could on a sofa in the room.

This hospitalisation lasted about two weeks, during which time the infection was treated and the wound (which looked like a raw leg of lamb) dressed and attended to by my superb female doctor. I insisted on being discharged although I still needed daily treatment, and therefore Nong found a small one-roomed apartment nearby which, with her aid, I was able to be transported to and from every day in the wheelchair she had bought.

This incarceration lasted another six weeks with Nong nursing me and dressing my wound twice a day. God knows where she found the patience; I am not a good patient and the small prison of the apartment was torturous. My strange dreams continued as though I was in another dimension, and are still vivid today; but I couldn't wait to get back to Nongkhai and home and my computer – and writing.

The cost of my incarceration had been phenomenal, exhausting my small savings and loans from friends and a few relations. Nong again had orchestrated this worrying problem by begging for help; her family helped enormously, so demonstrating once again the togetherness of Thai families. But for them, I would have died – although this strange experience had convinced me that I had already done so. Nong's two brothers and their families visited frequently to keep her spirits up, and to bring me a TV to occupy my time and stop me going mad!

The brain is a strange instrument; for, during this time, and for some time afterwards, I recalled my weird dreams in another world and I can still visualise it as though it were yesterday and reality; but it *was* a dream, no doubt manufactured by the massive doses of morphine I had absorbed.

I had this time in which to consider the past and to ponder the future and the words of my old artist friend in London, Zeesh: the artist whose sole reason for living was his art. What is my main and necessary preoccupation in life? With seventy-four years on the clock I had to engage in something that could be realised in the next ten years. Could I possibly capitalise on the half-dozen scripts and TV series I had developed during this last crazy period of my life? My six or so scripts/ideas/formats/two or three novels had to be the focus of my work from now on. Polishing and rewriting and presenting and maybe producing them – if I could raise the necessary finance and physical energy.

Reaching the ripe old age of seventy-odd is a watershed: the time when one realises that one's youth has long since gone, and even middle age is a dim and regrettably distant memory; when grey hair has turned to white, and once supple and agile limbs and muscles have atrophied like old vegetables. Growing old is an unavoidable degenerative disease reflecting the mistakes of past life and creating regret for those mistakes. Unfortunately there is no going back and therefore one must suffer with as much grace than one can muster.

All seemed to be going well with my office now fully equipped with my computer, scanner and super colour printer and air-conditioning unit. I began working and editing previous notes and scripts in earnest.

During my time in the Bangkok hospital, despite frequent appeals to the British Embassy, I got not one offer of help or advice or indeed a call of sympathy from the Consulate. Neither have I since had any assistance from the UK government in my appeals to return to the UK for NHS attention (for which I paid for sixty years or more), being told only that I would have to return and stay for a full six months, at my own expense, before being granted 'residency' again. That's what the British government thinks of its OAPs: they steal our contributions for years, and when our pension is due they nail it down to the rate that was granted when applied for, simply because I decided to move out of the UK when I was sixty because I couldn't afford to stay there! On top of that their mismanagement of sterling has seen its value drop almost fifty per cent. So my old-age pension was ten years out of date and diminished in value by half! Some blasted government; if I ran my finances in that way I wouldn't live another five years!

I want nothing from the British government more than that which I have paid for: my pension and access to the NHS if I could ever afford to move back there. Gone were the days when a gentleman's word was his bond. Those who created the old-age pension scheme and the NHS must be turning in their graves! The real nanny state is long gone; instead, it is a 'thieves' kitchen' with everyone but those who have paid their dues dipping their fingers into the pie!

The big difference between families in the UK and in Thailand is that in the latter there is a respect for age; parents are revered by the families, some of which may amount to fifty people or more, and all are concerned for their other family members. I am only 'family' by marriage but, when in need, I was respected and supported. In the UK, families have split up as soon as the children leave the nest. When my help is needed by my Thai family then, of course, I give it. In the UK, generally speaking, a call for help falls on deaf ears, as it does with the government departments. Selfishness and greed pervades.

The company I had set up in New Zealand with Johannes, my computer animation partner, could not be financed there, since it is a small country with little independent finance available; and to persuade finance from anywhere else in the investment world was impossible; although great skills in the film business exist there, it is too far away to exert any kind of control over. I did, however, manage to set up a sale of one of Johannes's animation series with the USA, and support for this with a financier in London on the guarantee of the sale producing enough finance to make the series – some $400,000. The financier was also considering financing my bundle of three movies. Unfortunately Johannes contracted a fatal illness and sadly died before I could complete.

My attempts to finance my movie or TV projects, whilst living and working from Thailand, were also an impossible task; and with the British pound losing ground and the cost of living in Thailand going up, Nong felt that if I had any more health problems we just wouldn't be able to afford to live. The visiting tourist industry had fallen off drastically, owing to the big bank collapses around the world and the consequent effect on the cost of living, which meant that tourists had less money to spend; and the business in the restaurant fell off so badly that we had to close up shop. There was then no alternative: I had to plan on returning to the UK.

Chapter Twenty-Four

TAIL BETWEEN LEGS BUT HEAD HELD HIGH

THE THOUGHT OF LEAVING THE country and people I had come to consider as my home and family and returning to London did not appeal to me at all, particularly as I would have to leave Nong behind in Thailand. I would have to stay for a minimum of six months to re-establish myself as resident again.

My relationship with Jane had remained cordial and friendly and she kindly offered to allow me to stay with her, as I planned to return to Thailand once I had finished my business which included some film financing. I also planned to pursue my case with the BBC regarding my copyright of *Doctor Who* and UNIT. I made an interim settlement with the BBC which enabled me to buy an electric wheelchair, in order that I could get around locally and to the various hospital appointments I had to attend.

When the six months were up, the movie deal still hadn't finalised so I had to search for a flat. This, as it happened, was fortuitous since I would be required to work all of the movie business from London and not Thailand. My daughter Kate tried to set me up with some accommodation, but as an English citizen again I managed to get the local council to provide a flat. My pension had been upgraded and this would assist in keeping Nong cared for in Thailand – but it meant I had to stay in London. It was in the midst of winter, with the temperature well below zero, and a visit to Thailand with temperatures of around thirty degrees was too hard to resist – and in any case I had to see how Nong was coping.

Nongkhai was as unbearably hot as London was cold! I settled Nong as securely as I possibly could, packed as much of my paperwork as the airline would allow and headed back to freezing London and work.

I had bought a new computer, settled myself again in London, been commissioned to write this autobiography and invited to the fiftieth anniversary celebration of *Doctor Who*. Uppermost in my mind, however, is trying to get Nong to join me here in London. My life is once again devoted to writing and producing – alone again. My deal with the financier was still on the cards and depended on a bank deal which I had helped engineer and which I would participate in. This would provide enough capital for Nong to join me, or for me to commute between London and Nongkhai. I had been working with my friend the broker for over a year, and the deal is due to complete as I write.

'What's it all about, Alfie…?' – damned if I know!

It is about time my fortunes changed. Tomorrow is another day!

NEXT!